CORPORATE FAILURE BY DESIGN

CORPORATE FAILURE BY DESIGN

Why Organizations Are Built to Fail

Jonathan I. Klein

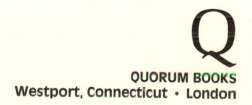

QUORUM BOOKS
Westport, Connecticut · London

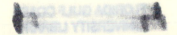

Library of Congress Cataloging-in-Publication Data

Klein, Jonathan I., 1950–
    Corporate failure by design : why organizations are built to fail / Jonathan I. Klein.
      p. cm.
    Includes bibliographical references and index.
    ISBN 1–56720–297–7 (alk. paper)
    1. Organizational behavior. 2. Management.
  HD58.7.K547 2000
  658—dc21   99–046053

British Library Cataloguing in Publication Data is available.

Library of Congress Catalog Card Number: 99–046053
ISBN: 1–56720–297–7

First published in 2000

Quorum Books, 88 Post Road West, Westport, CT 06881
An imprint of Greenwood Publishing Group, Inc.
www.quorumbooks.com

Printed in the United States of America

∞™

The paper used in this book complies with the
Permanent Paper Standard issued by the National
Information Standards Organization (Z39.48–1984).

10 9 8 7 6 5 4 3 2 1

TO MY PARENTS

Contents

Preface

Truth is stranger than fiction, but not so popular.

—Anonymous

An information technologist at a law firm develops a software program for quickly, thoroughly, and accurately completing routine forms. His supervisor orders him to destroy the program because she had not authorized it. Instead, the technologist sells the program to a rival company, resigns shortly thereafter, and starts a lucrative consulting practice.

Officers of a manufacturer of computer hardware, desperately needing an operating system, schedule a meeting with the CEO of a small software company in order to discuss an arrangement through which the latter might develop one. They arrive at the CEO's home for the meeting, only to be kept waiting all day while he and his wife dither over the correct procedure for such an arrangement. Eventually, they leave without ever having had the meeting in the first place. The hardware manufacturer then approaches another software company that quickly agrees to develop the operating system, and enjoys tremendous success in doing so.

The vice president of Human Resources for a huge telecommunications corporation pleads guilty to charges of insider trading, for which he is fined almost a million dollars. He had previously pleaded guilty to a scheme in which he received kickbacks from profits earned by sixteen of his friends, from insider information he had provided. This is the individual responsible for developing and administering companywide ethical development programs, one purpose of which is to warn employees about the illegality of insider trading.

In almost every branch office of an industrial manufacturing company, the general manager has used his position for personal gain, in effect embezzling company funds to purchase expensive items for personal use, extravagant office decorations, elaborate security systems, and the like. In each case, the GM has purchased the silence of employees with gifts, time off, and other favors, and has gained the complicity of immediate supervisors by landing lucrative contracts for them. Corporate headquarters, unable to halt the waste by any other means, is forced to shut down almost every branch office.

A computer hardware consulting operation found itself devoting a tremendous amount of time and effort bidding for a project with a prospective client. It turns out that its most serious competition was presented by bids offered by two other divisions of *the same company*.

Organizations.
Built to fail.

Acknowledgments

As an exploration into the "dark side" of organizations, this study pene-
trates issues that some organizational decision makers no doubt would prefer to conceal or ignore. To protect my sources against such efforts,
information supporting the study was obtained by guaranteeing confidentiality to informants.

That guarantee extends to this section, from which, depending upon their
choices, informants could be excluded altogether or in which they could be
included without identifying their specific contributions. To both groups, I
extend my heartfelt gratitude for data that both informed, and helped to
present, an unprecedented and critical study of organizations.

Within the more fearless of the two groups, I would like to acknowledge
the valuable contributions of the following individuals: Peter Alsberg, Joan
Anderson, Jeffrey Boxer, Laurie Boxer, Kenneth Brousseau, Henry Chan,
Michael Glasberg, Stacey Griffin, Ron Hagler, Charles Hanlon, Jennifer
Hein, Derek Kimball, David Lesser, Jacqueline Lopez, Jean Maki, Charles
Maxey, Michael Pirrault, Meyer Pollock, Amy Powers, Kim Robinson,
Anne Wiedenweber, Joan Zielinski, and Eric Zirnite.

Introduction

Death borders upon our birth, and our cradle stands in the grave.
—Joseph Hall

Countless words have been written on the subject of making organizations succeed. We have been admonished to "empower" employees, develop a "strong corporate culture," maximize "total quality" and "excellence," "stick to the knitting," "manage by walking around," and "get close to the customer." We are assured, in the title of a recent book on the subject, that the value-driven organization is *Built to Last.*[1] Admonitions such as these have proven to be informed, constructive, and even inspiring.

However, a critical insight is excluded from all of them, and implicitly denied by their optimistic tone. Representing this omission is the very problem that must be addressed in order to make any organization succeed—to ensure that it is "built to last." The problem:

Organizations are built to fail.

Yes, fail. Miserably. All organizations.

As a result, organizations in fact *do* fail—and well before the long term, wherein "failure" may be excused as simply a reflection of massive societal changes, and may even be characterized as the successful completion of a mission.

No—organizations tend to fail *quickly, prematurely,* and *without having achieved their goals.*

The reason is that *organizations are undermined by the very things they do in order to exist.* Hence, organizations are built for demise by their complete dependence upon sources of demise.

This is not to say that some organizations are uniquely predisposed toward failure, while others are not. Rather, *all* organizations are so predisposed.

Also, this is not a statement that is intended simply for dramatic effect. Rather, it is meant to be taken literally. Additionally, this is not a statement that organizations deliberately design themselves in this fashion because they want to fail. Organizations want to succeed.

Finally, this is not mere speculation. Rather, it is an assertion that is strongly supported by all available evidence.

THE FACTS OF THE CASE

The most persuasive evidence that organizations are built to fail is their astronomically high mortality rate.

Even defined by Dun and Bradstreet as narrowly as possible, to include only companies in arrears at the time of their demise, failures claim almost half of U.S. businesses within five years.[2] For a broader range of reasons, the most widely-accepted estimate is that failure claims *an overwhelming majority* of businesses within five years and *almost all businesses* within ten years, according to such disparate researchers as the Business Team business brokerage firm,[3] the consultant Douglas Gray,[4] the Small Business Administration,[5] the authors of the SOHO business guidebook,[6] and the academician Timothy Bates of Wayne State University.[7] As a result, typical attrition in a recent year "left nearly *$30 billion* in unpaid bills and threw thousands of people into our unemployment lines" (emphasis author's).[8]

As another indicator of organizational attrition, the number of business start-ups is annually approximated or even eclipsed by business closings of all types, and is *greatly* exceeded by terminations that are aggregated with acquisitions by other companies—a figure that is relevant due to the incapacity that invites at least some takeovers. In the table below, note the relationship between start-ups on the one hand and, on the other hand, (1) terminations and (2) terminations plus acquisitions.[9]

Year	Start-Ups	Terminations	Terminations Plus Acquisitions
1990	769,000	844,000	990,000
1991	726,000	821,000	959,000
1992	737,000	819,000	957,000
1993	780,000	801,000	937,000
1994	807,000	803,000	940,000

Although the table appears to cover a recessionary period, the researchers take pains to assert that annual terminations of at least 800,000 represent the norm. They also suggest that the tabulated data may reflect the earlier expansionary period, since "failures lag the national economy, meaning that they don't start to go up until we're well into a recession." The bad news, then, is that the depressing data may actually present a *deceptively rosy picture.*

The news may get even worse than that; indeed, the most powerful organizations in human history may have ultimately proven to be helpless in the face of their own failure. In his classic work, Edward Gibbon attributed the fall of the Roman Empire to such organizational infirmities as poor leadership, divided authority, the exploitation of the industrious by the recalcitrant, corruption, insensitivity to the environment, ambition, political behaviors, poor management qualifications, nepotism, internal conflict, usurpation by underlings, and jurisdictional disputes.[10] Thus, the Roman Empire itself may represent nothing more than the collapse of a failed organization. Given the scope and scale of its victims, then, it is not surprising that our own mere corporations cannot escape the clutches of organizational failure.

For reasons that will be presented shortly, this generally dismal record is an issue that has rarely, if ever, been seriously broached. However, this oversight is about to be corrected. For the time has come to face the sobering realization that *organizations are simply not doing their job.*

THE MYTH OF THE ETERNAL ORGANIZATION

If failure is so universal, why then are there so many organizations? The obvious reason, of course, is that they are continuously replaced—more or less, as we have seen. In this sense, the reassuring presence of organizations is comparable to the illusion of eternal youth created by the "beach blanket" film genre—the illusion that youth persists, against the reality that individual youths do not.

Not unlike biological death, then, corporate death is made to seem highly unusual by: (1) the disappearance of victims, (2) the plenitude and seeming typicality of survivors, and (3) the resulting invisibility of the entire phenomenon. Corporate death is in fact so commonplace, as well as efficient, that it is often mistakenly localized to small business, and identified as a "small business problem," simply because start-up firms perish so rapidly that they never receive an opportunity to grow.

THE ELEMENTS OF FAILURE

Easing Into Failure

One reason why organizations fail is that it is easy to fail. As Aristotle observed, "It is possible to fail in many ways . . . while to succeed is possible only in one way (for which reason also one is easy and the other difficult—to miss the mark easy, to hit it difficult)."

Aristotle may have been a bit reductionistic: "equifinality" is a term that refers to, and denotes recognition of, multiple routes to success. Examples of equifinality include highly successful sports coaches with wildly different leadership styles, ranging from the professorial John Wooden in college basketball to the high-strung, even dictatorial Vince Lombardi in professional football.

Nevertheless, Aristotle's point is well-taken; multiple though they may be, "success factors" remain few in number, are highly interdependent, and interact in complex ways. Hence, they are only as strong as their proverbial weakest link, and their complex relationship requires careful management. By comparison, failure can come through innumerable instances of neglect.

Inner Failure

So one might argue that, yes, organizations fail in large numbers. However, culprits seem to include forces, such as macroeconomic or technological events, that are extrinsic to rather than inherent in the organization. Thus, one might conclude that failure is not something to which the organization is "prone."

As an example of this argument, University of Connecticut researchers observed that, among respondents to a family business survey, "poor management was not usually cited as a reason for failure of the family business," and that greater importance was assigned instead to financial planning, conflict, succession, market factors, and the environment.[11] Also illustrating this argument were reasons cited by DRI, the consulting firm, for business failures reported by the SBA: these included more internal but, from a human resource perspective, still seemingly nonmanagerial issues such as "inadequate accounting systems, lack of reasonable cash/finance management, inability to cope with growth, and—most of all—the lack of strategic business planning."[12]

The problem with both analyses is that they tend to belie the full magnitude of the management function, and the full range of activities for which managers are responsible. Many management activities, almost by definition, are intended to account for issues that require attention due precisely to an intractability that reflects their external origins—which also makes them appear to be extraneous to management. Overlooked in the aforementioned University of Connecticut study, for example, were such clearly managerial responsibilities as financial planning, conflict-resolution, succession planning, market research, and strategic analysis; neglected by DRI was management responsibility for control, system development, and strategic planning.

The Organizational Nature of Organizational Failure

It fell to a third researcher to fix accountability where it belonged, by concluding that "a thorough review of the Dun and Bradstreet Corporation statistics indicates that *roughly 88.7% of all business failures are due to management mistakes* [emphasis added]."[13] Management mistakes cited by the researcher included inappropriate motives for entrepreneurship, disdain for procedure, underestimation of resource needs, insensitivity to the environment, infatuation with the product, and unrealistic projections of the future.

As shall be shown later in this discussion, these "mistakes," while properly attributed to management, encompass a multitude of sins that are often far more purposeful, complex, and unavoidable than the term suggests. Because such activities are typical of management, it will be shown that management *causes* organizational demise. In the language of social science, as a result, *the process of organizing is a self-limiting one*—one that initiates the very forces that undermine it. In practical parlance, this suggests that *organizations are built to fail.*

THE NATURE OF SUCCESS

On the other hand, some organizations do manage to survive, age gracefully, and even prosper. How can this be reconciled with the claim that they are built to fail?

It can be said that, as with any rule, there are exceptions to the claim that organizations are built to fail. Given the data on organizational mortality, these exceptions really are exceptional. It turns out that there are good reasons for them.

On Borrowed Time

One reason is that, while an important arbiter of long-term survival, organization itself represents but one of many contributors to short-term competitive success. To distinguish it from other entities, "organization" may be defined for our purposes as a configuration of purposeful *relationships* among its members, and the *responsibilities* assigned to each of them. Despite organizational limitations, much mileage can be gained from a marketable product, and from the resources it produces—at least in the short term.

The Relative Nature of Success

In the long term, the competitiveness of a flawed organization may perhaps be better explained by the relative nature of competitive success.

For example, a large number of organizations that succeed do so *not* because they are good but rather because the competition is worse: the proverbial one-eyed man in the kingdom of the blind. Examples include many sports franchises, political campaigns, and production companies specializing in daytime television shows, but there are plenty of others.

The Extracurricular Nature of Success

Some organizations continue to enjoy success that owes little or nothing to product quality. Sources of success instead may include entry barriers that are created through limit pricing (i.e., prices too low for the competition to afford), forward integration (i.e., purchase of customers), patents or copyrights, or other such tactics. The celebrated Internet "browser" war between Netscape and Microsoft, for example, will probably be won not on the product development front but rather through efforts to monopolize access to the marketplace, through proprietary arrangements with service providers.

Missing Competition

Other organizations remain successful because competition is absent altogether: examples include public, heavily regulated, or otherwise monopolistic organizations. For these organizations, incompetence is unlikely to jeopardize success because the marketplace, with nowhere else to turn, cannot respond by withdrawing support. Poor customer service at the Department of Motor Vehicles, for example, is unlikely to be effectively remedied by greater patronage of the post office, or to produce massive customer egress to private airplanes.

Resting on Laurels

Some organizations are sufficiently sustained by resources from an earlier success to maintain the appearance of success indefinitely, with minimal effort. Examples include record companies reaping royalties from the hit songs of retired but still popular recording artists. For other organizations, "success" may not require much in the first place: examples include student organizations, charities, and, again, sports franchises.

Failure to Acknowledge Failure

Still other organizations appear to succeed, but only due to their belatedness in acknowledging failure. Reasons for this reluctance are not difficult to imagine: failure may prohibit the attainment of cherished goals, undermine public image and self-esteem, create sunk costs, and necessitate the start-up costs of a new enterprise. As a result of reluctance to acknowledge it, many organizations that appear to be surviving have in fact already failed. The organization's *appearance* of survival may reflect any of the foregoing possibilities: a competitive advantage that is relative at best, artificial, easily attained and vulnerable, or vestigial and temporary.

THE PROBLEM OF ILLUSORY SUCCESS

In sum, then, long-term survival is possible, but may not require much. On the one hand, such modest requirements appear to be rich in opportunity—after all, if success is so easy to attain, why complain? The problem is that this same golden opportunity is also available to rival organizations, who can exploit it to their competitive advantage, by offering an unexceptional and only marginally superior product.

The result may even be the elimination of a seemingly impregnable monopoly, examples of which include U.S. automakers who found themselves fighting for their corporate lives against more efficient foreign competitors. Because of the opportunity it presents to rivals, success-cum-mediocrity represents an ultimately dangerous indulgence.

Despite the minimal requirements for staying in business, organizations tend to receive inordinate credit for it. As we will later see, this tendency is fueled by the organization's belief in, and the willingness of others to cede, a privatized, almost mystical understanding of its craft.

A CONSPIRACY THEORY

Many, if not most, egregious management excesses that account for organizational failure go unreported, because victims are reluctant to jeopardize either their current position or future marketability by sharing information about them.

Clearly, whistle-blowing about current misdemeanors poses a risk to job and career that few are willing to take. However, witnesses remain reluctant to talk, even about past events, and even after relocating to a new organization. The reasons are that, for the benefit of their new employer, they don't want to appear malcontented, vindictive, prone to externalize responsibility, untrustworthy, or encumbered by past problems that might require further analysis and verification.

As a result, organizational abuse largely remains a secret. One consequence for this study was its incorporation of information that was obtained only by assuring either confidentiality for those who desired it or the use of pseudonyms, indicated in the text by the use of quotation marks in denoting names. One consequence of this secrecy for all of us has been an ongoing inability to even recognize a problem precisely because it has been a critical one: critical enough to intimidate its victims, *until now*.

On the other hand, one unanticipated benefit was the enthusiasm with which information was proffered, even to the point at which respondents

actively sought additional interviews and presented extraneous information, indicating that this effort was "onto something."

MISSED OPPORTUNITIES

There appear to be other opportunities to discover the objective truth
about organizations, one of which is personified by the organizational scientist.

Curiously, however, it is the very objectivity on which science prides itself
that renders it unequal to the task of such analysis. This is because an
organization is a product of choice, and scientific analysis at its most
searching would raise fundamental questions regarding the merits of that
choice. Such questions can be addressed only through personal values—for
example, regarding the appropriate social objectives of organizations—and
personal values are expressly banned from scientific analysis, albeit with
only qualified success. Because they raise such value-laden questions, the
fundamental merits of organizations tend to escape scientific scrutiny.

This holds true for scientific analysis of *any* social phenomenon. As a
result, for example, science is applied to the task of explaining economic
forces, rather than to the task of recommending one economic system over
another. Similarly, the viability of organizations in general becomes as sci-
entifically absurd, and imponderable, as the "right" of a planet to exist. By
contrast, problems of maintaining such existence are fair game, since solutions can be justified "objectively" by their instrumentality to the organization's survival.

Thus, the organizational scientist focuses on problems for organizational
effectiveness, including employee motivation, interpersonal conflict, and organizational change. However, the organization itself is placed beyond
question, and reproach, as a seemingly naturally-occurring phenomenon,
rather than a product of choice—as an object of naturalistic wonder rather
than fundamental critical evaluation. The result, again, is protection for
organizational pretensions, against what is potentially the most credible
source of dissent.

AN ARGUMENT IN GOOD COMPANY

At first blush, the statement that organizations are built to fail may sound
like a radical departure not only from objective reality but also from accepted convention.

In actuality, however, this statement simply represents the logical implication of theory that has become "mainstream," if not downright ortho-
doxy, reflecting the thinking of such management icons as James March,
Herb Simon,[14] and Karl Weick.[15] In a nutshell, this line of thought is that
decisions in organizations are "nonrational," because they do not reflect

the organization's interests and are largely intended for purposes other than organizational advancement. Reasons include the information-processing limits (i.e., the "bounded rationality") of decision makers, resulting in decisions that, at best, meet minimal requirements (i.e., "satisfice") rather than optimize.

The logical implication explored in *this* discussion is that if decision purposes and inputs depart from organizational benefit, so too might decision consequences or outputs. Hence, the organization is built to fail by the limitations of its members.

The argument that organizations are built to fail is so consistent with mainstream scholarly thinking on the subject that it has already been internalized by academics, if implicitly so. To questions regarding their field of study, scientists in this field tend to reply with some variant of their "love" for organizations. This exchange is reminiscent of a reply by a human factors consultant, to a similar question by the author, that he "loved" work.

If the human factors consultant "loved" work so mightily, he would be doing it, rather than watching, reporting on, and assiduously *avoiding* it. Similarly, if organizational scientists were sincere in their love for their objects of study, they would be happily employed in them.

We find, to the contrary, that organizational scientists work either well to the outside of organizations, as consultants, or in an academic domain so well protected by tenure that their jobs and expected level of diligence approximate civil service positions. To organizations fighting for their lives in the marketplace, organizational scientists give the widest possible berth. And the reason is a sound one, if advanced disingenuously: "experts" on the subject do not trust their intellectual charges to do anything but fail.

To recapitulate: Inherent organizational self-destructiveness *sounds* like a radical concept only as a result of failure to explore the implications of conventional thinking. The concept also sounds radical only if one overlooks an equivalent but less ambitious one, and one that certainly captures the reality of entrepreneurship—the obvious, noncontroversial fact that organizations face an uphill battle to survive. The reason—and a point appreciated by the management scientist, consultant, and practitioner alike—is that the organization will perish if simply left unattended, and can survive only with serious, committed, and sustained attention to the problems that it inevitably presents. Left to their own devices, in other words, *organizations are built to fail.*

THE ORGANIZATION AS CULPRIT

The argument that organizations cannot be left to their own devices implies the fundamental purpose of this book, which is not to carp about organizational shortcomings but rather to *do* something about them. The good news is that such organizational problems are ultimately tractable because they are internal, close at hand, and the product of the selfsame organizational choices and actions through which they can be solved. And the most effective stimulus to solving these problems is the dire and inevitable outcome of failing to do so: a stimulus confronted only by recognizing that organizations, left to their own devices, are built to fail.

The statement that organizations are built to fail can perhaps be further clarified, and made less daunting, by specifying what the statement is *not*. Specifically, the statement does not altogether foreclose the possibility of organizational success. However, as an exception to a rule, success has exceptional sources, as explained earlier.

In Praise of People

Lasting success, where it occurs, is generally creditable to *people*—to their inner resources, to their willingness to apply them, and to the additional resources they acquire as a result. For example, the stunning success of Microsoft is creditable to the focus, brains, and energy of Bill Gates, and not to any organizational systems. The very *best* that an organization can do is to give its people the tools they need in order to do as well as they can—and then get out of the way. What often *passes* for an effective organization is one that simply addresses the problems created for people by organization itself: for example, by reducing political constraints on power, the effects of "learned helplessness" on creativity, and "status effects" on communication. In other words, an organization is effective to the extent that it *leaves people alone*—leaves essential resources unrestricted, creativity unstifled, and communication unimpeded—allowing people to do the things they would have been able to do in the absence of organizational impositions in the first place.

This is a point well-understood by the organization's founder—the generally extraordinary individual by whom organization, whether in the form of "professionalization" or formalization, is often violently resisted, to the uncomprehending exasperation of offspring or others. Dealing with this difficult individual is the subject of many a sober, analytical, and often patronizing tract on succession. Rarely addressed, however, is the need to understand the founder, and the issues that he or she may be unable to articulate, but is left alone to face: the sense that in the process of "organizing," something will be lost, and lost forever.

Because of organizational constraints on members, failure is likely to reflect the purely *organizational* rather than human aspects of an organization, reasons for which occupy the rest of this discussion. To paraphrase Douglas MacGregor, success comes from the human side of enterprise.[16]

Organizational failure, of course, may also reflect the limitations of its members, for example, its key decision makers. Ultimately to blame, however, are the organization's function and its failure to overcome such limitations—for example, through selection, performance appraisal, and reward systems. Directly or indirectly, then, organizational failure is indeed *organizational*.

IN PRAISE OF ORGANIZATIONS

This is not to say that organizations lack any redeeming qualities whatever. To the contrary, shared by countless observers is the recognition that organizations offer otherwise unavailable advantages, including the following: (1) the concentration of human resources on a scale needed to accomplish complex or large-scale tasks; (2) the coalescence and coordination of multiple specializations, to the benefit of competence and economies of scale; (3) synergy, defined as group output beyond the amount predicted simply from summing participant competencies, due to ideas that are generated through interaction; (4) social rewards, which are particularly motivating for highly "affiliative" individuals; and (5) social controls over nonproductive behavior.

To achieve all of these benefits, it is understood that organizations are not simply desirable but rather indispensable, at least in our current economic structures. In fact, it is the very importance of organizations that prohibits any tolerance for their dysfunctionality, and necessitates the present effort to surface and redress it. What distinguishes this effort from others is profound respect for its difficulty.

A few words about other such efforts may help to clarify the nature and role of this one.

IN THE WORDS OF OTHERS

Organizational problems do not represent some bizarre fixation: rather, they have occupied organizational scientists since time immemorial, just as social problems occupy social scientists and medical problems occupy medical scientists. There is nothing morbid in this: rather, science represents a problem-solving enterprise, so that its focus, appropriately enough, is a problem focus.

Organizational Problems for the Rest of Us

Representing the target of many organizational critics, for example, are the dysfunctional effects of the organization upon others, including the individual and society. Individual dysfunctions, for example, were attributed by Emile Durkheim to "anomie," an absence of guiding norms,[17] and personified by William White, Jr., as the highly mechanized "organizational man"[18]; societal dysfunctions were ascribed by John Kenneth Galbraith to a veritable host of organizational efforts to manipulate and control consumers and others.[19]

However, these dysfunctions are a far cry from the organizational infirmity proposed here. To the contrary, these dysfunctions may even indicate that organizations do what they do all too *well*, effectively subordinating individual and societal interests to their own.

The Organization as Its Own Worst Enemy

Closer to the focus here are problems that the organization presents for itself. Examples include the technically accomplished but interpersonally inept manager, the degradation of group decisions by "groupthink," and the excessively short-term focus of the "work hard, play hard" sales culture. Such problems provide the content for management textbooks, for applied articles and books targeted to practitioners, and for the bulk of academic research: a massive literature indeed. The issues raised in this literature, while certainly to the potential detriment of organizations, are generally distinguished from the ones presented in this discussion by their idiosyncratic rather than systemic nature. As indicated earlier, such issues are not likely to include the organization itself as a problem.

The argument here, that the organization is the agent of its own demise, is perhaps most closely approximated by various analyses of the "dialectical" process through which an organization is likely to sow the seeds of its own destruction, by provoking insurrectionary social forces. One example of such a process is the use of Scientific Management to legitimize control, provoking resistance from workers. Contributors to this literature stream include Ken Benson, Jurgen Habermas, and Wolf Heydebrand.[20]

In contrast to the approach in this discussion, the dialectical approach is typically applied simply in analyzing the organization, rather than in evaluating its merits as an institution. In addition, the dialectical analysis is limited to selected processes; others are better depicted as accretionary, interactive, or self-negating. This book is intended to account for *all* such processes, dialectical and otherwise.

LESSONS TO BE LEARNED

In contrast to other approaches, the claim of organizational self-destructiveness has several intended practical benefits to our knowledge of organizations.

One benefit is simply to account for the high rate of organizational mortality. Another benefit is to account for other, seemingly more remote events, including the poor performance widely ascribed to government programs and institutions. A third benefit is that the argument represents a perspective that is sufficiently extreme and underrepresented to invite rebuttal and counterargument—in essence, to approach Truth by creating a dialectic, in process if not in content.

And so, to recapitulate: This book is intended to demonstrate how *organizations are built to fail*, an argument that is supported by overwhelming evidence, is consistent with current thinking on the subject, and represents an addition to our knowledge of organizations that is ultimately essential to their success.

BON VOYAGE

And so, with this purpose in mind, we embark on our exploration of the failure at the heart of our organizations. Our journey promises to be disquieting, disillusioning, and in reference to previous conceptions, even perilous. But it is a journey that must be made, because *only by understanding organizational failure can we take the steps needed to eliminate organizational failure.*

And so, keeping in mind the ultimate benefits of doing so, and knowing that we will not return the same as we were before, we journey into organizational terrain that may be well-traveled but will soon be perceived in an entirely new way.

As something that is built to fail.

We make this journey not to mourn organizations but rather to save them. Because only by acknowledging that they are built to fail can we hope to attack the problem, and to make them succeed.

Let the journey begin.

PART ONE

FAILURE IN PURPOSE

1

The Corporate Suicide Mission: The Emergence of Organizational Purpose

> There is no refuge from confession but suicide, and suicide is confession.
>
> —Daniel Webster

The failure of most organizations doesn't require an excruciatingly long wait. Webster's Dictionary defines "fail" as "to be unsuccessful in obtaining a desired end." Assuming that their "desired end" is to survive, most organizations oblige the definition of failure, and our prediction that they will experience it, by giving up the ghost within a couple of years.

Generally, organizational failure is *not* one of life's great mysteries; reasons for it tend to be pretty straightforward. On occasion, the organization's strategy aims at the wrong market, or incorrectly at the right market. More frequently, the market is not even considered. According to previous writers, most corporations tend to be riveted not on the market but rather on a particular product or service.

Given this priority, it is not surprising to find that many products or services have no client base. A product or service with no clients represents both the beginning and end of the story: built to fail, indeed.

Examples of companies lurching unawares into the marketplace tend *not* to spring to mind, simply because they are short-lived, disappear rapidly from view, and in their short lives hardly became household names. However, there are exceptions: examples among established companies with the resources to survive their gaffes.

CORPORATE COMEDY

One example is the baby-food manufacturer exporting to Africa, where, in order to communicate to illiterates, companies routinely present pictures of a product's contents on the label; in this case, customers must have had an interesting interpretation of a packaging label picturing the company's trademark smiling baby.

Another example is the fast-food company's slogan "it takes a strong man to make a tender chicken," which was translated for Spanish customers as "it takes an aroused man to make a chicken affectionate." Also showing its sensitivity to Spanish-speaking customers was a major airline that advertised its first-class leather seats in Mexico by translating "Fly in Leather" literally into Spanish as "Fly naked!"

In most cases, the market is neglected by companies without the resources to survive and amuse us with their marketing antics. In most cases, therefore, we are unaware of this as a problem.

CORPORATE TRAGEDY

Failure has proven to be more protracted and visible for companies that were initially successful but experienced failure by neglecting market changes: again, by focusing exclusively on their product or service.

Representing the classic textbook example is the U.S. railroad industry, which thrived during the nineteenth century but during the twentieth century found itself fighting a losing battle against such alternative forms of high-speed transportation as those presented by the trucking and air industries. Had railroad companies defined their mission not as providing rail service but rather as meeting the customer need for reliable, high-speed transportation, they would have developed alternative forms of transportation, rather than having left this lucrative opportunity to competitors. But they failed to do this, and eventually succumbed, surviving today only as a picturesque but highly expensive welfare case.

Other, more recent examples include IBM, which during the early 1980s was so wedded to mainframe computers that it failed to notice a sea change in customer demand to personal computers that virtually represented an operational definition of "paradigm shift"—until it was almost too late, forcing IBM to rescue itself only through its tremendous assets. Less endowed and thus less fortunate was WordStar, a company that lost its word-processing monopoly, and ultimately its corporate life, by ignoring changes in customer expectations about word-processing features that instead were thereupon exploited by WordPerfect and later by Microsoft Word. Representing another example, according to a management consultant, was the Swiss watch industry not realizing "that a timepiece on a watch doesn't have to have gears and jewels, that it can have a microchip and can be just as good a watch, so they lost tremendous market share."

According to another management consultant, while on a project for a client who manufactured physical plants for weapons,

the VP of Marketing and Sales walks in and says "I got such-and-such a problem fixed: I told him that they were wrong" and he was talking about a customer who was purchasing $200,000 worth of equipment and the Marketing and Sales guy was telling him how he was wrong and that the customer had to listen to the manufacturer about how to take care of this problem.

And I knew right then and there that, when they were talking about customers as being wrong and we told that customer about "how to fix this problem," I said this is a company that is in dire straits. . . . And now they're out of business.

PERSONALIZED CORPORATE STRATEGY

In general, another management consultant observed of the organization that

the way it actually does business has a lot more to do with the personal needs of the people who are in the position to make the decisions about how things are done and a lot less to do with the strategy of the organization. . . . It's done in such an unconscious way; the presumption is that there's an external need that's driving the strategy when in fact it's the whim of the people who are deciding on the strategy.

THE ALLURE OF OUTPUT

This observation is supported by the personal reasons for focusing on a product or service, and not on the market.

One such reason is *precedent*: a product or service represents a traditional way of defining a company, often by inclusion in the corporate nomenclature. As a result, a company tends to be viewed simply as in the dry-cleaning, restaurant, or overnight delivery business. As an established product or service, it may be assumed to come with a ready-made market.

A second reason is that key personnel tend to be self-selected due to some predilection or *affinity* for the product or service. Affinity may include previous experience, perhaps self-styled expertise, or maybe even a desired self-image somehow connected to the product or service. Note that none of this has *the slightest thing to do with the market.*

As a result of this subjective affinity, key personnel tend to have a direct hand in creating a product, so that *self-esteem* emerges as a third reason for attachment to a product or service. For example, in a software-manufacturing company in Los Angeles, an ex-employee recalls that the President . . . had come out of the labs; she was a developer to begin with. There was a specific product that she wrote and that product, in her mind, was absolutely perfect the way it was; it needed absolutely no revision and there was no sense looking into acquiring a company that made a competing product that was maybe more leading edge because hers was perfect.

She was totally blind on that particular thing. . . . That may be part of the reason why [she] is likely to allow the push on some of the products that are the mainframe products because those are the ones that she created, as opposed to steering everyone into the newer ones: things that are the newer technology-based products. Because now she can point to the things that she helped create and say "xyz product has brought in hundreds of millions of dollars in revenue stream to this company. That's the one I created."

Output is treasured not simply as a vehicle for self-esteem but also because it represents a personal creation that can outlive its creator. Hence, representing a fourth motive for identifying with output is a desire to exploit the independent existence of a product, or the independent function of a service, in order to satisfy a need for immortality. For example, according to an advertising manager, a manufacturer of radio and TV parts, when asked why he suddenly wanted to consolidate his various dispersed operations into one facility, replied, in his idiomatic Brooklynese, "When I'm gone, I want people should know I was here."

A fifth reason for identifying with a product or service may be summarized as ready *access*; a product is tangible, and a service can be planned and organized, so that both, as a result, are action-ready.

A sixth reason is that output makes it easy to define a mission based solely on *imitation* of the competition.[21] According to a management consultant, a company in the high-tech computer industry

got a little bit side-tracked because the competition was attempting to go into wireless communication. They tried to get into it, and it really cost them a lot of money and it really fragmented their operation. It caused them to take their eye off the ball of producing a high quality product that they knew worked instead of going into this kind of risky field.

THE NEGLECT OF INPUT

Regardless of whether output is viewed as a response to demand or as an end unto itself, organizations often neglect the very things needed to effectively make that output available in the first place. According to another management consultant, organizations

don't get it. They don't see that. So if they don't, then you've got to have a very simple statement of strategy so that everybody in the organization can understand what difference it makes to their job. If they don't understand that, how are they going to do it?

Because they define themselves in their role in terms of what they understood what people like them are supposed to do and they're not willing to say, "I'm just going to look at this totally fresh." [Instead they say] "this is what a President does. That's what the President thinks. This is what a Vice President of business affairs does. That's what he thinks." They're comfortable in that; they like that.

So if you extend the logic of that . . . everybody says, "What I'm supposed to do is execute this specialization role that I have." What binds them together? What's the thing they have in common? Nothing. There's no sense of direction. There's the presumption about responsibility because of a role.

Summarized another management consultant,

the greatest single failing I see in an organization is the failure to link the way things are done in the organization to the strategy that they're pursuing. Strategies are concocted without any awareness of the profound implications they have for how things are done in the organization. . . .

They don't fundamentally look at the way things are done . . . "How is this strategy going to impact the people we have now?" "Are we going to need to change the mix of people?" "Are we going to need to retrain people?" "Are we going to need to put new rewards in to motivate new behaviors?"

So there's this disconnect between the strategy of the organization and the way it actually goes about doing business. . . . In many cases, there's no awareness that one impacts the other.

THE HIDDEN PROBLEM

The problem goes even deeper.

Strategy represents an organization's explicit or "official" goal. As noted, this goal tends to be a reflexive expression of other goals, including but (as we shall see) not limited to the fulfillment of personal needs. Strategy is *rationalized* by sounding sufficiently desirable (and also vague enough) to enlist support from the full range of its "stakeholders," or interest groups, who otherwise have more specific and often mutually incompatible goals.

The organization's *real* goals are its implicit or "operative" ones.

It is from its operative goals that the organization gets into trouble. Operative goals may be *revealed* by the problems discussed so far, but originate in hidden sources.

To understand these sources, and the full extent of their effects, we need to look more closely at the subject of our discussion.

Welcome to The Organization.

INTRODUCING THE ORGANIZATION

Organizations can do many things.

They can make automobiles, medicine, or war; they can transform economies, the environment, and the political landscape; they can rule us, oppress us, or help us develop as individuals. They can dominate us, and, as we are beginning to see, they can perish in droves.

There is, however, one thing that is beyond the repertoire of organizations.

Organizations do not exist.

Existence is reserved for their members, who may include salespeople, soldiers, or soldier ants. An organization itself refers only to, and is defined by, a configuration of purposeful *responsibilities* assigned to, and *relationships* among, its members.

The organization's nonexistence is a crucial point, because as a result, its nature, purposes, and function necessarily become matters of conjecture.

To assist us with this conjecture, the organization's responsibilities and relationships can be represented by its design, which in turn can be clearly presented through the organization chart: the familiar, orderly-appearing array of boxes, solid lines, and dotted lines that serve to delineate the responsibilities and interrelationships of members.

However, while the organization chart is clear, it is hardly accurate; it is in fact much *too* orderly, typically omitting or distorting vital information, through inaccuracy, misconception, or neglect of the organization's informal relationships. For this reason, the actual design of an organization, along with everything else about it, must be inferred.

Like the organization chart for presenting it, the organization's design appears to be highly logical. This orderly characterization is the thrust of "expert" thought on the subject, which is that an organization's design evolves for some sound, lawful reasons.

To sum up these reasons, each part of the organization develops at a level of size and power commensurate with the size and power of the external, environmental stakeholder group (e.g., customers, potential litigants, and so on) for which that part is responsible. As a result, the organization is managing each part of its environment with the internal capability needed to do so effectively. It all makes perfect sense: the organization develops as it should.

ORGANIZATION AGAINST ITSELF

Unfortunately, expert pronouncements are no less conjectural than ignorant ones: closer inspection of the typical organizational design reveals that there is something *terribly wrong* with our organizations. What we find in our analysis opens a veritable Pandora's box of organizational disaster that will occupy us for the remainder of this study.

In analyzing its design, we find that an organization often assigns power to its personnel in a manner precisely *opposite* to the manner that would best serve it. Thanks to this allocation of power, the greatest influence over the mission may be enjoyed by work units whose contribution to the organization, and version of that mission, are *least* likely to be productive.

STAFF ÜBER ALLES

One reason is that the lion's share of the organization's power is assigned to individuals and departments with skills, tasks, and goals that, as we shall see, are *least* essential to meeting long-term market demand.

These tend to be staff personnel, operating to facilitate the line or production capability, and occupying professional positions in Advertising, Finance, Legal, Computer Programming, Engineering, and Research-and-Development, among others.

The heavy hitting staff units in most organizations tend to be marketing and particularly sales. According to an employee in a Southern California door manufacturing operation, "Our company always caters to sales . . . because they're like God." A less charitable employee in a healthcare company headquartered in New Jersey concurred that, "Every company I've ever worked for the sales team and marketing, they do the least and they benefit the most. . . . In my current company, it's definitely related to the company's goals." Due to their commonality, many of our succeeding examples will come from sales.

Have Skills, Will Travel

One source of their advantage is that staff skills tend to be extremely portable, which means that they are readily applicable to other organizations, so they can provide considerable job mobility. By giving substance to the threat of egress, staff skills produce considerable leverage in negotiations with the organization over salary, benefits, position, and responsibilities. Due to the power they enjoy for the same reasons over other organizations, replacing staff tends to be costly.

As a result, according to the marketing director of a Southern California mortgage banking firm,

We're always afraid to let salespeople go, because we think they're so important, that everything they bring in is so important. It may not be important; often, the business they bring in is not profitable.

A few terms need to be defined. "Power" has been defined as wherewithal, as the opposite of dependence, and as a dimension of a very specific relationship between "social actors," which means individuals or groups. Hence, power is maximized if in that relationship dependence (1) *on* the other party is minimized and (2) *by* the other party is maximized.[22] In the case of staff, then, one clear reason for their power is their use of skills that are minimally dependent on the organization, since they can be readily applied elsewhere.

Simple Pleasures

One reason for the portability of staff skills, in turn, is their *generic* quality, since they do not have to be customized to any organization. Another reason is their application to discrete tasks, which can be easily credited. A computer programmer designs and is credited for a complete software program; a financial analyst compiles an entire investment plan.

Staff skills are portable also because they can be applied to simple tasks, facilitating their adaptability elsewhere.

Illustrating the simplicity of sales tasks, and in a rare refusal to kowtow to the power that comes from it, a manager in the aforementioned mortgage banking company, facing threats to quit from salespeople pulling down $500,000 per year, responded "Don't let the door hit you on your butt on your way out. . . . I could replace all of you with shoe salesmen," and he promptly did just that, obtaining the undiminished level of performance he predicted.

Revenues without Costs

In addition to the simplicity of their tasks, staff require almost no physical plant, incurring as a result limited costs and appearing instead to operate a profit center. In the case of sales, this perception is enhanced by a task that is directly if not magically juxtaposed with the appearance of revenues. In relation to revenues, sales represents a "proximate cause."

Thus, staff may derive power not only by minimizing their dependence on the organization but also by maximizing the organization's apparent dependence on *them*, by performing tasks that are the direct precursors to revenue-generation. The organization seems further dependent on staff personnel because of their ready, individual creditability for the simple and discrete tasks they perform. Finally, this dependence in turn is deepened by the organization's prior investment in production and production capability, costs that can be assigned elsewhere and recouped, again, only through sales.

The Mystery of Staff

Additionally, while they certainly produce measurable outcomes, staff positions require tasks and skills that are, for the most part, unmeasurable, if not entirely invisible. Advertising and research-and-development require creativity; marketing demands social manipulation; finance, legal, and computer programming entail esoteric knowledge; and sales activity stipulates interpersonal suasion. Despite their inherent simplicity, then, the resulting mythology provides staff activities with a patina of mystery, and staff skills with qualifications that are virtually impenetrable, adding to the perceived rarity and value of the craft. Enhancing this value is the fact that staff skills come prepackaged and cannot be acquired by training, dispensation from which enhances the apparent cost-effectiveness of staff to the organization.

Sales as a Popularity Contest

According to the employee in the aforementioned Southern California door manufacturing operation, a source of power unique to sales is that

some of these guys have got such a niche in the area. We've even had customers say, "If you don't keep this certain salesman, we won't buy from you anymore, because this is the only salesman we'll ever deal with." So even the salesmen somehow have got this rapport with their certain customers. They're just locked in there. If we got rid of that salesman for bad service, or whatever, half of our clients will go, too.

I'm sure part of it is all their wining and dining.

Observed a strategic planner for a Florida eyeglass manufacturing company, "the salespeople learned how to wine and dine because that's how they're treated by the hierarchy, by the President who you otherwise never saw." As a result, sales benefits from (1) customer dependence on the perquisites they make available, and from (2) the organization's dependence on customers, both of which for salespeople produce (1) the perks in the first place and (2) valuable alliances with customers that create further concessions by the organization.

THE DISPOSSESSED

Contrast the power of staff with the very different situation confronting other, line or "operational" work units. Operations, of course, entail different things in different organizations. In a manufacturing firm, operations include manufacturing itself, along with such functions as materials management, procurement, and distribution. In the mortgage banking industry, by contrast, operations encompass functions like underwriting, processing, funding, auditing, and customer solicitation.

Dependence

In contrast with staff, operational areas have almost *no* leverage with the organization, and therefore *none* of the power that leverage would bring. The reason is that Operations are utterly dependent on the organization, since their skills tend to have been developed in a way that has utility only where they are developed and currently applied, but nowhere else. For example, the job of assembling a central processing unit represents a task and skills that are indigenous to the computer operation that manufactures that CPU.

No Appreciation

In addition to their "indigenous" quality, the tasks performed by Operations tend to be the complex ones of developing and creating products. Complex tasks are hard to credit to any individual because they (1) diffuse decision making and other functions over an entire team, individual contributions to which may be indistinguishable from others, and thus hard to credit; (2) have a slow turnaround time, making project completion perhaps indeterminate and further impeding individual creditability for it; and (3) produce organizational benefits that are long-term, hard to quantify, and equally difficult to verify, much less to credit to any individual. Due to the unlikeliness of receiving credit for them, operational tasks endow their performer with neither independence from, nor dependence by, the organization, minimizing both the employee's external job mobility and internal power, respectively.

Costs without Revenues

Due also to the complexity of their tasks, operational areas require a huge infusion of physical equipment, facilities, and physical plant that, along with uncertain, long-term benefits, makes them look like cost centers. These uncertain, long-term benefits, of course, rest entirely upon staff, particularly marketing and sales.

According to the strategic planner working with the Florida eyeglass manufacturer, "if sales are not up to quotas, the blame is generally attributed to some failure of the product rather than to the salespeople's inability to sell it." The expense required to fix the product exacerbates the perception of operations as a cost center. For several reasons, then, operational areas are penalized *by the very importance and complexity of their tasks.*

Familiarity Breeding Contempt

Furthermore, unlike staff, and in contrast to their own individual outcomes, the skills and activities of operational areas tend to be eminently measurable and visible, based as they are on a product's nondefectiveness and conformity to specifications. Training, which for the most part is eluded by staff activity, can and, due to the complexity of operations, *must* cover virtually *every aspect* of operational activity, which also magnifies the expense of operations and reduces any mystery associated with it. Thus, where staff activity from the perspective of the organization appears to be almost cost-free yet heavily mythologized, operational activity seems to be expensive while fully manifest, if not mundane. As a result, operational areas enjoy none of the power that comes from the mystery of what one does.

Corporate Wallflowers

Finally, operational areas certainly enjoy none of the customer contact that produces for individual salespeople the alliances that can be parlayed into the extraction of concessions from the organization.

THE IMBALANCE OF POWER

As a result, the allocation of power between staff and operations tends to favor staff: the units that on behalf of the organization and for the benefit of operations perform the *simplest* tasks and the *least* important functions.

The strategic planner for the Florida eyeglass manufacturer observed that "from the meetings I went to, the glamour boys were the salespeople and especially the sales manager. During sales meetings, the atmosphere was that of a carnival or football pep rally. The production people were almost persona non grata: regarded as a necessary evil by the salespeople, easily replaced."

Confirmed a marketing director at the Southern California mortgage banking firm, the perception of upper management is that "salespeople bring in the money; underwriters, processors, funders, and auditors send money out. Therefore, management regards sales as the more important group."

ORGANIZATION GONE AWRY

How exactly does this misallocation of power undermine the organization?

Firstly, the internal purposes of work units are naturally expressed in their performance goals. Operational work units tend to have the long-term goals of product quality, and the task of maximizing it, that would doubtlessly best serve the organization. However, these are less powerful units, ultimately pursuing goals superimposed by more powerful units. For example, the information technology department in the Southern California door manufacturing operation had little alternative to authorizing the "wining and dining" by sales.

For more powerful departments, goals may come from their considerable options on the open market.

The Suicide Mission

Secondly, purposes of individuals and work units can be advanced by dictating the overarching mission of the corporation in a way that supports those purposes. Thirdly, influence over the corporate mission is provided by power over the organization.

Due to their power, staff personnel can be expected to influence the direction of the organization in a manner *very friendly* to their function, in a way that enhances their individual, open-market value. Given this value, and the portable skills and individual credit driving it, staff can readily escape any organizational costs of their goals, even catastrophic costs, by landing on their feet elsewhere, unharmed and none the worse for wear. As a result, this organizational expense can climb to the absurd degree observed by a management consultant in a very large, East Coast pharmaceutical company, making household and off-the-shelf medical products: specifically, within

the research and development department in one of the divisions . . . the research became so esoteric and they got so caught up in doing the research and even one researcher tried to outdo the other [so] that they *had not developed, however, a new product and brought a new product to market in 24 to 27 months.* So despite the fact that they had this really fast-moving high-tech R and D effort going on it wasn't producing anything for the company. They had won some awards for some new synthetic fibers and so forth but it wasn't getting into products. . . ."

One Detroit automaker apparently marched to disaster to the beat of a financial drummer. According to a management consultant,

Finance became the dominant path to power, and you had the succession of CEOs who came up on the finance side. Because they were managing the money all the time, they were blindsided by the Japanese car thing, whereas if they'd been a customer-driven organization and not tried to maximize income by planned obsolescence and not tried to sell style changes and tried to sell quality cars they wouldn't have gotten into so much trouble.

THE UNIVERSAL LANGUAGE OF SALES VOLUME

Volume Over Income

Many organizations march to the beat of their dominant Sales units. According to the marketing manager in the mortgage banking firm, we depend on huge sales volume. We had a situation where we handle people who aren't the cream of the crop. What happens is that the sales force accepts less than desirable loans from their customers, and when the company resells these things we lose our shirt. . . .

That meant that, when we lost a loan in default, couldn't sell it because it was a lousy loan, or whatever else, they still got paid. So they weren't tied to profitability at all.

Confirmed a manager in a nationwide communications company:

Sales objectives are measured based on quota attainment. Each unit of product is associated with a quota amount and possibly an additional bonus amount for strategic products.

The sales department is interested in keeping track of the quotas, *but not the revenue* [emphasis added] as registered by the billing system. Sales always looks for ways to compromise revenue and profit in exchange for sales volume.

Volume vs. Income

Thus, sales volume is certainly not the same thing as revenues, much less profitability.

Furthermore, sales volume can be pursued *at the expense of* revenues and profitability. For example, one ploy for maximizing volume is to harvest existing customers rather than develop new ones. As described by an ex-employee of a software developer in Southern California:

For the division I was with, their meat and potatoes comes from mainframe software. And sooner or later mainframe software is going to peter out. They really need to be developing other areas and other products. . . .

Salespeople will spend a lot more time as they put it "playing software police" than they would spend out there finding new customers and developing new sales on new products because those are easy sales. If they walk in and find that they've installed the product on a larger box (they call it) which is just a larger mainframe computer, now they owe us more money.

And the long-term goals of the company should be to develop new customers that will perpetuate more sales in the future rather than just try to suck as much out of the existing customer base as you can.

Volume without Income

It gets worse. In the Southern California door manufacturing operation,

they'll sell the product and then they'll end up giving no charges, they'll give them samples, or . . . it's a special customer who gets a special deal and basically they'll give them the biggest discounts I've ever seen. They have no discount structure. So they get the bonus on the full price, but we as a company are losing money or they'll give it away free.

Sales volume receives the highest priority because it is readily translated into a language universal among businesses, including future employers. By contrast, revenues and profits are too easily seen as "funny money," easily manipulated and thus untrustworthy. Thus, individual sales performance receives credit from high volume, while the firm is encumbered by neglect or even the sacrifice of revenues and profit.

In general, then, staff positions benefit from the portability and mystification of their tasks and skills. Accordingly, staff have ready access to the open market; prefer the short-term, narrow goals that afford them entree; and have the wherewithal to hoist these goals as the corporate mission.

We therefore find that for staff units the power to dictate the corporate mission is derived from open-market value that has little, if anything, to do with the importance to the firm, of either the environment they manage or the tasks they perform.

Due to the goals of its empowered work units, the organization may find itself, very quickly and irrevocably, deeply in trouble, along with its highly dependent, immobile line units.

FRIENDS IN HIGH PLACES

Short-term goals play very well at upper organizational levels that "officially" sanction the corporate mission. One direct reason is that staff and administration may in fact be the same people; at the Florida eyeglass manufacturing company, as elsewhere, "the guy who was being groomed as the heir apparent to the CEO position was the guy who rose from the sales force into management. Likely future promotions of salespeople by the next CEO perpetuate the myth that salespeople are infallible."

Other forces for supporting sales volume include the "selection" of compliant staff, through either the disenfranchisement or the elimination of sales or other staff supporting other goals. For instance, a cosmetic saleswoman working for a pharmaceutical company driven by nutritional sales was a strong advocate for expanding rather than milking the market. As a result, she indicated that "it was very frustrating working for them. . . . In the long run, the cosmetics department just dissolved. . . ."

Upper Management in Cahoots

Another reason for upper-level pursuit of sales volume is that it makes possible short-term revenues, which, for upper managers, maximize open-market value, an enticing goal because they enjoy and can exploit at least the same high degree of external job mobility as staff. Sources of job mobility for upper management include their expertise regarding organizational and so-called people skills, skills that are portable because they are esoteric, easily mystified, and applicable in virtually any functional area of any organization.

The Complicity of Owners

At higher levels still, particularly in this age of mergers-and-acquisitions, owners as well may focus on the short term, although their position directs their lascivious attention to short-term *profit*: an orientation that reflects opportunities both for profit-taking and to "beautify" the firm in order to market it for acquisition. The latter consideration is one good reason for the sudden lack of organizational interest by the CEO who had just sold the Florida eyeglass manufacturing company, as well as the nervousness of employees and customers of one nationwide insurance company

that has always been a mutual company, which means they've been owned by their policyholders.

They've made a decision to go public. A man was brought in to make the company public. Is this in the best interest of the employees or the key officers in the company? We've gone through reengineering to go public. The President/CEO can stand to make a lot of money, due to the stock options, from which he can benefit. Stock prices can go up. A lot of policyholder advocacy groups point out that they are getting a paltry number of shares. . . .

THE UNHOLY TRINITY

As is the case with staff positions, then, upper management and owners may place a high priority on short-term goals: the source of the short-term focus for which management has become legendary. This was precisely the focus of a particularly peripatetic individual described by a management consultant:

A guy that I've worked with, and I traced his career on three different assignments. He's on his third now, that I've seen. In all cases, he got out before the stuff hit the fan. He did some things, made him look good, but it was all built upon a foundation of sand and it fell apart, but he was gone before he could be tagged with the blame.

To summarize, then, crucial goals include short-term *volume* for staff, *revenues* for upper management, and *profit* for owners: our first but certainly not last look at disparate goals among corporate powers-that-be. While short-term volume is a matter of urgency to the staff pursuing it, equanimity to management, and indifference to owners, it receives upper-level toleration as a tool to keep staff happy. That is pretty much all that we need to know about the trappings of intraorganizational power.

To reiterate, then, based upon its very definition, power is assigned by the organization to its members in the most paradoxical, self-destructive, and perhaps even cruel fashion. The *greatest* power is assigned to members based precisely upon their *minimal* personal investment in the firm, *limited* basis for long-term loyalty to it, and *low probability* of defining productive goals for it, while the *least* amount of power is allotted to members from whom the firm is likely to receive the *greatest* personal investment, long-term loyalty, and productive goals. Given that power equates to influence over the organization's goals, then, it is small wonder that such goals are likely to be suicidal ones, and that organizations are built to fail.

THE FORGOTTEN WORKERS

Relative to the unholy trinity of staff, upper management, and ownership, the dependence of the forgotten operational employees was driven home in a particularly pithy way by a machinist, according to a management consultant working with a machine-tool manufacturing firm in the upper Midwest. In a meeting with upper management, the machinist said,

I don't want this plant to go out of business. I know everybody complains about me because I mouth off all the time, but I have a lot to lose if this company goes out of business. . . . I'm not going to find another job. You guys, you'll all be able to find another job. You have degrees; you have this; you have that; you have the other thing. That's why you hear me complain so much—because I want this place to work.

I want our machines to work when they get out there and they don't. That's the flat truth; the stuff we ship off our floor doesn't work. Because I know: I have to go out and fix it in the field; I have to repair it out there.

According to the consultant, the machinist "got to the core of what the issue was in that company: that people didn't listen to those who actually had their hands on the equipment. They were very isolated."

Inasmuch as all corporations are managed in this fashion, each enjoys the "success" of surviving against competition that is at least as bad, so the cost to product quality is confined externally, to customers. Costs are felt by the organization itself when the competition wakes up. This is precisely what happened to the U.S. auto industry in the 1970s.

ORGANIZATION AGAINST ITS MEMBERS

In one sense, the point of the discussion so far is that the goals that would best serve the organization are undermined by the goals foisted upon it by the individuals and groups most able to do so.

However, the more general and even more frightening point is that the organization's "ideal" goals, while subverted most immediately by its most powerful members, are ultimately unmatched by the individual goals of virtually *all of its members.*

Relative to its long-term needs, we will find that, in addition to the excessively short-term goals at upper levels, management at other levels tends to be too conservative, and that they along with supervisors can be depended upon to fob off purely work-unit goals onto the organization.

Neither can the organization count on its line and support staff. While these groups seem to take the long view, this view is contingent on their continued employment, which for them has the highest priority due to their lack of open-market value. Thus, their long-term vision for the organization is confined, understandably enough, to one in which they continue to play a role.

Moreover, virtually everybody has, through his or her position, a sufficient stake in current directions to resist any changes whatsoever, including those producing short-term disruption but long-term benefits to organizational survival and prosperity.

Finally, individuals have individual needs: for instance, social approval, power, or control. Given the priority of these needs over organizational ones to the member, the organizational interest most assuredly takes the proverbial backseat, as we will see in the next chapter.

It is clear that, at any given moment, the organization's "ideal," long-term needs depart from those of at least some members. We have seen that long-term profitability is ill-served by the short-term objectives of its powerful goal-setters. At other times, the organization may be best-served by a risky decision that would undermine middle managers, a technological change that would downsize some line and support staff, or other changes that would subvert the individual needs of some member or alter current power arrangements for everybody. Thus, at any moment, we can expect "ideal" organizational goals to fly in the face of some internal interests, and thus to be resisted from some quarter.

Since there is a permanent yet invisible divide between the purposes of the organization and those of the very individuals who comprise it, nobody within its membership is willing to, as it were, stand up for the organization. In contrast to its members, an organization is at a permanent, and fatal, disadvantage.

The problem for the organization was noted early on: the organization *does not exist.* Existence is reserved for the real people who, relative to their nonexistent organization, can monopolize the formulation of its goals, entirely to their own benefit. Hence, the nonexistent organization is on its own, with no help from the members on which it depends. Since it is built entirely from its members, and depends on unflagging support they will never provide, it is once again time to point out that the organization is *built to fail*.

Moreover, an organization requires a division of labor, both to provide its product or service and to perform the other functions needed to sustain itself, like administration and human resources, for instance. As we shall see, a division of labor is a source of conflict incompatible with an integrated organizational purpose and resolved, in the absence of an organizational voice, only by individual power, and not by organizational need.

As a result, like newborn turtles massacred on their way to the sea, most organizations don't make it beyond their infancy. Those that do, for reasons about to unfold before us, tend to live short, violent lives.

As we have just seen, the most immediate reason for the organization's demise is that it is built to fail by its very purpose: or, rather, by the purposes pursued by members to meet their needs. Of course, nobody is to blame for the multiplicity of individual needs, since they reflect the diversity needed to accomplish the tasks that justify the organization in the first place.

And nobody is to blame for the permanent divide between the needs of members and those of the organization: members are members *only* to pursue their interests. To more fully understand their motivation, and to look more closely at the organization's march to ruin, attention is now directed specifically to the organization's members, to the reasons for a misplaced faith in the organization's ability to rely upon them, and in particular to a science that has insisted upon ignoring them.

PART TWO

THE STRUCTURE AND CONTENT OF FAILURE

2

The Enemy Within:
Organizational Members
and Their Jobs

Self-interest speaks all sorts of tongues, and plays all sorts of roles,
even that of disinterestedness.
—Francois, Duc de La Rochefoucauld

There is an entire discipline devoted to the study of organizations. How
can this discipline turn a blind eye to the fact that organizations are designed to fail? One way is by neglecting the motivation and resulting
behaviors of organizational members: the very building blocks of organizational demise. In order to ultimately understand this demise, our purpose
in this chapter is to focus upon these individuals, and first of all upon the
reasons for prior neglect of them.

ORGANIZATIONAL SCIENCE, AND SCIENCE FICTION

To delve a bit into the philosophy of science, the study of people often
reflects social functionalism: the belief that *any* social arrangement, including our organization, develops because it *must* serve some social function.[23]
As an example, the function of youth gangs, as a surrogate family in the
absence of the real thing, provides a nonobvious and interesting explanation for an otherwise purely destructive social arrangement.

Because the appearance of such arrangements is automatically explained
by some social function, their functionality is assumed, and the validity of
functionalism itself is beyond evaluation and verification. If need be, a func-

tion can easily be concocted; if nothing else, organizations serve the "function" of keeping employees off the streets. To put it bluntly, functionalism explains nothing.

Functionalism derives its staying power from the belief in the ultimate survival and thus the social function of any social arrangement it describes. Regarding the subject at hand, functionalism rests upon the blissful unawareness of the fact that organizations are built to fail. One reason is concealment of various dysfunctionalities by blinders from none other than beliefs like functionalism itself. As a result, we are given the "political functionalist" argument that power arrangements within organizations are somehow adaptive to the environment, and, as we have seen, the results of these arrangements, in corporate mortality, that give the lie to this assertion.

The logical vacuum of functionalism may perhaps be best understood by looking at its underlying assumptions.

The Unreasoning Belief in Reason

Functionalism is the engine that drives the prior assumption of "teleology": the assumption that events collectively pursue, and achieve, some inner purpose. In this discussion, teleology is expressed in the belief that workplace events somehow advance organizational survival and prosperity.

Teleology is an expression of faith in advance and in the absence of any verification. By accepting and proposing consequences for this absence of verification, teleology is an implicit admission of ignorance.

Teleology tends to be expressed in the superstitious cant that "everything happens for a reason" and "things work out for the best." Everything *certainly* happens for a reason. However, whether things always work out "for the best" most assuredly depends upon one's point of view. Bankruptcy works out best for the pawnbroker; car accidents, for an HMO; death, for the mortician; and organizational demise, for the corporate raider.

The assumption here is that there are other interests in the organization. From their perspective, teleology is a distraction at best and, at worst, an invitation to inaction, if not connivance in disaster.

PERCEPTION AND POWER

Misplaced faith in the organization's innate purposiveness rests upon the widespread treatment of power, a term that, in general, tends to be bandied about rather loosely. As we saw, power is defined as the opposite of dependence within a very specific relationship between social actors. At first blush, it *seems* that the organization is well-served by an allocation of power that allows the empowered to handle the dependence of others.

However, since we are discussing human beings, we are discussing behavior *not* in response to the outside world but rather in response to a *perception* of the outside world. Thus, power is enjoyed *not* from creating dependence for others but rather from creating their *perception* of that dependence.

For example, salespeople enjoy power from an optical illusion created by their direct proximity to the creation of revenue, fostering in turn perceived dependence by others, which may have little or nothing to do with *actual* dependence. As a result, power may be ill-deserved for its individual beneficiary and dysfunctional for the organization. We may plunge into the perhaps intellectually intriguing but also ultimately circular discussion concerning whether perceived dependence is *itself* dependence, and whether the power from creating it is *itself* power. By entertaining these possibilities, we have succeeded only in further divorcing the organization from an allocation of power based upon the capacity of the recipient of that power to transact with the environment, and therefore from any lingering notion of functionality.

SCIENCE AND STATUS

An underlying reason to neglect the actual sources of power may have something to do with the social scientists who are guilty of such neglect.

Social scientists necessarily deal, in the speculative fashion required, with variables, like organizations themselves, that, to reiterate, *do not exist*. Speculation, in turn, is the prerogative of all participants in, and self-proclaimed experts over, the social process: lay as well as professional. Physical scientists, by contrast, deal with things like chemicals and falling apples that most certainly *do* exist. As a result, exploiting the realism that goes with the territory, physical scientists tend to claim, and social scientists tend to envy, the luxury of certainty and an exclusive grip upon "hard science" itself. To validate their own enterprise, social scientists often traffic in the unambiguous, causal vernacular used by their self-styled, "hard science" counterparts.

For this reason, organizational and other social scientists tend to cite unshakable causal relationships among equally ironclad variables; thus, "power" is lawfully related to "dependence," and the organization's "design" is dictated in no uncertain terms by its "environment." Reference to "perception" and "illusion" in the formula only muddies an otherwise elegant and simple relationship, invoking concepts with complex, uncertain, and often unpredictable mutual effects. Such effects clearly do not lend themselves to the high degree of certainty exuded by scientific laws.

To avoid revealing the uncertainty it would otherwise convey, we find that the human perceptual process is neglected in some of the world's most authoritative work in the field of organizational design. Instead, we find the implication that the organization, in some way, objectively "sees" and "knows" the environment.

It is this bedrock assumption of organizational omniscience that supports the patently insupportable belief that organizations are built to survive. To invalidate this belief, then, one of our tasks is to disprove this assumption.

In fact, we have already taken a giant leap toward doing so. As we have already seen from the formulation of a corporate mission, the organization responds to its environment not from some knowing essence but rather in ways dictated by individual members. We can recognize the distorted perceptions that govern the power of these individuals. To understand their *behavior*, our attention is now directed to those individuals themselves.

SELF-INTEREST AND DECISION MAKING

Sports fans can probably recall instances in which they or their peers greeted an adverse referee decision with howls of protest: and then listened with glee to hear the reversal of the decision greeted with equal venom by opposing fans. If questioned about their reaction, both groups of fans would probably respond with equal and uncompromising conviction in the correctness of their positions.

How can this be? How can the same set of information elicit two sincere, conflicting, and utterly self-serving reactions?

We begin with the assumption that all behavior is motivated: an unverifiable statement, since the appearance of behavior automatically implies some prior motive, but that is the nature of an assumption.

We can also make the general, reasonable, and in fact equally unremarkable (but shortly purposeful) observation that behavior is performed when conditions support it: for example, social behavior certainly requires other people. Thus, behavior requires both a *need*, from motivation, and an *opportunity*, from these supportive conditions.

Representing one example of a behavior is a decision. Representing one example of a decision, in turn, is the judgment by the sports fan.

If we want to understand the motive for a behavior, representing an excellent place to begin is by identifying the purpose of the behavior. Representing a *bad* way to identify this purpose, on the other hand, is by asking the person whose motive we want to understand.

For example, if asked about the purpose of making a decision, most people would probably respond "to make the correct decision." That response represents a "socially desirable" response: a response that plays well with the listener and accords with the decision maker's self-esteem.

RATIONALITY VS. RATIONALIZATION

Unfortunately, although (or, more accurately, *because*) a socially desirable response feels good to all concerned, it is also a delusional response; this is the problem with self-reported purposes and motives in general. If the purpose in making a decision is to arrive at some objective verity, we would see consensus between fans of opposing teams, based on their common application of a single set of objective criteria.

Instead, the conflict we observe between them suggests that the actual purpose in making a decision is to make not the *right* one but rather only the objectively justifiable one that can support other, personal goals that have a higher priority to the decision maker. For a sports fan, the other, higher-priority agenda is the success of his or her favored team.

A decision can accomplish objective justification along with other goals because (1) it relies on the information-gathering process of perception, (2) perception allows for considerable discretion, and (3) discretion can be exercised to advance these other purposes.

Perception allows for discretion in many ways. As a prior process by the time we respond to it, perception can be reenacted simply by imagining the event. Imagination is discretionary simply because we can choose what to imagine and how to imagine it. Moreover, the difference between imagination and the event itself is directly proportional to the *uncertainty* of decision information.

In the case of the sporting event, information may be uncertain due to its speed, the questionable physical position of participants, the uncertain effects of their actions, and so on. Since uncertain information can help perception achieve various perceiver goals, it is small wonder that sports fans invariably "see" what they want to see.

Research as well as our own experience suggest that decision making, like behavior in general, is highly motivated. For example, research subjects have expressed high regard for the intrinsic merits of undercompensated tasks; the purpose is to elevate their self-esteem by characterizing their role as voluntary and empowered, rather than constrained.[24] Group members have expressed clear, sensory misjudgments to gain acceptance by other members.[25] Personnel have morally espoused socially irresponsible behavior to pursue organizational profit.

Let us return to the observation that a specific behavior requires a *need* and an *opportunity*. To recapitulate: the *need* for discretion by the sports fan is created by team loyalty, while the *opportunity* is created by the uncertainty of decision information. The point that concerns us here is the fact that, regarding both the need and the opportunity to address the other purposes of decision making, the sporting event positively *pales* in relation to the organization.

Enter the Organization

As we saw, the decision agenda of the sports fan is dictated by team loyalty. In organizations, the agenda is to advance the job of the decision maker. According to organizational theorist James Thompson, the job provides the individual with an arena or *sphere of action* [Thompson's emphasis] in which to seek solutions to his career problems, and thus to meet the demands placed on him by the social system. Whatever value he places on occupational-career achievement relative to other dimensions of his life, these other dimensions can seldom be satisfied without some satisfactory solution to the occupational-career problem.[26]

The job is so critical, then, that it creates a set of needs that must be addressed before addressing other needs. We may summarily refer to these needs as "self-interest." This is *not* to engage in the patently circular notion that self-interest represents an element of "human nature" to the point that even altruism is pursued only to enhance self-esteem; rather, it is simply the claim that self-interest motivates career goal-orientation through organizational membership, and nothing more. From this, we conclude that organizations present a pressing need for self-interested decisions: certainly an obvious conclusion, but one with the dire consequences that will unfold in the remainder of this discussion.

The *opportunity* for self-interest is created by the massive uncertainty of information facing the organizational decision maker. This information is uncertain because decisions in organizations typically concern some aspect of collective effectiveness, which itself is subjective (see Appendix 2) and reflects in turn indeterminate: (1) *responsibility*, referring to the identity of performers, to their "inclusiveness" (e.g., group vs. individual), and their number; (2) degree of *performance* by those seen as involved; (3) *conditions* under which this performance took place; (4) *benchmarks* for comparatively evaluating it; (5) its *timing* and *duration*; (6) its *effects*, including interaction with other variables; (7) methods for *measuring it*; and (8) *evaluation* and *interpretation* of performance.

To reiterate, then, decisions in organizations have massive implications for job and career issues, along with a high level of uncertainty; due to this nexus of need and opportunity, these are largely self-interested decisions. As with all decisions, *explicit* motives for them most assuredly must be "socially desirable" ones. This is particularly the case within organizations, in order to persuade (1) others, and derive the external support needed to surreptitiously advance self-interest, as well as (2) the self, intent, as it always is, on a high level of self-esteem. To be self-interested, *while* socially desirable, individual decisions in organizations must appear to be, and therefore must be presented as, *not* self-interested: rather, as *organizationally-responsible*. In many cases, then, organizational responsibility is espoused in proportion to its absence as a motive.

In a nutshell, power is handed over to individuals ostensibly as some sort of subliminal exchange for pursuing the organization's interest, by handling its dependence on them. In reality, we now recognize that power enables its beneficiaries to pursue *self*-interest, by nurturing and exploiting the apparent dependence of others upon them. And as we saw in the opening chapter, self-interest can be made to undermine the organizational interest in direct proportion to the individual power to do so.

In so many words, then, the most committed and, as a result, probably the most successful aspirants to powerful positions are likeliest to view the organizational interest as a virtual plaything, to be manipulated to personal gain. And often, to maximize self-esteem, this manipulation is subconscious. As a result, the organization's leaders may be *the very ones who are the least likely to understand its interests*. The organization is therefore doomed by *the very reasons* for which its members join it and seek to advance within it.

This issue will bedevil us throughout the discussion. For our first, critical exposure to it, and despite their putative other-directedness, these self-interested decisions *form the basis for the design and purpose of the organization*.

OCCUPATIONAL CHAUVINISM

It seems that the picture painted here concerns some shamelessly self-interested machinations to distort the organization in order to suit individual purposes. In fact, that is *precisely* what is suggested: organizational members do in fact act in this fashion. However, they generally do so without realizing it.

The scenario probably begins long before the organization enters the picture, when its future member first decides upon a career. There may be many reasons for that choice, but included among them is the belief (or if the choice meets other purposes, perhaps the rationalization) that the career is important, both to society and to the organization trying to meet society's goals. Through education and other training, these beliefs may be reinforced and enhanced, if not introduced in the first place.

As a result, people enter organizations prepared to entertain a certain delusion of grandeur about (1) their career, (2) the job through which they will pursue their career, and (3) the work unit in which they will do their job. In a university, for instance, according to a department chairperson,

historians think that history is the be-all, end-all; the biologists think the same thing [about biology]; the humanities think that they're more central, that they're the core of the institution—they think the business school is just some Johnny-come-lately that doesn't have any real theory. . . . Fine Arts thinks that if we don't have a Fine Arts program then we are not a liberal arts undergraduate institution.

According to a consultant, demonstrating most sharply the chauvinism of various occupations, the classic war that gets fought in most organizations pits the functional people, who decide what gets done and how much, in what quantity, for how many dollars, against the product people. . . . If people are in the product organization they believe that all the decisions should be made by people in the product organization. You take those same people and put them in a functional job they'll think the function ought to decide what's going to be done. So it doesn't have anything to do with any objective reality out there in the world; it depends on where they are in the organization.

Due to "occupational chauvinism," other work areas seem to serve as either a source of input or a target for output, and are referenced in language that is entirely centered on the work area perceiving them. For example, to an Information Systems Department, everything else is a source of "data," while to Human Resources, everyone else is an undifferentiated mass of "incumbents," each with some sort of "job description."

Moreover, other areas are evaluated, and probably negatively, based on criteria that have importance to and favor the evaluator; for instance, humanities professors opine that their business school counterparts lack "any real theory," as we have seen, while business school faculty tend to deride the Ivory Tower irrelevance of their peers in the humanities and other areas.

Thus, each work unit regards itself as the Center of the Organizational Universe. Each work unit is also surrounded by other equally self-absorbed work units; as a result, it is unlikely to receive the obeisance it feels it deserves from others. Thus, each work unit has reason to assume that others lack full understanding of: (1) the importance it has assigned to itself, (2) the organizational function providing that importance, and thus (3) the organizational mission subsuming that function.

OCCUPATIONAL OMNISCIENCE

What this means is that we suddenly find ourselves entertaining the dizzying conclusion that each work unit honestly believes that it *solely understands the corporate mission.* Therefore, with any opportunity to do so, each work area *would claim the prerogative to define the organization's mission.* The result of this hypothetical opportunity would be a corporate mission that defers to the self-assigned importance claimed by the work unit. Hence, it is no surprise that the Fine Arts Department regards its role as pivotal if not definitional to the mission of a liberal arts undergraduate institution.

In the business world, of course, we now recognize from the previous chapter that the opportunity to define a corporate mission is more than hypothetical. We saw that work units are able to cash in on their own successful pursuit of power by hoisting individually beneficial purposes as, ultimately, organizationally suicidal missions.

We *now* see that this input: (1) arises not from contrivance but rather from the values that accompany career choice, (2) is inevitably self-interested because it is consistent with that choice, yet (3) is ultimately sincere because it expresses those values.

Thus, we find that the organization's mission is determined *not only* by the allocation of power among competing work areas but also with the right to do so experienced as a virtual *entitlement*. As a result, the organization is inevitably steered *in the wrong direction*, for *all of the wrong reasons*, by people who feel *entirely justified in doing so*, and *vindicated* for doing so successfully. Small wonder, then, that the organization's interest is so easily undermined by members, since the act *is concealed from the very people engaging in it*.

The search for evidence need extend no farther than our university business school departments. Meetings in these departments are for the putative purpose of enhancing educational capabilities, but their actual function reduces to pure political plotting: to what, from the departmental perspective, has been described to the author as to "serve our interests."

Accordingly, the output of these meetings includes curriculum proposals that meet an official objective of enhancing education but are dictated by departmental rather than educational priorities: a clear juxtaposition between the objective justification required and the hidden agenda actually dictating decision making. One can only imagine the generality of this chicanery if it enlists the commitment of the very organizations that are *devoted to understanding and improving our organizations*.

JOB AND ORGANIZATIONAL MISDESIGN

In sum, a corporate mission is defined to accommodate pre-existing departmental goals. Furthermore, the department is designed to enhance the designer's *individual* goals. This is the process for converting the occupationally chauvinistic, "operative" goal to an "operational" or actionable goal. According to a management consultant, "People tend to design their own jobs or their subordinates' jobs to enhance their positions." To accomplish this,

you've got to have a lot of people reporting to you; that's one way of boosting your job; that's another way of getting your pay hiked.

Or you might want to define the job in such a way that in fact other people are dependent on you. They have to come to you for permission . . . to get resources that you control. Or they have to come to you to get your buy-in, or your concurrence. There's a great deal of that. . . .

So people will tend to stretch their job descriptions as much as they can so that they are doing things that are seen as having some central importance. . . .

And usually this is done unconsciously. Most people don't sit down and deliberately strategize about how to design jobs for their own personal benefit; it's just that their own personal benefit colors the way they see the needs of the organization. So they can't distinguish between their own needs and what the needs of the organization are. . . .

As is the case with the corporate mission, then, job design becomes an expression of occupational values and priorities. According to the management consultant, it may also express more personal preferences:

There's a natural tendency for people to design jobs to enhance their own personal needs, as opposed to fitting the functional needs of the organization.

Their own needs for control, for example. So they'll have all these jobs reporting to them, because they've got big control needs. It's not because the betterment of the organization is served by having all these people reporting to me, centrally, or having to come to me to get the resources. But it does serve my needs to be central, in control.

Jobs are thereby designed not for effective task performance but rather only to satisfy the power and other needs of the individual designing them. The results cannot be to the benefit of the organization.

Moreover, with the intended growth in individual influence, we find an expansion in the number of dependent individuals. This has several paradoxical effects.

Specialized Incompetence

Consider the phrase "computer genius." Typically, this is an accolade, bestowed in recognition of getting computers to do what they're supposed to do, by someone to whom this skill is so esoteric that it represents a cause for superlatives. By "geniuses" themselves, this task is recognized as simply the application of straightforward knowledge, in more or less a "cookbook" fashion, that represents part of a day's work.

What this expresses is the general willingness to cede expertise over an unfamiliar enterprise simply because, to those lacking it, familiarity is so inconceivable that it is assumed to reflect singular abilities. Over a familiar enterprise, people are less charitable. Thus, for example, due to its visibility and familiarity, and despite the arguably greater difficulty of transacting with the technology, we never hear about a "television genius" or about an "air-conditioning genius," although perhaps we should.

In essence, then, this is a testimonial by someone who has no knowledge of the skill for which it is given, and therefore with absolutely no competence to give it. By contrast, those who *are* computer literate know that they aren't geniuses (although they probably keep that knowledge to themselves). Paradoxically, then, expertise is demonstrated only by knowing that it is *not* expertise. Everybody else knows too little not to be awestruck.

In an organization, the claim of expertise is relatively easy to come by: it derives simply from the authority to make the claim, and to compel deference by others. The collateral authority to design other jobs buttresses the claim by ensuring the dependence of other jobholders, so that they don't acquire enough information to *dispute* the claim. Designing other jobs further enhances the perception of this expertise, by suggesting the deep level of understanding needed to identify, organize, and allocate individual responsibilities.

Another, simpler, and more direct benefit of perceived expertise is the license to design other jobs to participate in procedures that force incumbents to in some way genuflect to the designer: in effect, honoring oneself, like awarding oneself with a graduate degree. Sooner or later, someone is bound to assume that the genuflection is deserved.

Thus, job design becomes a tool both in creating and in mythologizing the expertise of the job designer. Of course, given that the claim lacks any objective rationale or validation, this "expertise" becomes a guise for incompetence. Given overreliance on it, this incompetence is multiplied accordingly. And given the power of the person wielding it, it becomes incompetence run amok.

For the organization, job design is but one among many sources of incompetence. For the observer, this insight into job design provides an early window into the organizationally destructive effects of individual self-interest.

In the case of underlings, incompetence is more explicit, and intentional.

The Design of Incompetence

Researchers have long noted that decision makers inevitably tend to be dwarfed by the magnitude of the decision task, for reasons summarized earlier as information-processing limits or "bounded rationality."[27] The problem may be the disability of decision makers or the unpredictability and, according to recent thinkers, the chaotic nature of reality itself:[28] in either case, decision makers tend to view decision information as uncertain. Particularly disturbing is that information in organizations *inevitably* and *overwhelmingly* dwarfs the capabilities of decision makers because of *the very manner in which their jobs are designed and defined.*

Each job is designed as a narrow "specialization." This ostensibly serves the "rational" purposes of applying expertise, coordinating that expertise with other positions, and thus realizing the efficiencies of competence and routine.

The Multiplication of Incompetence

However, there are other intended effects, some of which will be explored later on. For now, attention is devoted to one function of specialization, which is to fractionate jobs in order to make them sufficiently narrow to maximize, in relation to the job designer, (1) the dependence of each individual jobholder and (2) the number of such dependent individuals. As a result, each jobholder becomes increasingly remote from departmental purposes and ignorant about how to facilitate their achievement.

Moreover, since jobs are designed in response to the needs of the job designer, growth within a work unit is dictated internally, and not by the needs of the external environment. Thus, a growing work unit is likely to confront an unchanged rather than an expanding environmental interface.

Within that unchanged interface, each member within a burgeoning population simply deals with a smaller and smaller portion. Thus, an expanding work unit constricts the information accessed by each member to deal with the outside world.

As a result, individual decision makers within a growing department are increasingly eclipsed by the requirements of the collective decision task. Lacking the necessary information, decision makers are forced to rely on one another to acquire it. We find, then, a high degree of interdependence among information-starved personnel.

The problem, as summarized by a management consultant, is that

you create these jobs—these specialized jobs. Therefore, you have to have a lot of interdependency. You reward people for doing their specialized tasks, and they lose sight of the big picture. They begin to do what you're rewarding rather than what's in the organization's interest because they're not asked to think about that anymore. . . .

I think the problem is that people don't see the big picture and they don't see the simple important realities about what they do. And so they go along with all the baloney because they're afraid someone's going to find out they don't know.

More profoundly, a department growing in this immanent fashion doesn't simply *conceal* the big picture: it *loses* its part of the big picture, by evolving into a veritable collection of unconscious automatons.

By viewing political infighting as a "war," the multiplication of jobs represents both a requirement for and a perquisite of any political "victory" by a work unit: in a phrase, along with promulgating their individual goals as organizational ones, triumphant units get to grow.

To reiterate, the reason for this growth is not the "rational" one of matching the importance of the external environment that it must manage;

the reason for this growth is simply that the work unit can now successfully insist upon it.

Domination by Incompetence

The organization thereby finds itself dominated by work units that grow to the point where its members lose all sense of their organizational purpose, are forced to rely on limited information for their day-to-day function, and are dependent for that information on other personnel who probably don't have it. One way to look at this is that the organization has in essence *grown into a state of ineffectiveness.*

Another way to look at this is that the organization is captained by work units who perform this function *badly.* For members responsible, this is perfectly acceptable, since the whole arrangement leaves their individual goals unmolested. Hence, for example, they have no quarrel with the pursuit of sales volume and abandonment of profit. For its part, however, the organization in the process has taken another step toward its own destruction.

Thanks in part to the pell-mell growth of dominant work units, and to the increasing volume of insistence upon their goals, other work units tend to develop as "support" units. Increasingly, the entire organization slips into an orbit around its dominant units. This is the origin of the organization's real structure: the one that is missing from the organization chart.

The employee in the Southern California door manufacturing operation observed, in reference to its all-powerful sales force, that

it's not so much that they dictate how or what to do; we budget a certain amount for sales and it's just kind of sales-generated. If they meet the quotas, everything's great, and if they don't, then everything's bad. It's up to them.

So they, basically, have a lot of power, meaning that, if they do extremely well, and they go over budget in a month, then basically they can do what they want or say what they want or ask for anything they want. But everybody else is supposed to make sure that we support them, so that they can meet our requirements.

It's almost like a presumed assumption that you just go along with what they want. Nobody ever contradicts them. It's like, if they want to go golfing and spend thousands of dollars that's great, that's fine, it's all approved, and it's paid for. But if somebody in the company needs a new printer and it's a hundred dollars, it's a major ordeal to get it pushed through.

In a nutshell, this captures the entire meaning of power, and its effect on the *actual* structure of the organization. By examining its actual structure, we understand fully that the organization is piloted by some of its least efficient or least organizationally responsible decision makers.

CONCLUSION

Within the first two chapters, we have raised many dispiriting and fore-boding issues, with many varied reasons. In the inevitable search for a single, "bottom-line" cause, one strong possibility is that there is *no position responsible for the design of the organization*: to repeat, *there is no one responsible for organizational design*.

This sounds like a horrific oversight; after all, its design is absolutely critical to the organization, and to its success. To an organization, its design is the same thing as is the physiology to a living organism. The design gives the organization its repertoire and its capabilities; it is both the current identity and the future potential of the organization.

On the other hand, while costly, neglect of organizational design is perfectly understandable. The organization forms in order to *do* something: not simply to display itself as a capable, well-qualified assemblage. Furthermore, as the organization develops, these purposes can change. Thus, the organization places a higher priority on the tasks that it sets out to accomplish than on the alignment or realignment of its components in order to accomplish them.

Nevertheless, there is cold comfort in one's understanding the neglect of organizational design; if anything, this makes such neglect a natural, if not inevitable, feature of the organization. And it is the naturally-occurring rather than aberrant status of its debilitations that dooms our organizations.

In the next chapter, we will look more closely at the amazing and destructive ways in which the organization designs itself.

3

Dressed for Success, Qualified to Fail: Staffing the Organization

Beware, as long as you live, of judging people by appearances.
—Jean de La Fontaine

THE PRIVATE WORLD OF THE FOUNDER

Along with its considerable promise, of course, a start-up firm requires a large and continuing infusion of cash. What distinguishes the start-up firm for the founder, therefore, is a tantalizing level of potential gain, along with the enormous risk that represents the evil twin of opportunity. As a result, The Founder, of course, is painfully cognizant of the *risk-seeking* nature of the new firm.

At the same time, The Founder probably has a personal vision about making the whole thing work. As the sole occupant in this intersection of vulnerability, promise, and wisdom, The Founder feels qualified to know what it takes to succeed and avoid failure, to know that others lack this perspective, and therefore to be *highly resistant* to any input from them: hence, we find the "micromanager" refusing to delegate responsibilities.

At the same time, delegation of duties is, at some point, likely to be loudly recommended by deteriorating task performance, reasons for which include an expanded interface with the outside world and too few people to handle that interface.

Furthermore, at this stage, the organization's "personnel" are likely to include The Founder's family members, close friends, or other associates, all of whom probably benefit from favoritism, given the organization's lack of alternatives, and who, themselves, have signed on to an uncertain firm perhaps due to their own disqualifications for more established (and more selective) operations. Thus, in addition to a steadily encroaching environment, another reason for the poor performance of tasks at this stage is the underqualification of personnel responsible for them.

One obvious source of dysfunction at this point is *nepotism*: favoritism based solely upon shared family membership. Nepotism may reward underachievement as well as underqualification. For example, according to an ex-employee of a radio parts manufacturing firm in New York,

the boss was an elderly man who had two sons, [one of whom] kept busy making himself look busy. He was always going from one part of the office to another, or to the factory, and he was never really doing anything. . . . Here was a guy occupying space, getting presumably a good salary, and not contributing anything— and only because he was a son.

Nepotism is maintained by family loyalty; by a desire to keep rewards close to home and thus available; and by overestimation of ostensibly shared traits due to familiarity with them or to The Founder's egocentric reasons to inflate them. According to various management consultants, nepotism is maintained also by trust, the ease of control, and of course, frugality.

Nepotism can remain a source of dysfunction well into whatever future awaits the organization; for now, however, the problem is that tasks are easily overwhelmed by the environment and by incompetence.

Regardless of its source, failure to adequately perform certain tasks has now transformed them into uncontrolled, urgent ones.

FORMALIZED INCOMPETENCE

So, sooner or later, The Founder, albeit reluctantly, begins the process of off-loading control over these functions. As a micromanager, The Founder is overextended by these other tasks, and probably too inundated with them to have much knowledge about or residual interest in them. Ironically, then, immersion in an overabundance of tasks ultimately reduces the very knowledge for which it is intended: relative, let us say, to delegation, and to systematic, informed consultation, coordination, and control.

Generally, in cases of ignorance, decisions tend to be aided by decision shorthands or "heuristics," which are rules of thumb, among which is reliance on *precedent* and *familiarity*.[29] In delegating functions, precedent and familiarity are provided by people who have been previously responsible for them, however informally.

Another result of ignorance in delegating responsibility is, of course, an incapacity for informed evaluation of the new hire. The new hire may exploit this inability by manipulating the perception of his or her previous responsibility.

Not surprisingly, people tend to claim credit for success and to disown responsibility for failure: a phenomenon called the "self-serving bias."[30] Obvious reasons for this bias in organizations include not only self-esteem but also future opportunities from a display of competence.

Given the lack of formalization at this stage, one's responsibility for poor performance may be disowned by claiming that it resulted from insufficient control, or lack of formal authority, which therefore must be increased in order for performance to improve. Given the credulity of The Founder over functions beyond a self-selected sphere of influence, this expansion of formal authority may sound like a perfectly reasonable request.

Therefore, one amazing and ironic consequence of poor performance is the tendency to off-load and extend responsibility for it to the very personnel who (1) were probably unqualified for their jobs to begin with and (2) are able to claim "previous responsibility" solely from their inevitable *failure to do their jobs effectively!* To repeat: incompetent task performance often results in authority *for the very personnel guilty of that incompetence!*

This is precisely what happened in a start-up healthcare company. According to a former medical management employee there, the company retained a consultant

to set up tracking systems for all of the doctors in the groups that we contract with and [she] did a lot of work on the regulation part, dealing with the department of corporations and stuff.

She implemented this whole project, planning, did all this stuff, and it *didn't work*. Everything that could go wrong did go wrong. It didn't get started on time; it didn't work; the systems were not designed properly. They paid the consulting company probably close to five or six hundred thousand dollars for her time plus other people's.

And then, they *hired her*! And she's still there; I just talked to some people the other day. She's still there, running the show. Things are still messed up. . . .

Astoundingly, then, the organization may formalize those responsibilities that it performs particularly badly, in sequential order of how badly it performs them. As a result, the organization is likely to *formalize its very incompetence.*

Institutionalized Incompetence

Furthermore, by incorporating these additional individual responsibilities into the formal organizational design, the function represented by these responsibilities has now been elevated to the status of a full-fledged "interest," representing, defended by, and thus maintained by, an entire "interest group." For instance, we can expect the aforementioned systems analyst to defend her position against any change, and along with that position, to maintain her nonproductive way of filling it.

Additionally, the organization has embarked on a process for making these responsibilities permanent, or "institutionalizing" them. The result is that, as part of ongoing organizational procedures, the inappropriate way of fulfilling this function will henceforth be transmitted explicitly and formally to future employees. The systems consultant will no doubt favor successors with her "knowledge," such as it is. Rather than transformed and made more effective in the process of receiving a formal home, as evidently hoped, this responsibility, and the inept way of fulfilling it, are instead, now and forever, *set in stone*.

The underqualification of personnel charged with the organization's most urgent tasks represents only the immediate problem. What makes this process particularly troubling is that this inept group represents what in effect is the organization's first layer of management. Eventually, these people will represent the organization's "upper management," with enormous policy-making power, and the ability to wield it not merely as an interest group but rather as the organization's "dominant coalition." Beyond that, they will represent the archaeologically deepest layer of the organization's culture, with influence, through cultural transmission, upon the values, beliefs, and attitudes of any future generations of managers: assuming, of course, that the organization displaying this sort of dysfunction lasts long enough to *have* future generations of managers.

Given the immediacy and profundity of its incompetence, however, an organization in this position is probably on borrowed time, and faces a mercifully rapid demise.

CREATING INCOMPETENCE

On the other hand, some organizations begin their lives by doing things rather well: quite commonly, in fact, which may be why they have survived to this point. Lacking essential incompetence, these organizations make up for lost time by *creating* incompetence. In these cases, the organization's survival, and perhaps prosperity, make its self-destruction highly visible, familiar to the rest of us, agonizing for the victim, and wasteful and tragic for all concerned.

Professionalization and Failure from Success

The process through which incompetence is created has been described by a management consultant:

One thing that destroys organizations is the failure-of-success syndrome, whereby companies that have developed a track record of success ... develop a myth ... that the reason we're successful is because of the way we do things here and therefore we won't change a damn thing because we're doing things right. ... "We're not going to listen to anyone. ..."

And they'll point to their past record as the evidence for that. And then, when the world changes, they fall on their faces.

As a process of rendering certain behaviors permanent, then, it stands to reason that institutionalization tends to resist change. The catastrophic consequences were summarized by another management consultant, according to whom IBM "almost failed in the personal computer market, because all of the internal planning and systems that it had institutionalized made it impossible for them to get from A to B in a certain amount of time."

The reflexive nature of institutionalization was captured in a perhaps apocryphal story told by an ex-employee about the head of a software manufacturing firm in Los Angeles:

His aunt used to cook roast beef and would cut the ends off, and always cut the ends off and never knew why. He never knew why and he finally asked her "Why do you cut the ends off?" "Well, that's how my mother used to do it."

Finally, he went and talked to the great-aunt and said "Why do you cut the ends off the roast beef? It doesn't make any sense. They're perfectly good." "Well, I cut the ends off my roast beef because my oven was too small and I couldn't fit it in." The process was perpetuated way past its useful life.

The Management of Incompetence

Apparently, a fundamental problem created by the process of institutionalization resides in the very definition of management itself. *Webster's Dictionary* defines "manage" as "to control the movement or behavior of." To demonstrate this control, the behavior subjected to it is defined as microscopically as possible. Hence, through institutionalization, management evolves as a process of identifying, authorizing, and monitoring highly specific behaviors. These behaviors have now become "procedures." It turns out that these behaviors may have had little if anything to do with the organization's success to this point.

It may have been that, while the behaviors at one point may have been appropriate, they were appropriate only for a previous context, denying them current suitability and lending weight instead to such behaviors as openness to, analysis of, and responsiveness to the organization's environment. Alternatively, it may be that the personnel performing these sacrosanct behaviors did so in a manner that resists such a microscopic focus, yet in fact deserves the bulk of the credit: for example, in a manner that was interactive, proactive, or creative. Or it may be that the behaviors were transient proxies for such creditable qualities as improvisation, spontaneity, serendipity, and other sources of resistance to procedure—resistance that would be *destroyed* by institutionalization.

A management consultant describes the process through which institutionalization destroyed the essence of the functions that were formalized, in "Pharmanox," a Southern California pharmaceutical company:

People are thinking about what is the "Pharmanox" way and "don't we need to make some rules and policies so that things are done the 'Pharmanox' way" and the result of that is that's *not* the "Pharmanox" way. The "Pharmanox" way is *not* to have lots of rules. . . . I've talked to people who say, "I want out now. This is no fun anymore. . . ."

It started a long time ago. When there were a hundred employees in the company, one day they made a rule, that when you were going on a sales trip and took a hundred dollars out of petty cash you had to sign for it, because you never had to before. And people said, "This is ruining the organization."

Summarized another consultant, an organization tends to

become increasingly rigid. What gets left out of the picture is that in the past, they have been very adaptive; they may have done things in a lot of different ways; there was no particular way that they did things that was responsible for their success. *But they felt the concept that there was*: that "we were successful because we're so good in the way we've done things and therefore we're not going to change anything. We're going to continue doing things in this particular way because we've always done things that way, and we've always been successful."

So organizations tend to routinize or codify or institutionalize things that end up being the wrong things.

Therefore, as one of its consequences, institutionalization may clearly obliterate the very behaviors responsible for the organization's one-time success. In addition, institutionalization as a result may devalue, disenfranchise, demotivate, and ultimately drive out the people responsible for those behaviors.

Moreover, institutionalization may select the very people who will help bring *down* the organization: the "Preservationists," charged with identifying, authorizing, and enforcing the organization's misbegotten procedures.

According to a consultant, a key element of institutionalization is that

the people who then advance are the people who don't rock the boat. They don't bring in new ideas. What they do is enforce the way things were done in the past: supposedly, the way things have been done in the past. What they do is they stop any innovation. They stop things from being done in a different way or a more adaptive way. . . .

So, systematically, there's a selection bias that enters into the organization that ends up staffing senior, powerful, influential positions with people who dislike change and dislike uncertainty and hold onto for dear life the tradition—the way they've always done things.

We have now opened a veritable can of worms.

Let us take a closer look at the organization's insistence on hiring its least qualified managers.

MANAGEMENT MYTHOLOGY

One way of hiring managers is through promotion. And, as we are about to see, one problem with promoting people into management is that the individual doing the hiring knows next to *nothing* about the responsibilities of the job. Truly.

Moreover, this ignorance is well-concealed, since the person doing the hiring is likely to talk a good game, by entertaining some popular misconceptions that pass for real knowledge about management.

The Myth of "Common Sense"

For one thing, management is often seen, generally by none other than managers themselves, as simply a matter of "common sense." If this assumption were valid, and given widespread managerial neglect of more systematic decision tools, we would be awash in wildly successful businesses, rather than picking through the carnage revealed in horrifying corporate mortality rates.

Management is a task that involves knowledge, of the many variables to be anticipated or recognized, relationships among them, results of these relationships, and how to intervene to get the best possible results. This knowledge is a far cry from the heavy-handed simplemindedness of "common sense."

The Myth of "Intuition"

Management is also seen as the product of "intuition," which represents a shorthand for failure to *learn* management knowledge. The results of management based on such lack of learning can be found in every harebrained decision that fails to apply the experience of others. Feeding this tendency is a view of management based only upon *personal* "experience." There is, of course, no gainsaying the value of on-the-job experience; however, in the absence of information from the experience of others, personal experience often becomes simply a guarantor of habit, bias, and ignorance.

The Myth of the Management "Artiste"

Finally, management has been characterized as an "art," which is the self-deluded lament of anyone venturing into a task while lacking any qualifications for it. As suggested earlier, and as seems to be the case with sales or for that matter any interpersonal skill, management skill derives considerable cachet from the mystery exuded by the fact that it is internal and invisible, and applied to unmeasurable interpersonal activity. Therefore, as is clearly the case with staff positions, management produces power solely from the perception and overestimation of it.

THE PRACTICE OF MANAGEMENT

In contrast to these half-baked qualifications, management is a serious practice, one that justifies an entire discipline taught in school and complemented with training in executive development programs; in the absence of such preparation, management is performed badly enough on the job to produce organizational failure on the grand scale we observe.

Probably no one has devoted more serious attention to the practice of management than Peter Drucker, according to whom the task entails

specific management skills which pertain to management, rather than to any other discipline. . . . As a specific discipline, management has its own basic problems, its own scientific approaches, its own distinct concerns. . . . Management is a practice rather than a science. In this, it is comparable to medicine, law, and engineering. It is not knowledge but performance. Furthermore, it is not the application of common sense, or leadership, let alone financial manipulation. Its practice is based both on knowledge and on responsibility.[31]

There are many ways of defining organizational management. The conventional, textbook definition includes the tasks of planning, organizing, directing, and controlling. To better focus organizational management on the response of employees, we may define this function as the process of motivating, coordinating, controlling, and representing the behavior of subordinates.

The knowledge cited by Drucker concerns the issues likely to be faced by the manager in performing these tasks, the complex and highly interactive variables these issues represent, and techniques for handling these variables. The skills cited by Drucker include the self-presentation, interpersonal, and organizational skills needed to effectively confront those issues, handle those variables, and employ those techniques.

The point, then, is that the knowledge and skills entailed by management are both specific and inestimable.

THE MALPRACTICE OF MANAGEMENT

The purposes of undervaluing management reflect the purposes of managers themselves, given, by dint of experience, their seemingly exclusive prerogative to define the management function. These purposes are to democratize and at the same time to monopolize the management function: to make it easily conferred and, thereafter, impossible to dislodge, which works quite well for the objectively unqualified manager. Moreover, as a function of experience, management decisions are made to appear immune from criticism by others: including the decision to define management itself in this uninformed fashion.

THE MALPRACTICE OF MANAGEMENT HIRING

Since hiring is itself a management function, this underestimation of management both opens up and yet confines the (1) function of filling the position to the person claiming the responsibility and (2) job qualifications to the candidate selected in this utterly uninformed fashion. The sad fact is that, as an underqualified manager benefiting from these selfsame, lax selection methods, the hiring individual is probably, and uniquely, ill-prepared to recognize management qualifications, or the dearth of them, in anybody else.

Management tends to be conceptualized in incremental, hierarchical terms: as a position of Lead Worker, occupying the first among qualitatively equivalent positions, rather than associated with the qualitatively distinct function assigned to it by Drucker and others. In sum, management is viewed as a first prize.

Accordingly, a common practice is to hire a manager through promotion, as a reward for performance. This is certainly a way to *motivate* a high level of performance, since managing rather than actually performing a task no doubt: (1) commands more respect; (2) requires less physical work; (3) is better compensated; (4) permits more input into organizational doings; (5) permits more indulgence of power, if one is so inclined; (6) garners more attention, if, again, one is so inclined; (7) allows more discretionary time; (8) allows more time off; (9) allows more time to do nothing, period; (10) permits more interesting tasks; (11) allows exposure to more varied, perhaps more interesting, people; (12) is an important step up on a career ladder; (13) positions the incumbent for even bigger steps in the future; and (14) permits entree into exclusive official and unofficial events.

Nevertheless, despite the motivation it provides for prior performance, promotion to management does not guarantee that the future behaviors it subsumes will necessarily be *productive* behaviors.

There is no better example of this than the use of a management position as a reward for performance in other positions. The reason is simple: *there is no relationship between the ability to perform a technical task and the ability to manage it,* a disparity immortalized by Laurence Peter as the celebrated "Peter Principle."[32]

According to Peter Drucker, management represents a set of discrete, practical skills. The technical requirements of task performance, by contrast, are as varied as the tasks themselves.

In a publishing company, for example, a copy editor reports on the harrowing consequences of working under someone promoted

based on technical skill rather than a person's ability to deal effectively with people. . . . Morale was frighteningly poor at the time. I survived my first few weeks there because I stuck close to another woman who was hired at the same time. We provided the emotional support we needed for each other. The environment was very negative because the boss had a chip on her shoulder and talked down to people. In a word: EGO. My friend ended up quitting.

Clearly, previous performance as a criterion for promotion is no guarantee of a qualified manager. However, events take a turn decidedly more ominous than envisioned by Laurence Peter upon closer examination of the "performance" for which a manager is hired. We are about to see, as suggested earlier, that the people who are hired to be managers are not simply unqualified but rather represent *precisely the wrong people for the job.*

As a result, the organization is doomed by the very disqualification, if not the outright malice, of *its most empowered personnel.* Illustratively, amusingly, and no doubt inadvertently, the superintendent of a Rhode Island school district, regarding a pseudonymous choice, announced that "after finding no qualified candidates for the position of principal, the school board is extremely pleased to announce the appointment of Arthur Patton to the post."

THE DISQUALIFICATION OF THE QUALIFIED

The problem of which we speak begins with the acknowledgement by the hiring individual that qualifications for a management position ought to include some specialized skills: so far, so good. These skills in turn certainly *ought to include* management skill. This skill may be divined from qualities like competence, respect from others, and influence upon them.

However, management skill tends to elude the people charged with hiring for it, who, remember, have their eyes on management as common sense, intuition, experience, and some art form. Moreover, there is a more fundamental problem: *the individual demonstrating any promising managerial qualifications may very well be the* last *person promoted to management.*

The reason for this paradox may reflect an inference, from the previous discussion of job design, that people hiring for the management position may have also designed the position with their *own* needs in mind. The *last* things they need are the obvious, multidimensional threats posed by a hireling with management potential: a threat to resist control; a threat to require little or no direction, revealing the superfluousness of anyone responsible for providing it; and a threat to think independently, marshal support and other resources, and successfully adopt contrarian positions on key issues. Perhaps most important is the threat to outperform superiors and usurp their positions, since they have benefited from the same lax standards they now seek to enforce.

We therefore have reason to believe that a job candidate is likely to be disqualified from the management position by the most obvious qualifications for it. And we have reason to marvel that, in perhaps no other way, is the organization earmarked so unmistakably for mediocrity.

Unfortunately for all of us, examples extend to some of our most critical organizations. According to a deputy district attorney employed in the DA's office in a major metropolitan area, competent employees tend to

be perceived as a threat by the administration. Instead of being placed in positions of power, they are given lesser assignments, with lesser responsibilities. They might head less important functions, where they don't pose a threat. Bigger cases are handled by people who are less competent because they pose no threat to administration. So the politics and the power structure are more important than the results that are sought through the DA's office. And the talents of the DA's office are being wasted.

According to the deputy DA, "a guy who won a big case was considering running for DA's office, so he was perceived as a threat by administration, and sent to run a minor office somewhere. So he quit."

The qualified are not punished simply in publicly maintained government agencies. For example, a large investment company in the Northeast

hired a very capable woman at a senior level to bring a marketing orientation to the organization, and they threw her out. She was brighter than her boss and had a better grasp of marketing. Her boss was so threatened by her that he started screaming at her in meetings. As a result, she had to quit.

HIRING THE UNQUALIFIED

If not the qualified manager, then who is considered for promotion to the job?

In searching for a qualified hireling, the powers-that-be search for somebody who is willing to deploy the full weight of management resources into supporting rather than challenging them. At the same time, evaluation of performance in order to identify a qualified management candidate naturally tends to fall within the purview of somebody on a higher level than

the applicant. Thus, this evaluation tends to be handicapped by the remoteness of the evaluator from the performance to be evaluated: a problem
that will resurface when we discuss performance appraisal later on.

To bridge this gap from the evaluated applicant, the evaluator constructs
for the applicant a performance *ritual* consisting of highly-visible behaviors
that clearly demonstrate and portend support for higher-ups. Such support
is promised through the ritualistic display of servility identified through the
single evaluation criterion of *service*.

"Service" is a criterion for hiring managers that was probably exploited
by the earliest members of the organization, since they have traded on their
loyalty, and perhaps little else, during a time of resource scarcity, risk,
inexperience, and the firm's unproven capability. Simply by being there,
early members demonstrated "service." At various, ritualistic simulations
of organizational commitment, aspirants to management will continue to
"be there." The table is set, then, for cultivation of service as a management
hiring criterion from the earliest days of the organization, from its deepest
archaeological layers.

For several reasons, service as a promotion criterion fills the bill of the
hiring individual.

Primarily, as a ritual, service entails pure symbolism displayed, for example, by participation in do-nothing committees, implementing do-
nothing programs, achieving do-nothing goals. A meaningless exercise of
this type, in genuflection to hierarchy and to its occupants, equates to nothing less than personal degradation. And the individual willing to defer to
authority so gratuitously is likely to apply that authority if need be to
underlings.

At the same time, service is a purely subjective criterion that, if evaluated
favorably, constitutes a favor for which the hiring individual can expect to
be repaid. For this repayment, the hiring individual expects the authority
of the new management hireling to be applied to the enforcement of procedures.

The "enforcement" part of the equation demonstrates control by the
hireling, while "procedures" demonstrate planning and detailed focus by
the organizational machinery. As both an individual responsible for the hire
and as a card-carrying member of the organizational machinery, the hiring
individual benefits from the enforcement of procedures in enhanced competence, value, and job prospects.

For all of these reasons, then, the organization has hired its "Preservationist."

For his or her part, the hireling has engaged in a display of service due,
no less, to expectations of repayment, for the following reasons.

Given the servility demanded, the promotion to management that constitutes the reward for this servility clearly has a uniquely high degree of
attraction for this individual. Chances are excellent that the applicant wants

the management position this badly, not from a sudden infusion of public spirit for the organization, but rather from longer-standing, personal goals. The chasm between those goals and the fabricated goals of the ritual in turn attest to a willingness to be utterly unauthentic.

The hireling certainly expects some reciprocity in exchange for this overweening display of obeisance, for a willingness to be utterly false to all concerned, and for a promise to continue doing the same thing in future support of hiring personnel.

We therefore find the applicant and the hiring individual locked in mutual expectations of recompense. As a quid pro quo, service requires participation in nakedly *political behavior*: behavior intended to maximize personal power. This is yet another turning point through which the management hiring process heads further into selection of the wrong people for the job, and draws the organization ever deeper into its own destruction.

QUALIFYING THE DISQUALIFIED

There is nothing inherently demonic about political behavior; we all do it, and would be crazy not to. However, it would be shortsighted to deny that problems are created by political behavior: as a criterion for promotion, its most salient shortcoming is that it represents, in fact, the very *opposite of merit*.

Perhaps to compensate for lack of external pressure, and despite all of its foibles, public bureaucracy is designed for "rationality."[33] Rationality requires evaluation and promotion based upon *universalistic* criteria, equally applicable to all, reserving reward for those who excel on an intentionally level playing field.[34]

By its very nature, on the other hand, political behavior is intended to tilt the field; it is conducted with the expectation of special consideration for *failure* to meet universalistic standards of merit. As a precondition for promotion to management, then, political behavior produces the very *antithesis* of merit as a criterion for hiring candidates for the organization's most important positions.

Despite their pretensions of rationality, of course, public agencies quite baldly make political appointments to their positions. According to its former director, commissioners of a state lottery are appointed "based upon political favoritism. One of them was the governor's driver; another was a used car salesman." In the DA's office, promotions are political rewards for favoritism, according to the deputy DA.

Of course, given their dispensation from external pressure, public agencies can forgive themselves for failure to live up to their self-imposed ideals of rationality, since costs are defrayed to the long-suffering public. On the other hand, despite their own risk from competition, private organizations tend to commit the same indulgence.

The reciprocal relationship between political machinations and merit was dramatized by a copy editor in a publishing house:

Currently, the operations VP is determined to hang onto a department about which she knows nothing. In publishing, the manufacturing department has little to do with warehouse functions and best belongs with production functions. Her hunger for power is preventing the manufacturing department from getting the leadership and direction it needs . . . and we all suffer as a result.

Moreover, the situation worsens when we recognize political behavior as a job mobility tool of last resort; it is used most profligately when a job candidate, objectively or otherwise, lacks any merit for the job. Moreover, if utilized effectively, political behavior can easily produce the *leading* job candidate.

The problem that upward mobility is localized to the most "political" and least meritorious managers has escaped the attention of neither researchers nor practitioners. For instance, the management researcher Fred Luthans (1988) posed the hypothesis, "Could it be that successful managers, the politically savvy ones who are being rapidly promoted into responsible positions, may not be the effective managers, the ones with satisfied, committed subordinates turning out quantity and quality performance in their units?" Luthans's subsequent research confirmed his suspicions.[35]

Regarding the problem he had documented, the researcher concluded that "the solution may be as simple as promoting effective managers and learning how they carry out their jobs." Unfortunately, as in so many cases, the problem tends to resist its own solution, since "successful" managers succeed because they tend to be the best at managing the *perception* of their effectiveness. Hence, in the job promotion derby, *lack of qualifications* produces the heavy favorite. The larger problem is that, as a result of such debilitating and self-maintaining problems, organizations are built to fail.

Thus, it is not sufficient to merely observe that promotion to management occasionally rewards political rather than meritorious behavior; rather, this policy selects *precisely* those candidates who rely on this behavior in toto because they are, in fact, otherwise and *completely unqualified for the position.*

THE POLITICAL ROAD TO MISMANAGEMENT

Moreover, political considerations award job candidates who are disqualified for management not only by lack of merit but also by some maladaptive personal styles and characteristics.

Projected Self-Interest

Someone who is rewarded and in effect trained for political behavior very often rationalizes this self-interested posture by projecting it onto others. Projection is, of course, a well-known Freudian mechanism, defined as the attribution of one's own motives to another, in order to legitimize them, among other reasons.[36] Thus, the political animal might well live by the mantra that "everybody is out for themselves," clearly in order to justify adopting that posture toward others.

By assuming that others are so motivated, self-interest is further justified for the person projecting it, not only through its newfound legitimacy, but also by denying to others alternative, selfless motives that would otherwise justify compassion. As a result, other people are easily viewed as resources that can be optimized for personal power.

The process of projection doesn't end there. Based on her experience with organizations, a management consultant concluded that "political" personnel "project their own insecurities" onto other employees. What this means is that the stimuli for those insecurities are assigned to others as well. Since these stimuli include low self-evaluation, and low self-evaluation responds to one's own perceived lack of qualifications, "political" managers can be expected to assign this inability to others, and *to see the very worst in employees*.

Management is defined as many things; one of them is the capacity to get the most out of others. Our political animal, by contrast, tends to approach others devoid of any understanding, appreciation, or empathy: qualities essential to motivating others. Clearly, then, our political animal is the *last* person with the capacity to manage. Yet this is the individual who is the odds-on favorite to be hired by rewarding "service" with a management position.

The successful advancement of self-interest is, of course, proportional to the *effort* devoted to self-interest. Hence, we are forced to conclude that, in organizations and elsewhere, concern for others is punished, and we are forced to agree with the truism that, indeed, "nice guys finish last."

Yet concern for others is a precondition for effective management. As a result, we find ourselves inching ever closer to the realization that many managers are the *last* people who should have been considered for their position in the first place: that the organization is directed by *its worst enemies*.

KEY RESERVATIONS

Two caveats are in order. First, others have advanced the argument that the political jungle tends to reward those who are *best* at handling the interpersonal interactions that, in turn, are most useful for the manager. For people making this argument, management behavior is likely to be *most* effective if management positions are used to reward political behavior.

On the other hand, as we can now see, the interpersonal skills rewarded by the political jungle are most decidedly *not* the interpersonal skills needed for the job: most notably, understanding and empathy. To claim otherwise may itself be a political tool. Often, the claim is advanced by managers themselves, to justify their own self-interest.

Moreover, in the hands of managers, this claim often becomes transmuted into an acknowledgment of both personal political skill and the political nature of the workplace: a juxtaposition that is made to seem adaptive by the argument that such skill is required to negotiate such a political jungle.[37] Overlooked by this argument, however, is that, in addition to omitting critical interpersonal skills, the argument itself can only enhance workplace politicality, if not make a self-fulfilling prophecy of it.

Secondly, it is not claimed that *all* managers are "political" and thereby inept. The problem is that those who fit this description influence the organization beyond the weight of their numbers alone, an issue that will concern us in the next chapter.

THE OVERRATED JOB INTERVIEW

The increasing functions for which the organization originally had to formalize itself and promote its managers also at some point necessitate hiring new employees. The selection technology is likely to be the job interview.

Research reveals that the job interview presents an opportunity that is *no better than chance alone* at predicting job performance, whatever that chance may be.[38] In other words, interviews would predict performance on a particular job 30 percent of the time if random selection *also* predicted that performance 30 percent of the time. Hence, the hiring task could depend, with reliability equal to that of a job interview, upon a coin toss, a table of random numbers, or a chimpanzee making choices by flinging banana peels in one of two directions.

In addition to underqualified applicants, the organization is beset by the virtual impossibility of the selection task itself: the task of projecting long-term performance based upon a short-term observation of someone doing everything conceivable to favorably bias the interview and favorably manipulate the decision.

Despite its poor record, nonetheless, the job interview remains the almost exclusive method for hiring a new candidate, largely because it represents the only familiar technology, and because it reassures the interviewer of a hands-on approach, which certainly seems warranted by its own unreliability. In fact, given its utter purposelessness, the entire interview is up for grabs, available for the applicant to appropriate. To the candidate who can surmise and respond to the "demand characteristics" or implied expectations of the interview, the process represents a wealth of opportunity.

Thus, as a result, jobs in general may well be given not to the most qualified applicants but rather to people who are simply the most qualified at *handling themselves during job interviews*. Not surprising, therefore, is a contingent of people who have built entire careers consisting of *interviewing for jobs*. Even worse, according to a management consultant, is the tendency to select, through the job interview, the "political" skill of mirroring the expectations of the interviewer, adding to the organization's already copious and ever-expanding capital of its self-destructive political resources.

ORGANIZATIONAL INCEST

Moreover, given the impossible subjectivity of selection, the hiring individual can easily rationalize hiring the most "likeable" job candidate, into the search for which the entire process has devolved. Confirmed an organizational researcher, "As you reflect on this interview experience, you feel you've just participated in a lottery of sorts. Your interview, the interview site, the length of the interview, the interview questions, and the recording and evaluation of your answers were all a matter of luck, not plan. No wonder that the traditional interviewing so often produces the 'halo effect,' in which an interviewer simply hires the person who seems to be wearing a halo similar to the interviewer's."[39]

According to an ex-legal secretary in Atlanta, for instance,

one law firm I believe I was hired at just because of personal preference. The gentleman that I interviewed with was one of the associates, and he and I just hit it off immediately, and we were both obviously attracted to each other. And he gave me a typing test which I completely screwed up and I was hired on the spot.

For the interviewer, a compatible employee may seem justified by the promise of a smooth working relationship, at least in the short term; in the long term, however, it promises nothing but trouble for the organization, as it proved to be for a university in Southern California:

Just before the old President is ousted, he elevates this guy from kind of a liaison to a Vice-presidency in a functional area that he doesn't know how to deal with. . . .

Suddenly we've got this guy off the street. Now we've got to find a CFO but we can't call him a CFO because the organizational structure doesn't call for two people at that level. So it's created this really awkward situation where the titular Vice-president cannot balance his own checkbook, let alone do the macro-budgeting and the projection for the institution. Well, it creates lots and lots of stress. It didn't have to be, if we hadn't had the elevation of this guy based on compatibility with the old President.

Based on the university's experience, one obvious problem from hiring a job candidate based on compatibility is outright incompetence, not to mention the bureaucratic snafu of sorting out the problem.

Another problem is that this process may be viewed as organizational "incest," promoting a uniform (1) perspective, with a poverty of *different* perspectives and the ideas they bring, and (2) style, with an inability to balance or correct it. Within a nationwide communications company, according to a company manager, the hiring interview

is highly dependent on the manager's preferences. If he already knows the person and plans for it the interview is basically not doing much of the task. . . .

Where the manager really liked an employee, he would tell the employee "go read this book tonight"—a book on some of the technical requirements in the interview—and then tomorrow, of course, a lot of questions are coming from that book, so the employee will know exactly what to answer.

The purposes of the sham interview don't take long to become apparent; according to the manager,

there are some kinds of dominating characters in the company who would select people who would . . . provide support, show some loyalty on an ongoing basis so if there are four or five that they hand-pick then they get some support in the meeting. And the other people would tend to conform because of this peer pressure.

Interestingly, available hiring technology can in fact improve immensely on the job interview in general. According to a management consultant, however, this progress tends to go for naught:

We do bring objective measures and personal characteristics and behaviors, behavioral competencies, and you look at the people the particular managers hire—big surprise. Who do they look like? They look like that particular person.

So it's this self-cloning kind of thing that goes on in organizations. Sometimes we have sat down with a manager and worked out the detailed behavioral description of what a job requires, and we put together a hiring profile, we've gone out and screened people using this hiring profile, we've gotten people who fit that profile very well. They come into the organization and they fail, because that profile doesn't fit the person who hired them.

Given that selection techniques favor the applicant who is compatible with the hiring individual, there is an enormous potential for procreating managers, institutionalizing their weaknesses, and "inbreeding" these weaknesses as organizational ones as well.

For instance, the manager who discourages new ideas is likely to hire new employees unable to generate them, who probably share a lack of appreciation for them, and who, upon promotion to management, are unlikely to hire job candidates who are able to generate them. Managers who have attained their position through lack of creativity or other lax qualifications will not risk usurpation by imposing more stringent qualifications in the selection process. And managers with a penchant for political machinations will select job candidates who are clearly willing to play ball.

As we have seen, these in fact are the very qualifications we can anticipate in managers who rise internally through the ranks. The selection process allows them to reproduce themselves: in effect, to *institutionalize themselves*. Thus, the organization promotes its "Preservationists," who preserve not only ongoing procedures but also, through the hiring process, the tendency to hire preservationists themselves.

To put it very mildly, it is extremely hard to see where the organization benefits from all this. To put it more forcefully, *organizational incest may well be the organization's most binding assurance of mediocrity and guarantee of self-destruction.*

These hiring techniques underscore, and our management consultants verify, the intended personal benefit of the hiring individual. In some cases, this priority assumes positively bizarre proportions. An ex-employee observed that a manager at a software manufacturing company in Los Angeles

hired only staff that in no way would show her up. They didn't have a CPA; they didn't have an MBA; they didn't have the education; they didn't have the experience; they didn't have anything that someone of her staff might actually be looked at and go "Oh, that person's really great and maybe they're going to jump over her." Her staff was all really second-rate, the people that she hired. And then, when she would fail, she would find one of them to blame for the failure.

According to a management consultant, a young woman working for a U.S. government military installation on the West Coast

inherited some poor performers and it was really quite frustrating to her.

What was interesting is over a period of time . . . she began to use the poor performers and in fact even hired another poor performer so that their work wouldn't get done and as the sterling supervisor she would ride in on her white charger and she would work overtime and she would clean up the backlog they had created by not getting their work done on time. So she would end up being seen as a star because she would come in on weekends and she would work and all of that.

Through "incest," the organization has managed not only to select unqualified managers but also to perpetuate this incompetence by selecting employees who in general (1) will aid and abet these managers currently and (2) replace them in the future in the same inherited spirit of and commitment to incompetence.

In the next chapter, we will see in full force the horror that has been loosed upon the organization. We will recognize the organization's leadership as consisting of the very *worst* candidates for their roles.

PART THREE

FAILURE IN METHODS AND FUNCTION

4

The Psychopathology of Leadership

An organization is like a tree full of monkeys, all on different levels, some climbing up, some falling down, most just swinging round and round. The monkeys on top look down and see a tree full of smiling faces. The monkeys on the bottom look up and see nothing but assholes.

—In the April 16, 1999, issue of the *Informant*, a newsletter written by and for district attorneys, in the county DA's office for a major metropolitan area.

THE BIRTH OF THE MICROMANAGER

As we have seen, one of the earliest incarnations of leadership in the organization is the "micromanager": the manager who refuses to delegate.

By definition, micromanagement entails stretching a single manager well beyond reasonable managerial limits, or the "span of control." The micromanager appears early on in the person of The Founder, due to the opportunities and risks unique to that role. Despite its naturally occurring origins, this managerial form, by its very definition, remains a bad idea.

Going It Alone

One reason for its dysfunctionality is that micromanagement precludes input by the people impacted by a decision, omitting the various advantages of their participation; these include their ownership over the decision, stake in it, commitment to it, and benefit to it from their knowledge, skills, abilities, perspectives, experience, and the capacity to "synergistically" interplay ideas.

Mobility without Facility

Another problem is that micromanagement represents excessive involvement in a task by someone who is probably not qualified in the first place to perform it at any level, to any degree, and in any form. One reason is that founding a firm *may* benefit from the legendary, unique qualities of the entrepreneur, including vision and fortitude; however, starting up a firm has *nothing* to do with leading it. The result is that leadership *includes* and micromanagement *excludes* the development and empowerment of followers; hence, the micromanager occupies a leadership role *without leading*.

For example, according to a department chairperson at a university in Southern California,

> the CEO is really out of his element in terms of knowing how to operate at that level and the result is that he's constantly tinkering in the day-to-day affairs of subordinates over issues that he shouldn't be concerned about. . . . He's constantly asking "how are you doing on that" or "how's that," as if these people are incompetent.

This is an example of "mobility without facility": occupancy of a role without the ability to perform it. As we saw in Chapter 3, this describes a founder's prerogative to plan strategy without the capacity to do so. The same may now be said for the roles of leadership and management.

Control beyond Control

A further problem is that micromanagement represents a frenzied attempt to establish the control that, for The Founder, has an understandably high priority, and, at the same time, creates its own control problems.

One obvious problem is unqualified and uninformed problem solving, which by itself can only exacerbate any lack of control.

A more specific problem is that, to underlings, micromanagement is not simply an intrusion but also clear lack of confidence, as demonstrated by the university President. In addition to stretching beyond the competencies of even a qualified manager, the micromanager is now saddled with the interpersonal issues created by a direct slap in the faces of subordinates.

In the military, we have, as an example, an officer who "was such a micromanager; such a negative person. At his staff meetings he would be-rate his people in front of everybody else." As a result, according to an observer,

people were so afraid that they were going to make a mistake, no decisions were made. When he went out into the field for a week, everything stopped. Nothing worked; just halted, 'til he got back, and then he made every decision, no matter what it was. And basically it's because his staff and everyone else would not make a decision by themselves because they were afraid of the consequences.

These problems are expanded by an ex-employee of a temporary staffing agency specializing in the entertainment industry. The ex-employee summarizes these problems as follows:

The founder/owner was so emotionally involved in the organization that he constantly wanted to know every detail about his employees' work. The owner took how the employees worked on a day-to-day basis very personally. This was largely due to the fact that, in this company, mistakes can really impact the bottom line. Therefore, employees were not allowed to make mistakes. And as a result, they were hesitant to make decisions without the owner's approval and oftentimes decisions employees made were based on how happy it would make the owner rather than on what they thought was best for the company.

Employees were not encouraged to use their own judgment in order to adapt to different situations. Therefore, employees were not truly empowered to do their work and their professional growth was stunted. I feel that as a result of this, the company wasn't able to adapt to its increasingly competitive environment and the growth of the company was stunted.

Although on a personal level I did get along with the owner very well, on a professional level I did not. I constantly felt that my professional judgment was in question and that I wasn't sincerely trusted. I became so frustrated with the situation that I quit.

In other cases, results may extend beyond abdication of decision making, to active resistance by subordinates to a subliminal yet offensive attack on their competence, in ways of which even they are perhaps not fully aware. For a qualified manager, these are difficult issues: for an incompetent one, well-nigh impossible ones. And as a result, *the micromanager has now created the very problem of control that the role was intended to resolve.*

THE FOLLY OF GROWTH

Control is also compounded as a problem by a particular goal pursued by many leaders, both of and within the organization.

It has been pointed out by innumerable financial experts that there are many paths to profitability; beyond a certain point, however, unilateral growth, unmatched by the environment, is *not* one of them.[40] Up to that theoretical point, growth enables the organization to exploit the various opportunities that, as we saw, are made available by group participation. Beyond that point, however, growth incurs control costs that exceed revenues.

Nevertheless, organizations cannot seem to help but wander well beyond that point, justified by the delusion that it is the route to greater and greater profitability. It isn't.

It seems a sure bet that profit represents only the most obvious motive for growth. For other researchers, a more plausible underlying culprit is the need for status, since it is far more prestigious to head up a large behemoth than a small and seemingly inconsequential department, division, or firm.[41]

Significantly, some researchers have noted that organizational growth multiplies the part of the environment with which the organization interfaces, which requires an increase in the organizational capabilities needed for that interface.[42] For instance, an expansion of a manufacturing capability may impinge on the local ecology, necessitating an Environmental Affairs, Public Relations, or Legal Department. As a result, we find that growth, once initiated, feeds upon itself. We therefore expect to find the problem of control itself spinning out of control.

MANAGEMENT BY ABUSE

It is as an attempt to restore the appearance of control that we find the emergence of the abusive manager. If we dig into possible motives, we may find frustration over inability to restore control, anger at subordinates for this inability, and heavy-handed domination to express this anger and restore control, at least symbolically.

Abuse is also made likely by some of the very reasons to seek a managerial position.

A Power Supply

One reason to seek the managerial role is the power need: a discrete, identifiable, and measurable personality characteristic. There are certainly other needs, but this is the one that, by its very nature, requires a dominant role.

The problem with power is that the individual attempting to satisfy it as a need does not necessarily wield it as a resource for the benefit of anybody else. Given the number of people impacted by the management position, this certainly victimizes a lot of people.

License to Mismanage

Another reason to seek the management role is that this position permits the authoritative management style through which (1) others may be disenfranchised and (2) the power motive may be satisfied *most fully*. This style certainly confers the advantage of license upon its practitioner; however, advantages are, to say the least, far more dubious for the quality of management and for the organization that depends upon it.

Unadulterated management license may serve to suppress subordinates to maximize not power but rather simply the latitude to exercise the manager's unique way of operating. Due to a particular (e.g., low information) cognitive style, for instance, the manager may be uncomfortable with or easily challenged by a different (e.g., high information) cognitive style.[43]

The Dark Side to Management

More disturbing possibilities are raised in a frankly dark side to organization and its management, by needs expressed in clearly pathological impulses to dominate, offend, injure, or otherwise penalize others. These hidden needs are created by personal characteristics, physical or otherwise, that are both visible and unacceptable to the manager experiencing them, and imply either some limitation to be overcome or some weakness to be disowned. Either may be achieved through a display of supremacy, which has the added function of expressing anger over this misfortune, by punishing those not personally encumbered with it.

Results of this darkly pathological management motive include all-too-familiar abuses of a powerful and potentially destructive position. As a result, for example, we find, in a large computer manufacturing company in Northern California, "a manager who was presented an issue by an employee, and before he gets clarity on the issue, blows up, starts screaming at the top of his lungs, uses profanity, and punches at the walls." Back down in Southern California, we observe a real estate CEO who would "scream constantly at the office manager, throw chairs at the wall, call people in his office and scream at them."

Furthermore, such pathologies may reproduce themselves.

The Etiology of Employee Abuse

It has been widely observed that the capacity for child abuse tends to be passed on to the victim. The same may be true, perhaps to some qualified degree, of "employee" abuse, by the manager.

A direct if simplistic explanation for both forms is that abuse is taught as an expectation for the role, and as a norm for the social context, eventually occupied by the victim. Perhaps, as we will see with performance appraisal, there is the belief that equity demands the imposition of past hardships on successors.

More complex if more speculative explanations for abuse account for the "affect" or mood of anger it creates.

It may be the case that the previous victim and current abuser may seek to re-experience the abusive relationship in order to somehow resolve it, but now from a position of power that affords such resolution through the expression of anger: in other words, through the abuse of a new victim.

The abuser may view the current victim as a focus for identification, and as a vehicle for symbolic retaliation against the previous abuser, now symbolized by the current abuser: in other words, by *the self*. The current victim shares with the previous victim *lack of power*: physical power in the case of child abuse, and intraorganizational power for the abused employee. Thus, any such retaliation, symbolic or otherwise, is futile, which only goads the current perpetrator to greater acts of abuse, in order to elicit retaliation and to punish the current victim for failure to provide it. This is why, for instance, violent criminals tend not to be mollified, and in fact are inflamed, by the helpless cries of victims. Thus, the entire re-enactment of abuse becomes an exercise in self-hatred.

The point for organizations is that the capacity for employee abuse is transmitted across generations of managers: assuming, once again, that an organization displaying this sort of pathology will last that long.

In sum, we can see that hiring methods are often designed to entrust many leadership positions to individuals with purposes that are markedly distant from those of the organization and patently inimical to the needs of others.

Of course, not all leaders are automatically disqualified for the task. On the other hand, *qualification* for leadership does not vouchsafe the *direction* of leadership, as we are about to see.

MANAGEMENT BY MIRRORS

History is replete with examples of great leaders, which demonstrates that history is highly selective; has a flawed memory, as do organizations, as we shall see; or responds to our need to believe in our leaders. The latter is the very problem we are about to explore.

There have, of course, been fine leaders who have provided fine leadership, but these may be pure accidents. Far more typical, and dangerous, have been leaders of another kind.

And there are good reasons for that: there is something inherently symbiotic and innately pathological in the relationship between the "born leader" and followers. In a phrase, followers *have no idea what or whom to believe*. Uncertainty pervades their entire existence, from the ethical content of their decisions through the origins and nature of their physical universe to their purpose within it. One conclusive verdict of research is that people despise uncertainty. Intimately aware of their own inability to reduce it, they look outside in an attempt to do so.

The Leader to the Rescue

Enter the leader. As a human being, facing the human condition, he or she is exposed to no less uncertainty than others are, and, like others, has plenty of reason to reduce it by utilizing external information. Uniquely, however, this is someone who has been assigned credibility by and over others, sources of which include the various personal and interpersonal characteristics identified as "charisma."

Thus, this is someone who has experienced, and therefore has reason to anticipate, external support for *internal* efforts to resolve uncertainty: someone who has been given very good reason to take himself or herself very seriously.

The exercise of charismatic leadership begins at some point with the leader's expression of belief, sustained by the "wish" that Freud assigns to all beliefs. This belief is delivered with a firm lack of compromise that evicts any internal uncertainty, is designed to do so by eliciting external support, and is buoyed by the *promise* of that support. For its part, sustained by the uncompromising quality of the belief and the authoritativeness of its source, the audience climbs on board.

Having been thus validated by the adulatory response of others, the leader's pronouncements are henceforth delivered with added conviction, producing further persuasion. The result is that the audience is convinced, and the *leader* is convinced by the fact that *the audience is convinced.* As observed in the letters of the pseudonymous Junius, "There is a holy mistaken zeal in politics as well as in religion. By persuading others, we convince ourselves."

What we have as a result is the symbiotic embrace of leader and follower in yet another misbegotten effort to find verifiable external resolution for one of life's little mysteries. The mystery itself may be some sort of creation, often to simplify a complex problem or add some luster to an otherwise drab existence. In either case, we find espousal by leaders and, across cults and continents alike, assent for such strange beliefs that mass-suicide will produce an afterlife on a comet; that exactly 144,000 white people will be elected to survive a black revolution; that Armageddon has once again been rescheduled and is now imminent; that it is essential that innocent fellow high school students should be massacred in the greatest possible numbers; that Jews should be exterminated because they are determined to conquer the world through both communism and capitalism; that all human affairs are dictated not only by Jews but also by Masons, the Trilateral Commission, and space aliens; that the earth is populated not only by space aliens but also by angels, devils, returnees from a previous life, and passengers to a better hereafter; and so on.

For our purposes, charismatic leaders have shepherded organizational marches into some of the strangest terrain extant. Examples range from such well-known and deservedly-ridiculed products as some junk bonds and car misdesigns to a decision, prompted by an engaging senior VP with a mortgage broker, "to open a call center that was destined to fail because we had no one with any retail experience whatever."

What this can teach us is that organizations can be most readily dominated by individuals with extensive leadership *capabilities* but with impoverished leadership *goals*: demonstrating, once again, "mobility without facility."

Like most elements of personality, the quality of charisma, and dependence on external affirmation, is not a Manichean, "either-or" characteristic: it appears in gradations, on a continuum. To the extent of its presence, we have: (1) the spectacle of a leader accepting external input only if it confirms a prior belief; (2) the supreme irony that this sort of leader resists *candid* external input due in fact to dependence on this very input, but in a less candid form, for internal validation; and (3) the paradox that the organization's perhaps *likeliest and arguably most qualified leader is also the likeliest source of resistance to external input.*

Additionally, organizations have ways to ensure that leadership is conferred on people lacking even the capacities for the role: *neither* mobility *nor* facility. By granting "legitimacy," the organization provides entree for a decidedly different stripe of leader, with consequences that are perhaps even more pathological and, for the organization itself, suicidal.

THE EXPANDING POLITICAL UNIVERSE

As we have seen, managers often assume their positions through political means rather than through their innate qualifications for leadership. As we have also seen, political activity by its very definition is often designed to redress the applicant's very *lack* of qualifications for management, or, for that matter, for any new position. That this lack of merit transfers to the new position was confirmed by an employee in a publishing company, who observed that

a publications committee, made up of power-holding individuals who have no contact with the direct marketplace, holds the ultimate veto power over whether a project is approved or denied. This publications committee makes decisions based on a number of other factors and often the people in the committee have no knowledge of the market in question. In fact, they often disregard the type of customer (academic, student, practitioner) and make decisions based on how compatible books have done in other disciplines.

As a means to garner power, political behavior is intended to produce dependence in others. By eventuating in promotion to management, political behavior has demonstrably produced some sort of dependence in the various people responsible for the decision. Hence, if it succeeds in its purposes, political behavior *has to have affected a large number of people.* In relation to the number of its sources, *political behavior has an exaggerated effect on the organization.*

Maximization of dependence is, of course, the fundamental purpose of power-seeking activity, calling for commensurately large-scale counteraction. The following dramatic instance was shared by the former CEO of an Illinois company:

I had an Executive Vice-President who was also general counsel for the corporation: a lawyer by education. . . . To him, it was really fun to do: "Why don't you and he fight and I'll watch." And there was something about him—he just liked to cause trouble and watch what was going on and then angle himself for a position by playing both sides . . .

The company is in a bit of a crisis position and people are disconcerted. Now, instead of saying to the people: "Yes, we have some serious problems and we have to go and address them"— . . . he goes and commiserates. It got a little out of hand. Because he wasn't passing on the information he was supposed to—he did it by information control.

I basically had to find brand new revenue streams. . . . So I'm out there doing all this stuff, I'm on travel and the Executive Vice-President is supposed to be communicating this stuff and he's not. He's commiserating with them that I've lost it. The trouble is—it got out of control, because these guys didn't stop to think "Maybe this isn't true." They figured it was all true, the CEOs lost it, and they went and orchestrated a *coup.*

[Upon my return] the top ten people in my company . . . show up in the room, and they arranged themselves in a little horseshoe around my desk. . . . One of the ring-leaders steps forward and says "We no longer have confidence in you; here is what we would like to have happen. We would like you to turn over the CEO-ship"—I, by the way, owned about 80% of the company at the time—"you are to turn over your stock to us also; you're to make the Executive Vice-President the President—he at least is rational" . . . and they wanted my response, then.

To fast-forward to the eventual result, the CEO shared the business plan concealed by the EVP, exposed the EVP's machinations, turned around his company, and deposed the EVP.

What this demonstrates is that, despite its modest sources, political behavior ultimately has a vast target. Furthermore, if it succeeds in producing promotion to management, political behavior has been *rewarded and reinforced,* which means that it will certainly continue. Additionally, having been safely ensconced in a management position, political behavior is now able to produce continuing if not accelerating effects on the large number of people impacted by a manager.

For example, recalls a printer mechanic of his manager in a Hollywood film laboratory,

once we realized that his education and knowledge were not valuable to the success of the company, the employees started rebelling. . . . He then tried using techniques such as if you ended up speaking your mind, telling him things would not work, he would then put you on the night shift where management would not hear your opinions or, basically, your voice.

So, he would then use scare tactics like that; he terminated, out of eleven employees . . . five. He got rid of the rest of the six employees who spoke against him. . . . Even to this day, he hires technicians who seem to be friends rather than knowledgeable, experienced workers. The company's success has gone down. Every development that he tries to prove is not working.

Political behavior can be resisted only in kind: by other political behavior. This is one reason why successful political gamesters may be few in number, picayune in focus, and yet with effects so inescapable.

According to "Mary," an ex-employee of a software company in Southern California,

"Doris," the Accounting Director . . . would out-and-out lie about how things were going. If she was in talking to "Candice," "Candice" would say "How is the new corporate reporting mapping project going?" "Oh, I'm very pleased with the progress. I think we're going to be doing very well."

. . . She had no idea what was going on. And it was my job to make sure that they were meeting the deadlines, and the next time I'd have a meeting with "Candice" and I'm saying "Well I'm very concerned because 'Doris' has not started at all the mapping project." "That's not true, 'Mary.' She told me that it's going very well." I said "She hasn't done anything" . . .

It would force me to send in emails or "I need a copy of your mapping sent to me no later than x time and copy every single person that needed to know whatever" which would then force her to either have to send something or to send what was not done. . . .

Soon you've got people sending emails back and forth, copying everybody on the planet, just because they're afraid not to send it, with a copy to prove that they sent it, marking receipts and saving all the emails with the receipts and printing everything out. . . .

Due to the countermeasures required, then, political behavior has not only a large but also *expanding effect* on the organization.

In sum, political behavior presupposes previous effects on a large scale, is likely to continue, will have large-scale future effects, and will expand those effects.

As indicated earlier, it should be clarified that nowhere is it claimed that the organization represents a glorified collection of political misanthropes. Thanks to its burgeoning effects, however, political behavior can easily be upgraded by a dedicated minority from a private indulgence to full-blown domination of the organizational agenda. As pointed out by organization theorist Jeffrey Pfeffer, "Once politics are introduced into a situation it is very difficult to restore rationality."

Organizational Effects

Political behavior by a manager certainly impacts the organization as a whole. Given that personnel are hired and promoted to, in the earlier words of one self-styled kingpin, "serve our interests," it has been observed that university departments want not teachers but rather *soldiers*. Thus, in effect, the political manager becomes a *military* appointment. The result for the organization is that a work unit already operating on the preconceptions of occupational chauvinism is likely to be further inflamed by a self-interested, battle-tested leader.

Indecision-Making

The impact of the political manager becomes a bit odder, but no less problematical, when we narrow the responsibilities of the role to decision making.

The job of the manager, first and foremost, is to exert control. Control is demonstrated by an absence of problems. One way to minimize problems is to do as little as possible; there are no plans undone, no expectations unmet, and no promises unkept: when little is attempted, there is little that can go wrong. The result is the conservatism with which managers have been widely associated, both by researchers and practitioners.

The avoidance of a decision represents, in its own right, a set of job skills. Specifically, the decision may be postponed, pending: (1) further analysis, (2) the acquisition of additional information, or (3) another decision on which this one is made to appear contingent or with which this one can be integrated. The decision may be elongated, due to some contrived need for deliberateness. Alternatively, in the interest of acquiring necessary expertise or authority, the decision may be deflected to someone else, or diffused among a larger group.

The efficacy of this tactic was demonstrated by a facility management department of a Southern California telecommunications company, in which, according to an employee,

management methods have been very successful in placing decision and planning into a group environment to first establish a process, goals, and limits, while holding on to linear management. They submarine any attempts of outcome by re-assigning subordinates out of and into the group settings, causing setbacks and delays, while laying blame onto the group and avoiding any personal responsibility for failure.

A good manager can stay within a job for five or six years, accomplish nothing and move to a new position before anyone is the wiser.

At "Lancelot" publishing company, according to an employee,

top managers at "Lancelot" have final sign-off on any Lancelot book that gets approved. In order to stall or buy more time, or slow down the decision process, top managers repeatedly request information that is extremely time consuming to gather so they can make the decision at a later time.

Many times once the information is provided, they still fail to make a decision for several weeks. This is extremely frustrating as many times the author is checking in on a regular basis to find out whether a decision has been made. This is very common right now at Lancelot because everyone is scared to make a decision and no one wants to take any risks.

In a management company within the healthcare industry in Southern California, a newly-hired staff accountant reports that

during the first couple of months I would question the final number on the balance sheet and address the supervisor regarding my observations. Although she has been doing this work for five years and is fully capable of making the decision (this I concluded from observations) she didn't want to be responsible for the final decision. So she would walk with me to the Director of Finance who would review the company's financial standing and give me direction.

In the entertainment industry, artist and repertoire (A & R) personnel responsible for evaluating new talent confess that their decisions tend to be avoided altogether in order to simultaneously reduce two opposed risks: personal association with, on the one hand, (1) a commitment to a poorly-performing act and, on the other hand, (2) rejection of a future star. When a noncommittal response isn't feasible, A & R personnel opt for the conservative posture of slamming the door on new acts.

In an article for the British publication *Sound on Sound*, a writer who goes by the moniker of "Big George" recommended a method he used in order to ascertain the interest of record companies in new acts; he sent them demonstration tapes or "demos" in the following way:

Send a blank cassette tape or CD to a company and see if they notice. Of the five record companies to which I sent blanks, two said they liked my music but it wasn't for them at this point, another said they would keep my tape on file until the next A & R meeting, and the other two didn't reply at all.

Send an early album track of a company's top-selling artist and see if they pass

on it. In the mid 1980s I was turned down by A&M on a Squeeze track, RCA on
a Bowie track and Warner Brothers on a Doobie Brothers track.[44]

> To reiterate: *these record companies turned down demos that either were
> blank or were recordings of their top-selling acts!*

Reasons include a subliminal (and probably justified) mistrust of one's
own judgment, deferral to that of others, and, as a result, virtually an entire
industry that relies almost exclusively on testimony (e.g., from agents and
previous clients) and "connections," including nepotistic ones. Results include the futile hopes and aspirations of artists, many of them potential
world-beaters. For *our* analysis, results also include a moribund strategy in
a highly competitive field. In general, according to a management consultant,

> [management theorist John] Deming says that "It's easier to do nothing than service
> a problem."
> When you've got people being measured by some quantitative thing, whatever it
> is, and you risk disrupting the creation of those numbers for the sake of trying to
> improve the thing, generally, it takes time to do it. In the meantime you can't meet
> your quota. So in the meantime you're dinged, so you don't do it.
> And the people don't take on the big problems. So however poorly the system
> works, as long as you can protect yourself, your little piece of it, that's OK. So you
> go along with it rather than doing the thing that's going to improve the system
> because it's going to hurt you in the short run.

Decisions for Their Own Sake

Representing an exception to but no improvement over its avoidance is
a decision that has as its only purpose a display of independence and analytical skill, typically through a counterintuitive, contrarian judgment. The
reason is to underscore the job qualifications that are strikingly absent in
the manager's political, nonmeritorious advancement to the position. According to a Hollywood screenwriter, such decision makers are

> validating their jobs, making unnecessary work for themselves. . . . The end result
> is to hurt the product, because they're wielding their power rather than trusting the
> people who know what they're doing.

Thus, management decisions tend to be either nonexistent or designed
as impediments to productivity.

In general, though, decisions tend to be avoided, and where unavoidable,
tend to be risk-averse in the short term. This accounts for our previous
observation that, at upper management levels and beyond, strategy prefers
the short-term safety of a focus on existing customers rather than the long-
term cultivation of new customers. Of course, short-term safety may easily

translate into long-term noncompetitiveness and, with it, organizational demise.

The Evaporation of Problems

Despite the avoidance of decisions, and often as a direct result of their neglect, unsolved problems can pose a threat to the carefully managed appearance of control. One way to restore the appearance of control is to make problems disappear: not necessarily to solve them, but rather only to contain and conceal them.

Superficially, the avoidance of decisions might sound like a good thing, as it seems to prevent a headlong and thoughtless invitation to disaster. On the other hand, in their avoidance of any problems, managers are often reluctant to address those problems that can grow to mammoth proportions.

An example of such a problem was a decision by a university vice president to approve shutting down all electricity on campus for maintenance work *during the week before final examinations*. Another VP petitioned the university president to override this mindless decision. The president's response was to avoid offending either party by replying, "Why don't you and the other guy work this out among yourselves?" Concluded a department chairperson, it is clear that "the CEO . . . will go to great lengths to avoid any kind of conflict or *resolving* conflict, for that matter, even at the expense of achieving goals—agreed-upon goals."

While an owner and a manager seem perfectly content with the subterfuge of banishing problems to some unknown fate, the organization as a whole has been kept in the dark about an issue that (1) may critically reduce morale and performance in one work unit, perhaps a key one; (2) may appear isolated but may sum to a larger problem affecting other areas; (3) if it doesn't yet, may soon affect other areas; and (4) may be kept from the personnel with the knowledge and the authority to solve it.

Most importantly, then, control is exercised, and management skill is demonstrated, simply by not involving others. The focus so far has been the cost of inaction or neglect of serious problems. An additional concern is that this self-reliance can also provide a clear sanction for *mismanagement*, since anyone who might intervene to halt it tends to be kept at arm's length. As we will see in later chapters, mismanagement is further supported by various arrangements and attitudes that disable or discredit sources of information about it.

At the same time, in exchange for this dispensation, the manager implicitly agrees to comply without question in larger areas of policy. The cost is to upward communication about these issues, and participation in addressing them.

THE IMPERIAL MANAGER

In a phrase, we have witnessed the development of an authoritative management structure, through the application of Management by Exception: an approach whereby managers intervene in the affairs of subordinates only in the case of problems. As we have seen, this approach may perhaps be better described as intervening only in the case of *problems with concealing problems*. Moreover, Management by Exception is distinguished and legitimized as a full-blown management "philosophy." Even though this is but one possible conception of management, and thanks in part to its legitimacy, this management style appears to be the rule, rather than the exception, as countless employees can attest.

We will visit Management by Exception in the following chapters. Of concern to us now is the carte blanche created by this "philosophy" for empire-building.

As the name suggests, empire-building is the process of creating an object of absolute, imperial rule. This process is permitted by the discretion that is, by its nature, beyond the control of others, so it is able to expand to include *designing the very domain of discretion*. What this means in practical terms is initiative not only for exercising authority over subordinates but also in effect for *creating* those subordinates, by designing their positions. This discretion is accorded under the assumption of the manager's expertise, as a result of the founder's early willingness to cede knowledge and an informed evaluation of the manager's function.

An extreme case, offered by an employee in the Southern California door manufacturing operation, presents, as one logical conclusion of empire-building, an officer who

had the accounting department under him, completely. Had no head person; there was him, and three clerks. And he basically told those clerks what to do, when to do it, and how to do it.

They didn't get any back-up, or any signatures. It was based on his signatures; he'd sign the checks, he'd approve invoices, and he was setting up vendors, fake companies out of Washington and Michigan, but they'd be cashed at a local bank, with his signature on the back.

So he was running this huge scam. . . . That's why the FBI got called.

He took care of all the petty cash, he took care of all the vending machines, he always had cash in his office from the vending machines. He'd hand people envelopes of money and say, "OK, you can have this."

And he was basically telling the girls, "Oh, here, take this. Thanks for not questioning what I'm doing." And these girls were oblivious; they had no clue what was going on. And when the FBI came in, they kept saying, "Oh, poor 'Luther.' We feel so bad for him; we feel so horrible." "You don't feel horrible; you just miss all the gifts he used to buy you when he'd go to Japan. You miss all the free trips to Vegas. And he'd give you gambling money. You miss the shopping sprees at lunch, the six-hour lunches, the mall" . . . It was like tax evasion, fraud; I think he embezzled over a million dollars from us.

In the more general case, empire-building is a ploy for increasing both dominance over and autonomy from the organization. Sometimes, the goals are more modest; according to an employee in an insurance company, declining organizational areas, "in an attempt to justify their existence . . . create empires around themselves. They take simple tasks and make them into projects that consume enormous amounts of time."

As a result of empire-building, the work unit becomes increasingly fractionated, with diminishing positions demanding supplementation by other positions. Fractionation thus begets fractionation, and reduces efficiency, as we've seen. And if all goes according to plan, the result is that the work unit becomes an even bigger player for political battles to come.

Thus, one consequence of the empire-building sanctioned by Management by Exception is the institutionalization of a political battleground. From its very inception, then, management hiring not only selects political animals but also creates a safe haven for the political behavior they prefer. For the work unit, results of Management by Exception include the political animal's familiar treatment of subordinates as objects for political gain, and otherwise their neglect. For the organization, results include waste, conflict, and orientation to personal rather than organizational goals: all ingredients of corporate suicide.

Empire-building represents a prerogative enjoyed by the manager within the work unit in exchange for the manager's loyalty and compliance outside of it. At the same time, the exercise of this prerogative requires the same internal loyalty and compliance from direct reports as demonstrated externally by the manager. In exchange for genuflection by these direct reports, the manager grants them discretion within their own private domains. In this fashion, Management by Exception is transmitted across levels of management, and eventually across generations of managers.

THE CORPORATE PATRIOT

Unfortunately, this microscopic level of discretion has a price; in contrast to other organizational interests, direct reports can very often be expected to bear the brunt of impact from our "political" manager.

Among subordinates, the manager can be explicitly moralistic and ideological. The morality and ideology likely to be espoused by this particular manager is corporate patriotism, to conceal self-interest with a veneer of responsibility to others. The corporate patriot represents an analogue to the heavy-handed national patriot whose overweening protestation of love for country is designed to conceal something decidedly different from love for its citizens, a sentiment expressed more piquantly through economic exploitation, racism, or class hatred.

Like its potential for the nation, corporate patriotism would be a good thing if expressed in genuine, other-directed responsibility.

Unfortunately, to conceal self-interest, it is strictly form over substance. Thus, corporate patriotism finds expression in ham-fisted demands for what might be summarized as duty, relative to which employees are deliberately maintained in a state of feeling inadequate, in order to sustain the manager's moral ascendancy and apparently monopolistic concern for the organization. To maintain this feeling, employees are exposed to demands that are excessive, erratic, impossibly subjective, vague, conflicting, or plainly abusive.

Results tend to be punitive, to underscore the seriousness of employee lapses and the manager's commitment to correcting them. However, in contrast to the stated purposes of punishment, the only thing that is learned is the *inability* to learn. Thus, in addition to the creation of organizational strife, an effect of political management within the work unit is the distraction and demotivation of the many personnel on whom the effect of the manager is actually intended to be motivating and developmental.

Within a religious organization, for example, according to a management consultant,

the married head of a department used "corporate patriotism" by preaching spirituality and the organizational mission essentially to conceal the fact that he was having an affair with his assistant. The person who caught them smooching in the photocopy room was paid $100,000 to leave her job without mentioning anything.

Based on observation of this corporate patriot's behavior, the consultant anticipates that he "will continue playing his political game and preaching love and vision while working his way to the presidency of the organization."

In sum, then, the organization has in the corporate patriot the kind of soldier predictable from an ostentatious display of service: the utterly self-interested one, which is to say the worst kind. Employees have in their manager someone far more interested in their exploitation than in their management.

MISLEADING THE ORGANIZATION

To this point, we have been given reason to suspect that leaders lead in ways that meet their own needs: by demonstrating the requisite self-interest to be hired, by selecting compatible new hires, by ensuring support for their own machinations, and by validating their own behavior, in ways that will maintain that behavior even after they have moved on.

None of this has escaped attention in the real world. Members of organizations have long noted, somewhat hyperbolically, that "the scum rises to the surface." As noted at the beginning of this chapter, employees of the district attorney's office referred to their supervisors in more pungent terms. Most tragic, in recognition of the utter self-absorption required, is the candid acknowledgment by a survivor in a World War II prison camp that "the best of us did not survive."

The foregoing discussion is *not* intended to foreclose the possibility that some individuals are capable of formulating a constructive direction for their organization. However, given that "mobility" is distinct from "facility," a constructive direction has at best a random opportunity to be expressed through charismatic leadership. And a constructive direction is excluded *altogether* from other, and likelier, forms of organizaitonal leadership, in which purposes are made counterproductive: either unintentionally, as a result of incompetence, or as a result of malign intent.

Hence, it is fair to say that inept leadership represents an organizational norm, rather than an aberration. Perhaps most problematic is that leaders can apply the influence that is definitional to their role in order to *perpetuate* their incompetence, by loudly and credibly deflecting blame for that incompetence onto followers. The performance of followers in turn is plausibly culpable because, relative to such incompetence, it tends to be degraded as a direct result, as well as *far more visible and measurable*. Examples range from unpopular political candidates who fire their campaign managers, and poorly-performing CEOs who point accusatory fingers at their staff, to overrated NFL quarterbacks who vociferously claim that their wide receivers "aren't getting open."

The fate of the organization is now firmly in the unfriendly hands of individuals using it to advance their own interests. In the next chapter, we will see specific procedures for solidifying the grip of self-interest upon the organization. Our attention is now directed to training and performance appraisal: procedures that once upon a time were intended to facilitate employee performance but end up instead, through their misuse, as reliable sources of individual incompetence and organizational self-destruction.

5

The Training and Evaluation
of Incompetence

By a small sample we may judge of the whole piece.
—Miguel de Cervantes

In the lexicon of organizations, "training and evaluation" tend to be linked, functionally as well as by nomenclature. One reason may be that evaluation not only concerns the effectiveness of the response to training but also continues the training process itself, by imparting information crucial to job performance.

The combined function begins with the initial training of the new employee. The training process represents probably the new employee's most thoroughgoing exposure to the new organization, and to its expectations regarding performance.

THE PURGE OF SKILLS

As we saw earlier, the employee learns a "specialization": an enterprise that promises expertise and the opportunity to both share and derive value from applying that expertise. In contrast to the promise, what is typically delivered through specialized training is anything *but* an area of expertise: rather, it is a rendition of what *not* to do, what skills *not* to develop, and what abilities *not* to apply.

Specifically, the new employee is introduced to a procedure, which reduces to a set of behaviors designed to detour from most applications. In short, what is delivered is "de-skilling," a term introduced by earlier writers and used since then to describe the actual nature and purpose of specialization.[45]

De-skilling has many purposes. From the vantage point of organizational design, de-skilling ensures that the job will remain at a level of simplicity and predictability that permits control, repetition, and coordination with other jobs. However, there are other purposes as well.

According to the Manitoba (Canada) Nurses Union (MNU),

American health care restructuring models . . . treat patient care like a factory assembly line, the goal being minimum cost and maximum profit. To these health care consultants, nursing care is simply a "series of tasks," and the objective is to delegate nursing work piece by piece to other health care workers who hospital administrators can hire for less money than nurses.[46]

Clearly, then, de-skilling is justified by cost reductions. Intended short-term benefits include the routinization of work and the various savings incurred as a result. Savings are envisioned from (1) "economies of scope," wherein each job is sufficiently narrow to permit a wide range of applications, much like a machine tool and (2) "economies of scale," where jobs, like product or service, are in effect "mass-produced" through their standardized position descriptions, the competence to train and manage them, and the resource requirements of each, including physical plant, equipment, and supplies.

From other perspectives, purposes may be more subconscious, and sinister.

For example, from the perspective of departmental design, de-skilling represents a tool to fragment the work area, expand its size, and maximize its power: a tool visited earlier. As we also saw earlier, de-skilling may in the context of job design serve to render the employee dependent upon others for tasks defined out of the position description, and particularly dependent upon the manager for coordinating these tasks. Based on the definition of power as the obverse of dependence, de-skilling maximizes the power of the manager relative not only to the employee (over whom the manager already enjoys authority) but also relative to the organization as a whole, which depends on the manager for control over the work area.

De-skilling in many respects mimics rather than applies the learning process. In its purest sense, learning provides a new, expanded way of looking at old things. De-skilling is the reverse: it simply narrows the application of current skills. For the employee, rather than the achievement of independence from learning new capabilities, de-skilling serves only to maximize dependence on the organization to realize any personal value. It is hard to imagine any organizational quarrel with that outcome.

Personal costs from this sort of training are material as well as developmental, including limits on power, confinement of a position description to compliance with a routine, elimination of any opportunity for excellence and uniqueness, and unexplored potential to achieve broader individual goals. As reported by the Manitoba Nurses Union,

according to a recent MNU study, deskilling was found to be one of the main causes of job-related stress. . . . Nurses are restricted from using their nursing skills effectively, and face limited opportunities for new learning or to develop their special abilities as individual nurses.[47]

As a result of de-skilling, then, training may appear to serve not the job, career, material, and psychic benefit of the employee but rather the utilitarian purposes of the organization (and perhaps the political purposes of the work unit and manager). However, we are about to find that de-skilling *fails to meet even the organizational goals that justify it.*

THE IMPRINTING OF THE EMPLOYEE

Despite its individual cost, the employee buys into a de-skilled position because it is typically received with a high degree of credulity, due to the employee's: (1) dependence on the organization for employment; (2) ignorance about the job; and as a result (3) perception of new information as objective, received wisdom.

Furthermore, the employee extends goodwill toward the organization, both reflecting gratitude for the job and as a precondition for accepting the job offer. The organization contributes to this process through implicit communication designed to secure the new employee's commitment. As part of this effort, the organization tries to present itself as favorably as possible: as caring toward the employee, thoughtful and efficient in its operations, and in relation to other organizations, as unique, competitive, and destined for success.

At this critical period, then, the organization is clearly in the process of "selling" itself to the new employee. Furthermore, to build the employee's commitment to internalize the new job, the organization makes its mastery an "accomplishment."

By committing to the task of learning the new position, and by deriving pride from mastering the task, the employee has been "co-opted" into accepting the new job design. Co-optation elicits commitment by providing some sort of stake: in this case, through behavior that presupposes acceptance of the new job. All of this takes place at precisely the last opportunity for critical analysis of the new position, before the door is shut forever by the increasing dependence of the employee's self-interest on the job as currently defined.

Thereafter, we indeed find that the employee develops a "vested" interest in the job, due to: (1) mastery over it; (2) infusion of sunk costs into it, including time, other resources, and satisfaction; (3) inexorable identification with it; and (4) acquisition of any status from it. Ultimately, then, the skills of the new employee, originally denuded by the de-skilling process, can at least in part be recouped only through the training process.

This, then, is the procedure for cloistering employees within narrowly defined jobs. Balanced against their costs, as we saw, are benefits intended for the organization, including efficiency. However, reality suggests otherwise.

Unintended Consequences

According to the MNU *Facts for the Front Lines*, and hardly qualifying as a surprise, quality and skill level go hand in hand. Based on a study published in the *New England Journal of Medicine*, "evidence shows that nursing care influences mortality rates. The richer the skill mix of care providers in acute care hospitals, the lower the patient mortality."[48]

Given that it depends on skill level, quality (also not surprisingly) takes a dive with de-skilling:

As nursing is delegated to the "multi-skilled worker"—usually a health care aide—the patient is distanced from the care of skilled and qualified nurses. As well, the holistic practice of nursing is lost in the process.

Nursing staff units and the delegation of nursing work to unlicensed health care workers contribute to the deskilling of the nursing profession. Both take nurses away from the bedside and both de-value the caring role of nurses.[49]

Furthermore, efficiency may also decline with quality and skill level. Based upon a study in *Nursing Management*, the MNU concluded that

staffing levels affect patient complications, lengths of stay, and cost. When comparing two units, one with inadequate nursing levels, the other with adequate nursing staff, it was found that the short-staffed unit had a higher incidence of complications, and in some cases longer lengths of stay. The longer patient stays cost the hospital $116,286.[50]

Hence, *de-skilling undermines the very efficiency for which it is intended.* On a departmental level, inefficiency reflects the insularity of these atomized jobs, designed and trained by those closest to them, producing interests unlikely to bend or to change to accommodate the needs of other units with which they are intended to be coordinated. In some cases, this insularity is to an absurd degree: it has been noted that jobs are often designed to suit the styles, tastes, and abilities of a previous incumbent, in effect *precluding effective performance by anybody now responsible for them*. In addition is the suffocating interdependency noted earlier.

Moreover, the employee's entire value has been force-fed into the job; therefore, the maximization of personal value requires the manipulation of that job in a way that imposes dependence on other people, in turn making it difficult for them to maximize their value, by producing value for the organization. In the long term and to its own detriment, therefore, the organization is setting the table for political machinations.

Also in the long term, finally, we find an employee, now fully "invested" in the job, who like the current trainer will henceforth be available to bequeath the same job to a successor, under the same, mesmerizing conditions. Thus, ever into the future, we anticipate the transmission of an unchanged job description across generations of uncritical incumbents, retention of perhaps already ineffective and increasingly outmoded ways of doing things, and an organization entrenched firmly in the past.

A FIRST LOOK AT PERFORMANCE APPRAISAL

As noted, performance appraisal in effect continues the training process by clarifying the use of performance standards. In addition, of course, performance feedback is invaluable as a tool to identify and resolve performance problems, substituting a constructive focus for mystery and threat, and in some cases providing reassurance. Furthermore, the employee performing at a high or improving level receives information that motivates even better performance.

As a result, according to Warren Bennis, "feedback is the breakfast of champions." For all of these reasons, and perhaps surprisingly to some, an effective performance appraisal has been consistently and strongly identified by employees as a *critical* workplace motivator.

In sum, performance appraisal is clearly one of the organization's most potentially valuable personnel tools. For this reason, its neglect or abuse is one of the greatest crimes by the organization against itself.

THE DISAPPEARING PERFORMANCE APPRAISAL

For "lower" employees, performance appraisal is honored more in the breach than in the observance.

One reason is that performance appraisal is intended to effect employee development, and this is a long-term outcome, with potential benefits that can, at best, be estimated, not validated. Moreover, these potential benefits tend not to be even envisioned for lower employees, given their assumed lack of the competence and commitment needed to improve.

The reason for even nodding attention to evaluating the performance of lower employees is that this function formally and parsimoniously connotes the modern-day manager's responsibilities for informing employees and communing with them. Reflecting prevailing assumptions about these employees, however, performance appraisal receives only the minimal attention commanded by a management obligation, rather than the serious attention warranted by a potentially critical management tool.

In a Southern California telecommunications company, for instance,

management performance appraisals are conducted by asking your friends within the company to fill out a job feedback form and send it to your boss. You also ask your immediate supervisor/manager to send the forms to subordinates (of your choosing) for similar feedback. By carefully arranging where the forms are sent people can shape their job appraisal.

In an insurance company in the same geographical region, an employee indicates that

the past performance appraisal tools have been extremely long and contain topics that are difficult to complete for certain employees who are not in a supervisory role. The company requires that each employee be ranked on each criterion regardless if it is relevant to his or her job description. Some of the managers admitted to rating the employee as "meets requirements" so they did not have to write comments next to items that were not relevant to the employee's job.

In some cases, performance appraisal is dispensed with entirely:

Nobody at Corporate ever got a performance appraisal. Rarely did anybody out in the field get a performance appraisal.

We went out to the field to work with one particular organization. They were really having some difficulties. The president of this particular facility, the plant manager, had been there for about four years and had never given a performance appraisal to anybody . . .

What ended up happening, interestingly, is that that whole organization basically ended up selling off all of its parts and no longer exists as an organization. Some people will tell you that part of the reason for that is that there was no developmental work done for any of the people in the organization.

In this case, the organization was directly cashiered by its inattention to things like performance appraisal. Often, costs fall on shoulders outside as well as inside the organization. According to an assistant director of human resources in a public school district out west,

employee evaluations are a huge problem in public education for both classified and certified. Many administrators do not properly evaluate substandard employees during their probationary period and as a result, the district gets stuck with that employee. The average cost to fire a tenured teacher for a school district is $250,000 and it is a cumbersome process. Terminating a classified employee for disciplinary reasons could cost a school district anywhere from $25,000 to $100,000 and is as equally cumbersome. This often leads to morale problems. . . .

A Function without a Purpose

One surefire indication that performance appraisals are not taken seriously by an organization, and representing a disincentive for employees to take them seriously as well, is their disconnection from key purposes. In the insurance company,

the performance evaluation is not directly related to the salary increases or the bonus distribution. The company distributes bonus and salary increases long after the employee appraisals are completed, distributed, and discussed with the employees and filed in Human Resources.

Some of the managers and the employees don't take the process very seriously since the performance evaluation process is not connected with salary increases, bonus distributions, or promotions.

Seriousness of purpose is reserved for problems with outcomes that, relative to performance appraisal, are more directly consequential, calculable, short term, and bottom-line or financial. In deference to these issues, performance appraisal is likely to be postponed to the point wherein further delay would jeopardize the evaluation itself as an evaluated performance.

At this late hour, performance appraisal tends to be conducted in a hurried, expeditious fashion, with little thought by the evaluator or value to the employee. As a result, the message to employees is that their jobs are routine, their performance is of no consequence, and they themselves are expendable, with predictable effects on motivation and commitment.

For example, according to the human resources manager in a California organization designing concepts and special effects for the development of themes in the entertainment industry,

the company conducted all non-exempt performance appraisals once a year, in November. Therefore, every manager had to complete many appraisals at the same time (up to 50) and did not put much thought or effort into completing the appraisals. Actually, many of the appraisals looked the same with the exception of the name. This led to the non-exempt employees feeling that their jobs were not very important to the company.

As a result of their neglect, any performance problems are often "resolved" by transferring the employee to other, luckless work units, at best perpetuating an organizational burden. In a telecommunications company in Southern California, for example, "a common problem of this company is blaming the union for the 'problem employee' [who] gets good appraisals to move on as somebody else's problem."

In the company specializing in design concepts and special effects,

there was an employee who had several performance problems that included not getting along with others in her team and not following instructions from her manager. She, of course, thought that she was an exceptional employee. Whenever there was a problem, she always put the blame on her coworkers and managers.

This employee was never given honest feedback. Instead, she was transferred to another division. It was not long after she was transferred to another division that she was again having performance problems.

Luckily, she resigned. Why was she transferred and not given honest feedback? Because she was the wife of the VP of the company.

What this story lacked in the equitable treatment of the employee it redressed with a happy ending for all concerned.

THE REAPPEARING PERFORMANCE APPRAISAL

Unfortunately, most such stories end far less happily: neglected performance problems tend to become urgent, either because their costs mount or they present rewarded behaviors that, as a result, become more extreme. This is the point at which honest performance appraisal may finally swing into action, to fulfill its one serious function: the legal function of notifying employees sufficiently in advance about the imminence of termination and other punitive personnel decisions that with honest feedback would have been unnecessary and have now become unavoidable.

Hence, the legal function waxes important because other functions of performance appraisal tend to be *otherwise neglected*, as are the ongoing problems it is intended to address, to the point at which these problems become urgent enough to require emergency treatment. To reiterate, then, the reason for the legal function of performance appraisal is that the procedure *has* no other function: a purpose that is justified by *its very exclusivity*.

As indicated by its legal function, performance appraisal of lower employees is generally intended to identify problems created by the employee for the manager. This is emblematic of Management by Exception, consistent with which it underscores the importance not of the employee but rather of the manager for whom the employee has created problems, communicating the fact that value equates to rank and reinforcing the message that the employee is expendable.

As a result of its problem-solving function, the feedback "target" develops the expectation of negative feedback. Furthermore, upon receipt, negative feedback is assigned the highest possible priority, since it is assumed to be (1) difficult to share and thus (2) significant if its source has under-taken the rigors of doing so. Positive feedback, by contrast, tends to be discounted because it is easier to deliver than negative feedback, for which it is assumed, and often correctly, to be sheer window dressing.

Thus, feedback in general tends to be perceived as negative, and due to the terminal consequences of negative feedback, as highly threatening as well. Understandably, then, performance appraisal is an experience that for most employees tends to be stressful and anxiety-provoking, rather than, as intended, developmental and facilitative: producing performance anxiety and related dysfunctions to be explored in later chapters.

It is too easy to conclude from this narrative that negative feedback is so plentiful that employees are likely to receive it in time to head off any performance problems. To the contrary, the opportunity for such a con-structive outcome is foreclosed by the manner in which negative feedback tends to be delivered. All too often, negative feedback, particularly to lower-level employees, is delivered in a manner that is easily construed as personal, patronizing, and ego-threatening, inviting a response that, rather than a problem-solving one, is instead equally personal, retaliatory, and ego-defensive.

Set in motion, as a result, is an interpersonal process in which the evaluator is driven to exasperation by the perception that previous feedback was ignored, creating an adversarial and contentious interaction that fur-ther convinces the employee of an attack by the manager and the manager of defiance by the employee. Not surprisingly, given their longtime neglect and eventual divisiveness, performance problems tend to expand, limiting productivity, furthering conflict, and hastening corporate annihilation for all concerned.

THE ILLUSORY PERFORMANCE APPRAISAL

Thus, as with most functions, performance appraisal leaves "lower-level" employees out in the cold. Regarding "upper" employees, performance ap-praisal reflects a decidedly different agenda, but one that is no more helpful.

In some cases, the evaluator deserves points for a sincere and constructive performance review. Where abuses occur, however, they are particularly destructive, given the prior investment in victims, their high degree of dem-onstrated potential, their clear and often justified sense of ill-treatment, and their availability of options to seek employment elsewhere. The result is the organization's abandonment of its best bets for the future. For upper-level employees, then, abuses of performance appraisal may be episodic, but can wreak havoc.

Most abuses reflect the fact that, at this level, the evaluation is itself so integral to the evaluator's own performance that it tends to be designed and conducted *solely for the benefit of the evaluator*. In some cases, the benefit is simply to appear professional, by taking part in the professional activity of evaluating employees. According to an academic dean,

I had a woman who worked for me once who was always very high on people at the interviewing stage and then what I learned about her was that two or three months later she's back in my office saying "So-and-so is really a problem. I'm trying this and I'm trying that, working with her."

What I found out was this was a way of drawing attention to herself. She just wanted attention. She wanted to fire them; she wanted my support. So she was enjoying transactions with the boss, and the only way she could really see much of the boss was to have problems with her employees.

The Free Ride of the Evaluator

In general, performance appraisal at upper levels of the organization confronts the fact that, to upper management, and in contrast to "lower" employees, an upper-level employee often is clearly somebody who is going places. For the evaluator, the possibility of tagging along for the ride, and directing it along the way, presents some opportunities, but also some problems.

One problem for the evaluator is that the high-flying upper-level employee is likely to have the perceived advantages of representing an unknown quantity, including at this point an indeterminate potential. The evaluator, by contrast, is typically an individual who is well-known by the organization, with strengths that, if not taken for granted, have certainly been fully calculated. In a phrase, the short-term problem facing the evaluator is *the appearance of superfluousness*, presenting the longer-term danger of *usurpation by the employee*.

As an example, a staff accountant reports on the reaction to her from the director of finance at a management company in the Southern California healthcare industry:

She offered no praise or appreciation of my abilities and I perceived she felt threatened, and had to prove her ranking above me. In actuality, my ambition to accomplish tasks efficiently and manage more accounts than any other supervisor had made me visible and a direct hit for the supervisor to complain to the controller. As I was scurrying about, getting answers from the director, redoing work processes in order to achieve task completion quicker and being proactive with work situations the supervisor was getting nervous.

THE SHAM EVALUATION

For the evaluator, on the other hand, the twin dangers of superfluousness and usurpation are offset by a position that affords considerable opportunity to suppress lower-level threats, imaginary or otherwise. One opportunity is provided by simple power. For example, in a lightbulb manufacturing plant in upstate New York, according to a management consultant,

it was the old manufacturing culture that in many divisions was in charge and the new, innovation-oriented, better-educated . . . number-crunching kind of people . . . people in the younger culture were often overly negatively evaluated because people in the old culture were afraid of them and didn't want to promote them because they felt at some point they'll take over.

In an oil company, according to this same consultant,

it was more like political parties. . . . Whoever became CEO, his party would take over all key jobs in the company and the other people would go underground for awhile. . . . So all your assignments and your evaluations would be influenced by politics so if you were in the in-group they'd be good and if you were in the out-group they'd be bad, regardless of performance.

Another ploy available to the evaluator is to design the performance appraisal to fulfill the highly respected roles of mentor, teacher, and gate-keeper. Performance appraisal can achieve this outcome through its three components of *observation, measurement,* and *results.*

The Power of Observation

One way to exploit the three roles of the evaluator is to conduct the performance appraisal as some sort of "test." As both the designer and the "proctor" for the test, the evaluator is clearly qualified for the three roles as an expert in the position. Moreover, a test raises the possibility of "failure," which signifies a performance problem for the employee but, for the evaluator, presents the opportunity to: (1) immediately fulfill the gatekeeping role and (2) if solved, eventually fulfill the mentoring and teaching roles.

While this richly benefits the evaluator, results are far different for the organization, from an evaluation of performance that is *wholly unrepresentative* of anything that might take place on the job.

For example, according to a former advertising Creative Director,

We had evaluations that for us were very important and very meaningful. These were industry-wide evaluations: the ad agency equivalent of Oscars or Tony or Emmy awards. We had competition for awards that were city-wide or state-wide in which a jury of our peers—our opposite numbers in other firms—were evaluating our creative work.

As copywriters, we evaluated copy; as art directors, we evaluated art. But we could have had an entirely different approach to what was used in the ad and would not have negated the effectiveness of the ad we were evaluating."

In addition to this inequitable subjectivity, observed the Creative Director, an important result of the evaluation was "copywriter's copy"—advertisements designed solely to impress peers and win awards, rather than to meet the one valid standard of effectiveness: whether the ads produced desired results, from customers, retailers, or other intended audiences. Hence, *evaluated performance had nothing to do with performance required for the job.*

A more extreme possibility is that performance is designed *solely* for evaluation. Those of us who matriculated in graduate school recall the Ph.D. qualifying examination that determines whether the doctoral student continues on to the dissertation or fails out of the program. The exam requires, in essence, writing an integration and analysis of research as rapidly as possible, and then orally defending it: tasks that will *never* recur in the student's later professional life. In fact, these tasks require a level of reductionism that if applied to later research would utterly destroy its value. Thanks to its dearth of value, the entire sequence is often referred to gamely by evaluators as a "hazing" process.

At best, then, the qualifying exam tests the ability to take a qualifying exam, and nothing more. And in general, like job interviews that evaluate fitness only for the interview and not for the job, performance appraisal that shapes the nature of performance simply tests the ability to undergo a performance appraisal, and nothing more.

Measurement and Marginalization

Logically bankrupt though it may be, the evaluation process forges ahead of its own accord. Measurement tends to proceed according to a standardized formula, with dimensions that are: (1) copious enough to seem exhaustive, (2) wide-ranging enough to appear as an accurate representation of performance, and (3) equitably standardized, in order to give the entire procedure a disinterested flavor.

The result is that certain types of performance are defined as "authorized." One obvious unintended consequence is insensitivity to the uniqueness of individual behavior defined implicitly, and residually, as "unauthorized."

Consider a hypothetical five-point performance dimension of "uses humor in interacting with clients." Nowhere is there the capacity to distinguish among the characteristics of an urbane, comedic genius; a cruel, sadistic practical joker; and a lighthearted, dim-witted buffoon.

Thanks to this insensitivity to uniqueness, another unintended consequence is to penalize the organization by marginalizing performance at the extremes, to which no "standard" dimensions apply, including the uniquely high performance that should be rewarded and encouraged, as well as the atrocious performance that should be curtailed. Moreover, to the detriment of both an organization and an employee who deserve better, the instrument often defines as irrelevant, inappropriate, or even destructive the very qualities that produce a welcome respite from the norm by straying from "authorized" performance, including originality, inventiveness, and unpredictability, justifying punishment for *excellence itself.*

Far more nefarious than its unintended consequences, of course, are the consequences *intended* for performance appraisal. One possibility is that performance appraisal is but a handmaiden to decisions rendered elsewhere. And representing a particular problem are the reasons for which a negative performance appraisal may be preordained.

One reason for the negative prejudgment is that, like the highly qualified employee who will never be promoted to management, the employee is *too good*: somebody who will probably compete successfully with upper management for bigger prizes. By entertaining this possibility, the organization has identified itself with, and has taken another quantum step toward, mediocrity and failure.

Regarding the aforementioned advertising awards, the Creative Director recalls that

I was very much involved in what we offered for presentation, and I was very concerned about how we scored and in particular how I scored, because these awards were very portable—we could carry a brief-case full of them anywhere in the country, and it was a door-opener for us. We wanted very much to come out with a lot of awards, because it made our agency look good: it put our agency in a very good bargaining position in the ever-present competition for new accounts.

And here's where the whole process was kind of a minefield: If I were on the evaluation committee—which has happened—I, being a normal human being, was not going to give an award to a firm that was most competitive with us, and at the same time I wasn't going to be very laudatory, to give a high grade, to some individual who I thought might become my own competition in my own agency.

Within the same organization, of course, evaluators are often likely to face competition from employees who receive highly favorable evaluations. To prevent this, evaluation results tend to downgrade any performance that could threaten the aspirations of evaluators. In sum, *performance evaluation punishes excellence.*

In this case, performance appraisal has become simply an abuse: as a ceremony intended to depict, as a product of deliberation, the in fact foregone conclusion, to punish the very qualifications for endorsement and promotion. In addition to punishing quality, other reasons for this particular abuse include the one that, according to an observer, victimized a woman who worked in a large cosmetics firm in the Northeast

for a married guy, and her appraisals were always A+. During an off-site conference, he confronts her, professes his love to her, and she politely and nicely replies that she's flattered, she regards him as a nice guy and respects him but that she's not interested. At this point he unprofessionally leaves the conference and afterwards she began to get poor performance reviews and he avoided her totally. She continually tried unsuccessfully to meet with him.

Eventually she confronted him, and he explained that he fell in love with her and resents her, that she was the root of his marital problems, that he had sinned in his heart and his mind and discussed the problem with his priest, and that he and the priest agreed to this unscrupulous behavior that eventually succeeded in getting her to leave the company.

Results

Rather than preordained in this fashion, a performance review often manufactures its own reasons to be negative.

One purpose of a negative appraisal is to demonstrate expertise and fulfill the gatekeeper role by foreclosing a blanket endorsement. Another possibility is to maximize the valuation of the previous achievement, and thereby the current position, of the evaluator who has traversed this particular path.

A third possibility is that the evaluator simply seeks to hoard credit for any subsequent "improvement," from a lucrative source. According to an ex-employee of a Southern California software manufacturing company, her manager "would not give an outstanding review to anyone. . . . She has taken credit for any employee who does well. She'll say she has developed that employee. And she does nothing. . . . And when they would get done she would say, 'Oh, that's because I developed my people.' "

Longer-term purposes may be *to create a need* for "improvement" that the evaluator can administer as a "mentor" and "teacher." To fulfill these functions, performance appraisal may be stage-managed to concoct a "failure" experience from which the employee can be "rehabilitated."

One possible benchmark for evaluation (along with hiring, as we saw) is similarity to the evaluator along key dimensions, perhaps to complete or correct the work of the hiring interview. According to a management consultant,

a ship captain was known as an aggressive people developer. But what that meant was he developed them in his own image, according to his own recipe. If they didn't fit his own image, he was brutal in his evaluation to the point that he destroyed them in the company.

For the evaluator, short-term results intended from this particular appraisal include personal validation through imitation by another. In general, longer-term results intended from a negative performance appraisal include the evaluator's benefit from: (1) an organization grateful for the rehabilitation of the employee; (2) given the evident difficulty of attaining it, the employee's gratitude for any favorable judgment; and (3) the transformation of a potentially formidable rival into a docile ally. And from any future role as a manager that may await an employee capable enough to require this level of suppression, the evaluator can count on wholehearted support. In a word, the evaluator benefits from *dependence*, both from the organization and particularly from the employee.

What the organization doesn't realize, in its lack of wisdom, is that it has created not only a chastened employee but also a victim of acquired, psychic dependence or "learned helplessness."[51] Through the loss of initiative and capability, and the costs of continuous oversight and authorization, the organization has in effect converted a human resource into a human liability. For example, to revisit the staff accountant at the health-care management company, we find that she has since learned that

I have to remain politically savvy in order to please the controller. I have gained a new posture in that I do not implement any change without a directive from above, seldom offer suggestions and I never complain about how things are presently being done. To do this would make me once again a target for negative communication between the supervisor and controller.

We find that initiative has been strangled in an otherwise fertile hotbed— the performer who is strong enough: (1) to require a level of diminution drastic enough to create an opportunity for the evaluator's intercession and (2) to promise improvement that is *dramatic* enough to place a *high value* on the evaluator's intercession. Any organization seeking to enforce its procedures, and initially lacking volunteers for the task, has now cultivated its "Preservationist" willing to do so. For example, according to an employee at "Lancelot" Publishing,

it is common within "Lancelot" for managers to look for a problem in high-performing employees so they can write something negative on the review. They are told that no one is perfect and that the ratings on the performance appraisal will be "average" for most people.

And so, once again to the detriment of an organization and employee who both deserve better, victims tend to be high performers. According to a management consultant, there are devious people who go to great extremes to cut down someone else who they know to be a superior performer in order to shift the balance of power in their favor and perhaps then ride along on that person's capabilities. I've seen that happen. . . .

Where I've seen that circumstance . . . is in the academic world, where there are tremendous egos involved. . . . Everyone is being evaluated all the time by everyone in terms of how "good they are" in some superiority scale. So, it is intolerable for anyone to feel that someone else around there is "better than them." So they'll engage in any kind of behavior in order to cut them down.

So if a young person shows up on the scene and really has promise and everything, you've got to put that person in their place fast. You've got to undercut them and put them in a dependent situation and see that they fail, in one way or the other by withholding information, or distorting information.

All of this is the best-case scenario: an ultimately favorable if unnecessarily punitive performance appraisal. In some cases, the verdict is to expel the high performer from the organization. Procedures can be implanted early on for such a purpose. Let us see how.

THE VIEW FROM AFAR

So far, we have more or less assumed that performance appraisal is entrusted to the supervisor, an issue raised to suggest that alternatives are not only possible but often desirable. Specifically: (1) *self-evaluation* can provide the most information about internal issues and situational constraints; (2) *direct reports* are the sole source of information about the management function; and (3) *peers* and *customers*, both internal and external to the organization, represent perhaps the most knowledgeable sources of feedback regarding the value of performance to others, including the interests that are most critical to the organization.

By contrast, from the perspective of the supervisor, evaluation information tends to be remote, episodic, not very representative, often the result of hearsay, and generally superficial. Nevertheless, the supervisor almost invariably reserves the prerogative to evaluate employee performance, due to (1) the assumed incompetence, politicality, and untrustworthiness of subordinates, self, and peers; (2) the unreliability of data from customers; and, perhaps most importantly, (3) the need to control the entire process for self-interested reasons.

Thus, performance is almost invariably evaluated by the individual who is *the most poorly positioned to acquire the information needed for the task*: a problem for management hiring, as noted earlier. In the case of the Southern California telecommunications company, for example, "occupational employee appraisals are performed solely by supervisors, who most often do not interface with the employees on a daily basis. In some cases, the supervisor may be 2,000 miles away." (!) A psychologist reports that her performance in a medical center was reviewed by an evaluator, the assistant chief of her service, who she saw "once every couple of years, and who had no opportunity to observe the performance of [her] duties."

PERFORMANCE APPRAISAL AS A MEDICAL "DIAGNOSIS"

To compensate for the remoteness of the supervisory position, the evaluator is driven to read as much as possible into scant pieces of information, to confabulate connections among them, to draw as many additional events into the mix as possible, and to atone for scarcity of data with apparent depth of analysis.

The Creation of Etiology

To achieve these purposes, performance is viewed merely as a symptom; "causes" are: (1) inferred, to offset the cursoriness of the review with the forensic skill to plumb the nonobvious; (2) defined in some overarching, inductive fashion, to counterbalance the imaginary nature of the problem with its widespread, critical, and potentially catastrophic effects; and (3) applied predictively to new instances, to demonstrate through novel usage the power and importance of an analysis that probably lacked even the flimsiest of support in the first place.

To the evaluator, and to anybody else willing to give the whole enterprise the time of day, performance has been "explained." However, to any observer with a working knowledge of behavioral science, the only occurrence worth noting has been the formation and application of garden-variety perceptual distortions.

Projectile Analysis

Applied to performance appraisal, *inference* is tantamount to attribution, and attribution is simply the assignment of unobserved motives to the evaluated individual. All too frequently, attribution is really *projection*, the assignment of the observer's own motives to the observed individual.

Moreover, projection often concerns motives so nefarious that they need to be disowned. It is more than coincidental that the greatest mistrust of subordinates is often displayed by Stalinistic types who themselves clearly deserve to be mistrusted. Ironically, then, the evaluated employee is impugned for impulses brought to the table only by the evaluator. The evaluator is in effect condemning and distancing the self; the evaluated employee is, for all intents and purposes, absent from the exchange.

The "Burglary" Effect

In some cases, inference may be deliberately opposed to an obvious conclusion, simply in order to appear in depth. As a result, according to a
strategic planner, excellent performance may be perceived as only a veneer,
or as exclusive to one dimension: at the expense, given the analytical powers now brought to bear, of putatively more important dimensions. For
example, an employee who is well-received by clients may be acknowledged
as an amiable sort but also perceived as manipulative or a lightweight. We
may call this the *burglary effect*, in which apparent performance "steals"
credit from performance along other dimensions.

Perceptual Set

As a result of the burglary effect or otherwise, inference regarding implied performance leads the evaluator to believe that he or she is "onto"
something. The result is a readiness to view *subsequent* stimuli in a manner
consistent with earlier stimuli, real or imagined. This is done by attending
only to, or excessively weighting, certain information now predisposed to
be defined as credible and valid.

In some cases, as a result, counterevidence can even be distorted into
providing evidence for expectations. For example, there was the case in
which a man, simply based on his unorthodox, home-based employment,
was accused of being a mobster by a teenage neighbor, who was even more
convinced after viewing the man's awards for advertising and other evidence of gainful employment, since, as the boy put it, "that's exactly what
the Mafia would do to convince people they're not in the Mafia."

In perceptual terms, this phenomenon is well-known as "perceptual set,"
or a set of expectations that unjustifiably influence subsequent perception.[52]
Perceptual set is a superimposition of value upon information that justifies
prior expectations. Reasons for valuating this information include its very
rarity, given which it is treated as a fortuitous and precious commodity,
particularly given the deceptiveness perceived behind the welter of conflicting information. In reality, information becomes "confirmatory" only by
distorting it in this fashion.

An Expanding Illusion

Having parsed this confirmatory information from other types of information, the evaluator feels free to use it to characterize other instances
about which information is even less forthcoming. The logical term for this
willy-nilly process is *induction*, which corresponds to the perceptual process

of "Gestalt": the construction of an imaginary pattern among actually un-related events.[53] Induction in turn is further generalized and degraded by *prediction* to *completely* unanalyzed and clearly unwarranted instances.

At this point, performance appraisal has become in effect a medical in-strument, designed to *diagnose* an underlying problem. The *overt* purpose is employee development, designed as we saw to fulfill the teaching and mentoring roles, the *covert* purposes of diagnosis.

Through its supporting cast in an ongoing medical soap-opera, the or-ganization: (1) assigns a great deal of gravity to isolated granules of data, since this gravity emanates from some onerous, underlying pathology, and (2) exploits the fortunate discovery of these data points with painstaking analysis of them. As presumed tips of a prodigious iceberg, these data are treated as if they are incontestable and conclusive: this despite their incon-sequentiality, controversy, and probable contradiction by other, undiscov-ered neutrons of information.

Thanks to these perceptual hallucinations, and to use a familiar phrase, the employee has now been *typecast*.

The Halo Effect

As we saw with the job interview, the organizationally consequential effect of these perceptual distortions is the highly-familiar, *applied* distor-tion called the "halo effect" or "halo error"[54]: in the case of evaluation, the intrusion of results from an analyzed dimension of performance to an unanalyzed one.[55]

As an unwarranted generalization from the particular, the halo effect is an indulgence that, in and of itself, is clearly unwarranted, based upon its very definition. The effect itself can be positive, in which case its victims include: (1) the organization that overestimates its employee and (2) other employees who are poorly evaluated in comparison. Providing an example was an artist in an advertising agency:

People regarded him as a good advertising man because he was a good artist. Well, he wasn't, and he fell flat on his face when he tried to create anything. Clients laughed at his efforts; he was pathetic. . . . People who did not work closely with him, who did not know how he functioned or malfunctioned, thought he was a genius.

If the effect is negative, it yields the following penalties for the evaluated employee:

1. Given the emphasis on the presumed problem, if not its absolute nonexistence in the first place, the unlikeliness of the evaluator to acknowledge, and certainly the inability of the employee to ever demonstrate, any required "improvement."

2. Punishment and discouragement, rather than positive reinforcement and encouragement, for acceptable, perhaps even exemplary performance along dimensions to which the halo error generalizes.

3. More emphatically, the fabrication of a generally poor self-evaluation. One possible and eventual result is the Pygmalion effect: the self-fulfilling expectations of performance, details of which will be explored later on.

A halo error is rather easy to come by, since it makes sense to assume that a personal trait has multiple effects. The result was illustrated by a "negative" error in which a psychologist acknowledged that her reasonable-appearing assumption that a coworker would be "unable to engage clients due to his otherwise depressed and withdrawn demeanor was not borne out, since the coworker engaged his clients in a very spirited way."

Reasonable-appearing or otherwise, then, the halo error not only reflects the aforementioned perceptual distortions but also represents a facile neglect of complexity or nonobviousness in human behavior. Thus, the halo error *is in fact* an error.

The important consequence of the negative halo error for evaluation is that it constitutes a conclusive tool for creating a performance problem so widespread that the only recourse is often to expel the employee from the organization. At "Lancelot" Publishing,

once an employee has been identified as having a problem, they are better off looking for another job. Once labeled, managers begin to scrutinize the employee's work to make them feel uncomfortable, so they will want to leave. This happens repeatedly throughout the company.

Moreover, at this point, termination seems called for in any event by previous mistreatment of the employee, and his or her transformation into an aggrieved, perhaps vindictive, and possibly dangerous employee, given the strong capabilities that may have earned the mistreatment in the first place. Put in the framework of street crime, eviction of the employee is recommended for the same reason that mobsters murder potentially vengeful relatives or friends of their gangland hit victims.

THE SYMBOLIC PERFORMANCE APPRAISAL

Lip Service

Whether its conclusion is favorable or unfavorable, performance appraisal performs, as another function, an expression of values to which the organization likes to *think* it adheres: its *espoused* rather than *operative* values.

Through this process, the organization hopes to communicate the very rigor that it lacks, and characterize its performance emphases as products of choice rather than as concessions to better-qualified competitors that they in fact represent. According to a manager, for example, a telecommunications company attempted, through the values promulgated through performance appraisal, to compensate for its knowledge "that its products/services offered to customers were not really in the technology forefront."

The problem is that an espoused value is simply what it says it is: pure lip service. The result is that performance appraisal excludes the features necessary to act on the espoused value, or to "operationalize" it: features that would otherwise include (1) systematic planning to produce an outcome; (2) mutual information by evaluators to validate the appraisal; and (3) feedback to the employee that in both tenor and content is calculated to secure an understanding and constructive response to the evaluation.

To legitimize espoused values, *observation techniques* may be especially elaborate, contrived to convey the very seriousness that, in fact, is missing from the entire procedure; for the same reason, *measurement* may produce a redoubled focus on "authorized performance"; and *results* are especially skewed toward failure, to signify the highest of standards.

In the long term and on a large scale, an organization forced to resort to this simulated performance review can expect the same level of collective failure that it contrives, through the appearance of rigor, to assign to employees who often deserve the very opposite.

None of this ought to come as a surprise to the authors of this charade, and it doesn't. The entire exercise is a bluff, and they know it. Organizational excellence is the farthest thing from their minds; its achievement is confined to its appearance, and its appearance is of interest only insofar as it preserves and advances their jobs.

The job, of course, is the focus of their concern. Self-interest concentrates this concern on the job and, at the same time, deflects any concern from issues of broader interest.

On the one hand, the job is the entire reason for being a member of the organization. On the other hand, a job is only a job.

Ironically, then, and not a little cruelly, broader aspirations, and a commitment to organizational excellence, may be localized *entirely in the high-performing victim of the performance appraisal atrocity.* With the loss of this individual, the organization has lost its best opportunity for this commitment, and from a veritable well of talent, that could otherwise be applied to its long-term benefit.

Bureaucratic "Achievement"

Another reason for a simulated performance appraisal, also intended to offset an abiding sense of inferiority, is to create internal, bureaucratic opportunities for achievement in the absence of more substantive, "real-world" ones. It is this priority that is reflected in enthusiastic congratulations for some aspect of performance at a committee meeting, or in horse-trading for some department priority. It is also this priority that makes symbolic service the kingmaker we found it to be in promoting managers.

A Paean to Procedure

A third and final focus through which a performance review is designed to offset a well-deserved sense of inferiority is upon simple compliance with procedure. By focusing on procedure, the organization elevates an easily attained criterion to the level of an "accomplishment." At the same time, the organization attempts to disguise, and blind itself to, its collective mediocrity, with the precision and care of internal control.

One problem is to exaggerate the tendency, noted earlier, to "authorize" performance and ignore it at high levels. Another problem is punishment of high-quality performance that violates procedures because it is deliberately unconventional. According to the aforementioned telecommunications manager, "works that are 'perceived' as not part of the department's mandate or politically incorrect are usually discouraged and much criticized. Thus, 'high performance' behavior is suppressed unless work is authorized—meaning it is aligned with managers' committed work plans."

Through its highest priority upon obedience, then, the organization in many cases has fully evolved to the status of a reform school.

FEEDBACK

Feedback represents the final element of the performance appraisal process, and opportunity for abuse.

Feedback comes in several possible denominations, including (1) traits, which are overtly favored because they are clearly evaluative, and (2) outcomes or results, which probably have a considerable covert effect since, as the bottom line, they are nearest and dearest to the organizational heart.[56]

For the recipient, however, both tend to be uncontrollable: traits because they are inherent, and outcomes because they may reflect remote sources. For instance, it is unreasonable to fault an employee for reduced sales that probably reflect a general economic downturn.

Traits

Additionally, traits, as part of identity, can if evaluated negatively threaten the recipient's ego, precipitating a defensive rather than constructive response. Traits are approximated by the value-laden wording (e.g., "excellent" to "poor") of many instruments, which as a result express at best an uncaring attitude and at worst malign disapproval.

Traits have also received more benign attention, through a focus on skills which, however developmental it appears, is more appropriate as a hiring rather than performance criterion. The underlying, practical utility of evaluating skills may well be that they are eminently measurable, through a competency examination. A more duplicitous purpose is to placate a restive employee with the assurance that a poorly-compensated, low-ranking, and routine position is but a brief way station on the upwardly mobile path to career success.

Goals

For their part, outcomes have often been presented, and ballyhooed, as motivating goals, but nevertheless introduce a host of dysfunctions: they can induce complacency if too easy, demoralization if too difficult, and can be made to be either through manipulation: of easy goals by the employee, or difficult ones by a supervisor seeking to justify the employee's termination.

If oriented to the individual, goals can impede cooperation; if collective, they can produce an inequitable distribution of tasks. They rivet attention on observable outcomes rather than critical (and, it turns out, highly motivating) processes, on symptoms rather than causes of problems, on visible short-term rather than abstract but perhaps more important long-term issues, and on measurable data rather than subtler but at least as important alternative outcomes. Finally, they encourage the belief that the end justifies ethically suspect means.[57]

As a result, goals may be useful for certain personality types (e.g., achievement-motivated) and tasks (e.g., deliverables, obviously). Nevertheless, responding to their shortcomings, the president of a headhunting company in Southern California told the author that "we do not focus on goals. We focus on process. If done correctly, the process makes sure that the goals take care of themselves." In spite of their costs, goals remain as the dominant performance denomination in many organizations.

There is, in fact, a single, measurable and controllable performance dimension implied in the use and development of skills, and in the achievement of goals. That single performance criterion is *behavior*.[58]

Behavior

For several reasons, behavior has been identified, by research and practice, as the performance criterion of choice. Behavior is controllable, separable from identity, and thus remediable by producing a constructive rather than ego-defensive reaction. In addition, a behavioral performance measure is easily integrated into a reward system, which, as we shall see shortly, is designed in part by identifying behaviors to be rewarded.

Moreover, behavior-based evaluation can help to clarify evaluation normally designed to be based on criteria *other* than behavior.

For example, the use and development of skills can be assessed, and enhanced, by treating them as the behaviors they in fact represent. Outcomes or results can be obtained by identifying the specific behaviors instrumental to them, for example, through a "Behaviorally-Anchored Rating Scale" (BARS).[59]

Perhaps most persuasive is that behavior-based feedback all at once represents, depends upon, invites, and thereby encourages, a constructive response by employees: a response to problem solving rather than to simply an evaluative procedure. This expectation was expressed in Douglas MacGregor's "Theory Y" belief in untapped employee skills,[60] in analyses of the Pygmalion effect, and in theory about adult and parent/child transactions, the latter two of which will occupy us later on.

However, there is a problem with behavioral feedback. The problem is that behavioral feedback, and self-fulfilling expectations of constructive responses to it, fly in the face of deep, insurmountable counterforces within the organization, including both an organizational structure and management attitudes that support the equally self-fulfilling expectations of very different responses by employees. Given the often political route to managerial ascendancy, these expectations may well be colored, on some level, by the lack of qualifications for those holding them and inability to conceive of these qualifications in anybody else: particularly at lower organizational levels. As a product of this structure, and expression of these attitudes, performance appraisal identifies employees as underlings rather than colleagues, focuses on paternalistic evaluation rather than collegial problem solving, forecloses the best chance at solving these problems, and, incredibly enough, instead of solving these problems, exacerbates or even creates them in the first place. In upcoming chapters, we will see these counterforces at work, in sharp detail.

IN DEFENSE OF THE INDEFENSIBLE

In addition to the organization that casts them aside, direct victims of performance appraisal include employees whose extensive capacities remain unappreciated, unexplored, undeveloped, and unexploited. For their brief tenure, these are the individuals with the greatest interest in abandoning this ritual altogether.

Not surprisingly, performance appraisal methods find unreserved support from upper managers who have survived this particular gauntlet and flaunt, as an award for achievement, what to them emerges as its "toughness" and to others is its utter lack of rationality.

To these individuals, furthermore, equity demands the imposition of their previous hardships on newcomers. For example, an ex-employee of a software development firm in Southern California observed that her previous supervisor's attitude toward any job-related rewards was "that we should somehow work hard to get it. Almost like she had worked hard to get that knowledge and sharing it would be like giving us a free ride."

Finally, in their roles as mentor, teacher, and gatekeeper, administration of the process enables its supporters to appear "managerial" and devoutly "organizational." The result of their resounding success is that, when the smoke clears, the only ones remaining in authority are boosters for the performance appraisal process: they now hold the only organizational positions with any control over the process, as the civil servants with seniority, professors with tenure, and directors on corporate boards.

Furthermore, the practice is eventually institutionalized, discouraging dissent, as unlikely as it is, to a voiceless, futile, outlier status. As a result, any explicit objections to a patently objectionable, organizationally suicidal practice come exclusively from lower-level employees with *absolutely no power to do anything about it.*

Construct Invalidity

When management is confronted with evidence that performance appraisal has not measured performance, the response is that ongoing methods of measurement *are performance*. Wished away in this response is an entire issue that continually haunts scientists: the issue of "construct validity," which is the ongoing question of whether measurement actually captures the to-be-measured variables. For organizations, the question is whether performance defined for evaluation purposes is the same as performance on the job. As we have seen, particularly at upper levels, the answer is often no.

For scientists, the question remains an open one. For managers, apparently, the question never even comes up.

CRIMES AND MISDEMEANORS

Utterly neglected, therefore, is the fact that performance appraisal exists in a realm separate from the employee's actual or ideal performance. The reason is that actual purposes of self-interest in no way resemble its purported purposes of enhancing performance.

As a process, utterly divorced from its purported purposes, the function of performance appraisal may be summarized in one word. It is a ritual.

In conclusion, performance appraisal, at best, represents an opportunity lost. At worst, it represents neglect of, or punishment for, an excellent employee and an organization who both deserve better. Its crimes may be episodic, but grievous, including the direct ejection of some capable human resources, adding to the mounting toll self-imposed by the organization.

For the organization, performance appraisal represents a lethal but perhaps only occasional implement for suicide. Our attention in the next chapter is upon a clearly endemic and thus infinitely more potent tool, used far more systematically by the organization in order to destroy itself.

6

Failure as Its Own Reward

Men of ill judgment oft ignore the good that lies within their hand, till they have lost it.

—Sophocles

The organization's reward system is, in every sense of the word, where the action is: it comprises management's behavior toward employees, the source of motivation for future employee behavior in response, and, through their future behavior, the behavior of the organization as a whole, to clients, shareholders, competitors, and other stakeholders as well.

From the perspective of the individual employee, the reward system demonstrates whether the organization puts its money where its collective mouth is. For the organization, as the source of its behavior, the reward system is the whole ball of wax, according to many thinkers on the subject: an organization's effectiveness is likely to be proportional to that of its reward system. We are about to connect the inevitable organizational failure to some hidden, surprising, and even frightening aspects of this clearly critical function.

OVERVIEW OF THE REWARD SYSTEM

It is always the case that behaviors are rewarded in an organization. An organization may reward some form of productivity, specifically defined as quality, quantity, efficiency, speed, or simply showing up and remaining conscious for much of the workday.

In the latter case, the organization in effect is giving rewards for doing nothing. Alternatively, the organization may reward seniority which, to advocates, is a reward for loyalty and to detractors is simply another reward for doing nothing, but over a longer period of time.

At one extreme, for example, a director indicated that her employer, a women's cosmetics firm headquartered in Texas,

ensures that people are rewarded for every step of accomplishment in the business. They even reward people just for helping and supporting other people. The reward is always something that women normally wouldn't treat themselves to.

That represents the sublime. For the ridiculous, we have the district attorney's office in a major U.S. metropolitan area. In that organization, according to a deputy district attorney working there, we have the example of a coworker who always

looked very busy, not doing any work, collecting a fat paycheck. He'd always claim that he had investigations to do, or he was busy working on his cases. He had a special case that he knew was going to end up pleading guilty, but it was set for trial, so he claimed he had all these investigations to do for this trial, and he had to go interview witnesses, taking all kinds of time off, couldn't do anything else that needed to be done because he was busy preparing on this case, knowing all the time that it was not going to trial and, of course, at the last minute it didn't go to trial.

According to the deputy DA, this particular preparation for a nonevent consumed "several months." Then there was the

employee who was sick all the time; you name it, she's got it. She was allergic to milk, was off for three weeks, until they found out what was wrong with her. A bone spur in her leg, headaches, tired all the time, weakness in the limbs, couldn't stay awake, sprained her arm while she was off for her bone spur, roller-blading and fell.

Not surprisingly, as a result, employees at the DA's office seem to have enough time to run other businesses on the public dole, including "security systems businesses, selling candles, elected officials running other businesses."

Employees feeding at the organizational trough aren't unique to the DA's office, or to public agencies in general. In an advertising agency in Miami, according to its former vice-president, the whole office was compartmentalized depending on your function. There were copywriters, there were account executives, there was an art department, there were production managers. I had occasion to walk from my office, I guess it was into the art department, which required me to go through a good number of different offices.

When I took this walk, I was truly amazed by the fact that each of the occupants of these offices was working on something that was noncorporate. "Phil" was working on a program for the Urban League, "Larry" was working on something for the Humane Society, "Tom" was working on getting a mailing out to his Air Force Reserve, for which he was some sort of volunteer secretary. I went to the art department and there were guys there working on freelance work: stuff that you're supposed to do after hours, on weekends—they were doing it on company time.

It was just that these personal obligations and responsibilities took precedence, to their minds, over the corporate needs. I thought that was kind of tragic and funny at the same time.

The women's cosmetics firm is clearly rewarding productivity, and is still with us. The advertising agency, perhaps not surprisingly, is not. The DA's office has also failed, but, as a government agency, is able to rely on public sufferance to maintain an appearance of functionality, much as a taxidermist can maintain the lifelike visage of a slain animal, despite inefficiency that would make short work of a private counterpart.

EFFECTIVENESS: DEFINITION AND SOME BAD EXAMPLES

To clarify our terms, a reward system refers both to behaviors that are rewarded and to the rewards for those behaviors. Since behavior is always rewarded, an organization always has a reward system; the only remaining question concerns whether the reward system is effective. *An effective reward system presents meaningful and desirable rewards for behaviors that are consistent with organizational goals.*

For an example of the very opposite, according to an employee, at least for motivating long-term commitment to the organization,

a Kansas City manufacturing unit was deemed unprofitable. They reorganized and streamlined their production to turn it around. The company newspaper applauded their efforts and the following year the unit was closed and the manufacturing was moved to Mexico.

Then there was, within a nationwide telecommunications company,

a new group created by a bright individual that succeeded, within two years of creation, to become the number three most frequently used credit card in the country. The third year the CEO asked for volunteers within the various business groups to participate in the "Baldridge Award Process." [This group] succeeded in streamlining their process and saved the company money, won the award and was promptly awarded by layoff of the now surplus employees as a result of winning the award.

What this demonstrates, with painful eloquence, is inevitable conflict among interests, both within the organization and between it and some of its members. In addition, in his classic *On the Folly of Rewarding A While Hoping for B*, Steven Kerr provided a veritable laundry list of substitutes for the pursuit of organizational goals through reward systems: these include rewards for objective and visible behavior, for hypocrisy, and for morality rather than efficiency.[61] Clearly, something is amiss with the design of this critical system.

DESIGN BY HAPPENSTANCE

One problem is that there is probably *no reward system that rewards the design of a reward system itself*, along with the lack of support for this function through other systems, for hiring, training, or evaluation: reward system design is not included in any job description.

One reason is that the function would be too costly, at least in the short term. To be effective, a reward system must be designed to support the integrative, overarching operations consistent with organizational goals. This requires the tasks of planning, monitoring, and control, which must be conducted at higher organizational levels wherein such tasks do not come cheaply.

Furthermore, the task is probably impossible to evaluate, since its consequences are probably too remote to trace back to their cause. By itself, unlike flawed janitorial or food services, faulty reward system design does not emit a distinctive "pain," finding expression only through remote symptoms, perhaps not before organizational demise itself; hence, a misdesigned reward system is not likely to be sought as a culprit for its crimes.

Therefore, since evaluation is unlikely, benefits cannot be verified or anticipated, so the considerable costs of designing a reward system are hard to justify. As a result, we find no responsibility for the design, and no feedback concerning the performance, of perhaps the most crucial organizational system extant. In the absence of this accountability, reward system design is entirely piecemeal, fortuitous, and serendipitous.

Thanks to its emergent quality, a perverse reward system is virtually inevitable, and thereby unavoidable and dangerous.

In analyzing this particular organizational disaster, we will focus in turn on both its rewards and rewarded behaviors. Attention is first directed to the rewards.

NEGATIVE REINFORCEMENT

The reward system adopted by an organization originates on the open market. Out in the real world, labor supply fluctuates; for "lower" positions, however, it tends to remain at high levels, due to disqualification from other jobs as a result of inexperience or discrimination. The result is a buyer's market for labor who as a result (1) command low wages and (2) can therefore be cheaply replaced.

It follows that the organization has the luxury of minimizing its human resource costs. In most cases, this means rock-bottom employee salaries and an absence of any supplemental bonuses, with or without which, given market forces, employees aren't going anywhere. In the language of economics, employees are treated as commodities.

In the language of operant conditioning or the more familiar "behavior modification," organizations tend to rely on *negative reinforcement*, in which desired behavior produces no reward, inviting only the consequence of punishment in its absence. (For additional background on this and other concepts addressed in this chapter, the reader is referred to the reward system primer in Appendix 1.)

For managers, reliance on negative reinforcement has a straightforward advantage: in the short term, it is *easy*. The manager becomes involved in the affairs of subordinates only if there is a problem: in particular, only if the problem is extreme enough to cause personal inconvenience, and only so long as it takes to threaten punishment if it continues or recurs.

MANAGEMENT BY EXCEPTION

In this fashion, the reward system spawns Management by Exception. For the organization, this arrangement has the following advantages:

1. The manager's time is conserved for tasks that have a higher priority than employee motivation that, for a captive audience, certainly requires no attention and no concern.

2. By confining the manager's intervention only to problems, and specifically to higher-level inconvenience from them, the organization is spared the costs of monitoring employee performance and evaluating its subtle gradations.

3. Of course, the organization is also spared the cost of resources that would otherwise be used as rewards.

Thus, the organization can cut costs directly, by saving on monitoring and rewarding employees, and indirectly, through efficient use of the manager's time, by relieving responsibility for supervision.

COSTS

These are short-term savings. However, there are also costs. Training under the aegis of Management by Exception has a character all its own. According to a staff accountant at a management company in the Southern California healthcare industry, her supervisor's

inability to be available for questions and answers became a frustration.

I found myself as a new employee standing by her desk waiting for her to acknowledge me and when she did, I would be told to wait, that she was too busy at the moment to answer any questions. In addition when I was given an opportunity to ask questions she would reply with statements attempting to discredit my question: answers such as, "I have already told you the answer to that question" or "you didn't listen to what I said to you this morning."

Thus, short-term costs include the inefficiency of neglect during the training procedure, wherein such neglect is particularly hard to justify on the basis of efficiency. In the long term, there are more serious, and mounting, costs of Management by Exception and reliance on negative reinforcement.

Costs to Employee Effectiveness, Efficiency, and Development

Firstly, negative reinforcement equates to an absence of reward for exceptional performance, providing no incentive for efforts to excel. According to a director of transportation for an organization specializing in geriatric care in Chicago,

my experience in a managerial position was an unpleasant one, specifically, primarily because my superior never ever offered official praise. He found my mistakes to be glaring and his response to them was also glaring. He never, ever once told me that I did a good job on anything, but he was sure to tell me that I did a lousy job on something that was much [better] than lousy—it just was not as excellent as he expected.

My morale fell very early in my experience there and because of it my performance also declined. I felt "What was the purpose of doing a great job and really sticking my neck out if I was going to receive only criticism for the first time it may have been wrong?"

I also feared him. Not only was he a vile person, I knew that the only conversation we were ever going to have was only on a negative note, because there was never a conversation on how well I did at my job, but only mistakes that I had made.

At "Lancelot" Publishing, negative reinforcement

is a big problem company wide. The turnover is particularly high because the salaries are low, the work load is tremendous, and there are very little rewards for doing your job well.

In 1998, 12 out of 13 people in the marketing department left "Lancelot," and the primary reason was feeling devalued, overworked, and underpaid.

One problem is that the individual needs otherwise met by recognizing job performance do not, of course, evaporate; rather, they are met by rewards provided by other, unsanctioned behavior. These behaviors pursue personal and interpersonal goals that from the organization's perspective represent a waste of time and effort.

Very often, this interaction focuses on the source of neglect for work performance. According to the Chicago director of transportation,

while my morale was going down because of my superior, I found myself bonding more with my coworkers, and by the end of my term there, which was a little more than a year, found that we had bonded so closely—we were all like glue—and the main topic of our conversation was our superior.

But we had a good time doing it; we found pleasure in talking about this man and the things that he did to us and the way that he never did praise us but always criticized us and here we knew that we were doing a good job. But we definitely bonded together for strength.

Another problem is that negative reinforcement provides for no employee development. Thus, the employee remains frozen in time, acquiring no ability to parlay work experience into added value to the organization.

Management by Neglect

Thirdly, by discriminating only from acceptable behavior, reliance on negative reinforcement presupposes an exclusive concern with failure to comply with some standard. This implicitly defines a task as routine, by giving no substance to excellent performance and by ignoring any qualities that would create this excellence, including originality or initiative. A task defined as routine reduces motivation and commitment because it implicitly defines its performer as nonessential, inasmuch as he or she is replaceable by the limitless number of people able to do the same thing.

Fourthly, as we saw, the manager's attention is warranted only by a problem *for the manager*. This equates rank with the value of one's time, further eroding the employee's self-image.

Fifthly, by focusing only on others for whom the employee has created a problem, reliance on negative reinforcement expresses absolutely *no* organizational or managerial interest in the employee. There is abundant research demonstrating the demotivating effect of supervisory indifference, dating back at least as far as the "Hawthorne" studies, wherein performance was invariably enhanced by any change in physical illumination, negative as well as positive, simply because employees regarded such change as an expression of interest by researchers.[62] Absent such interest by the organization, we certainly have every reason to expect employees to reciprocate with the lower performance that preceded the Hawthorne effect.

Lack of interest in the employee is expressed by devaluing the employee's purpose. In a heartfelt and eloquent condemnation of the Management by Exception she had experienced in a previous job, an ex-employee characterized the approach, and the manager implementing it, as

a very caste-oriented idea of how life should be, and once she reached a certain level she felt that certain tasks were beneath her. She would say things like "I can't be bothered with something" which I think is just a horrible thing for any manager to say to anybody about anything because every task should have value to it; otherwise, why would that person want to do it?

Costs to Initiative and Creativity

Furthermore, by stipulating consequences only to problems, the organization imposes a risk-averse posture on employees, who are understandably reluctant to hazard blame for mistakes made through initiative. Upper management may feel that this is precisely what they want: that routine tasks are not the occasion for innovation and uncertain outcomes. Created as well, however, are various unanticipated consequences.

Upward communication may be chilled, even where it concerns a problem and, in the absence of attention, potential disaster. Creativity may also be a casualty, even in proposing solutions to those problems. In general, employees are reluctant to act without authorization, reducing flexibility and burdening the organization with the costs of continuous oversight.

In some cases, risk-aversion is exactly the outcome sought by the organization. According to an employee in an oil company that prides itself on "achievement-related" evaluations,

guidelines to our projects are presented in a way that promotes or encourages risk-aversion. Our corporate society is based on risk-aversion.

One purpose is to allow the company to make the best evaluation decision. It transfers to employees' own lives in how they approach risk. Because managers pick safer projects, it leads employees to predict safer projects. They remember the mistakes you make. I'm evaluated based on how profitable the project was and how close I was to predicting it.

Interestingly, then, a company can in effect *create its own captive audience*, by nurturing a fear of the world outside, including other job opportunities.

A NOTE ON PUNISHMENT

Negative reinforcement is a veiled threat to punish, and has credibility only with willingness to deliver on the threat.

There are certainly abundant examples of employee behaviors so clearly egregious and unreasonable that they appear correctable only through punishment; however, as we saw with performance appraisal, these are often likely to be ignored until they have recurred or progressed to the point of intruding on others. Another cost of Management by Exception, then, is ongoing toleration of, and in effect negative reinforcement for, *unacceptable* behavior, to the point at which it becomes problematic enough to warrant a threat of punishment.

At this point, the only attention-worthy threat is to terminate. Often, the employee retaliates with a counterthreat of litigation, which may be too expensive for the organization to risk, particularly if employee retirement is imminent.

The futility of threats to punish at this late point is demonstrated by the frequency of recalcitrance or so-called retirement on the job. Another problem with Management by Exception, then, is that it may succeed in producing a level of "exception" ultimately beyond the ability to manage.

The more general problem is that punishment, on which negative reinforcement depends, has a host of costs to the punisher, raising not only the threat of counteraction but also the following issues, many of which have been noted by previous researchers:

1. All else being equal, punishment creates an aversive, contentious environment: threatening and humiliating for the target and for the punisher a source of guilt and conflict.

2. It imposes the heavy burden of dispensing it proportionately and equitably.

3. Just because it implies clear undesirability to the punisher doesn't mean that the target will necessarily agree; in some cases, punishment can be positively reinforcing, for example (a) by providing attention that even if negative and extreme is preferable to its absence, or (b) by contributing to the notoriety of the target that will earn social rewards from peers.

4. Although it may be presented as developmentally useful to its target, punishment is likely to be designed simply to allow the punisher to express anger.

5. It may punish not the intended behavior (e.g., lateness) but rather getting *caught* at the behavior,[63] leading to a more sophisticated, evasive, and thus more problematic form of the behavior (e.g., getting a coworker to punch one's time card).[64]

Summarily, negative reinforcement used predominantly by organizations ultimately relies for effectiveness upon the threat of punishment that has credibility only if it may actually be dispensed, in which case it can create more problems than it solves.

TURNOVER

A final cost of Management by Exception is turnover of employees who tire of all this benign neglect. Turnover, of course, implies the costs of training replacements, and of tolerating their suboptimal performance while they ascend the learning curve.

The neglect of employees through Management by Exception may seem unconscious, but very often, in fact, it represents a deliberate choice, reflecting the implied calculation that the benefits it provides from managerial efficiency are assumed to outweigh the costs it incurs from turnover. However, we have observed many costs additional and prior to egress from the organization. Furthermore, turnover is likely to sap the organization of its most qualified, marketable employees.

NEGLECTED BENEFITS

Moreover, Management by Exception implies a gross underestimation, of both *benefits* from the motivators it eschews, as well as its costs.

Specifically, one finding from the Hawthorne studies is that employees are rewarded and encouraged by the most inexpensive of all possible resources: by simple recognition. In making a command decision against it, Managers by Exception miss an opportunity for a plethora of benefits, including short-term motivation and productivity, long-term commitment and development, and thus enhanced capabilities for long-term productivity: all outcomes procured on the cheap.

In the Texas-based cosmetics firm, for example, its director suggests that "rewards are sometimes just praise and recognition": but apparently they are sufficient to be noticed, and motivating.

That their absence is also noticed was expressed by an employee of a Southern California aerospace company, who worked

in a field lab, testing rocket engines. A rocket launch was aborted due to an anomaly. A test team was required to work for five days, sixteen to twenty hours a day, to find and test a fix for the anomaly. This included a weekend or a "launch window" would be missed. Through an extraordinary effort the deadline was met. When a supervisor was asked to comment on the team's effort, he said "You're getting paid, aren't you?"

Apologia

Management by Exception does have its real-world apologists, including "professional" employees who take pride in their comfort with its implication that simply doing one's job is sufficiently to be expected that it goes unremarked by management. For example, engineers on an oil tanker exhibited tremendous pride in their qualifications for the job, in the job itself, and in their refusal to countenance constant management expressions of approval.

Nevertheless, one should not overlook the positive reinforcement, perhaps taken for granted by professional employees, of advanced degrees, awards, promotions, and recognition from equally well-qualified peers. When employees lack such reinforcers, replacements, given their efficacy, must be found.

Management by Exception deserves all this attention not only because it is dysfunctional but also because it is typical: as employees attest frequently, most organizations are managed in this fashion. Thus, the organization doesn't wander inadvertently into ruin: it is deliberately *led* there by its managers.

ZERO-SUM RESOURCES AND THE GENESIS OF POLITICAL BEHAVIOR

The tendency for the organization to husband financial resources by denying them to employees will probably elicit little sympathy, since it represents a choice, as is justification for this choice by alternative uses of these resources, like extravagant executive compensation. Less discretionary and worthier of our sympathy is the fact that organizational resources are finite, or "zero-sum."

Zero-sum refers to the property of finiteness wherein a gain for one application is offset by an equivalent loss for another application, producing a net change with a sum of zero. Because they are zero-sum, the amount of resources to reward one individual reduces by that same amount their availability as a reward for another.

Most organizations dance around this issue by pretending to have zero-sum resources in above-zero supply. There are exceptions, including a Boston-based semiconductor manufacturer who explicitly does what others pretend not to: evaluates and rewards based on rank. Less candid and more problematic, according to a manager, was the inevitable response to this issue in a nationwide communications company, for the benefit of an engineer who

was given an evaluation for his job performance in 1998 and received an overall excellent rating. His manager later told him that the evaluation would have to be revised downward because the Personnel Department did not agree to the high percentage of employees in his group receiving an excellent rating.

He learned that the company had allocated budget for performance award based on a bell curve. The result of the evaluation did not conform to a bell curve;

therefore, upper management wanted his manager to adjust the ratings to avoid a budget overrun. He has written a letter to his manager to refuse his award because the practice violated his principles. . . .

Clearly, one direct result of zero-sum resources is inequity for high performers, at least in reference to the open market. Inequity in turn may be redressed through conflict, which is waged through political behavior. As a result, whereas the organization might get no sympathy for the consequences of its miserliness in making resources available, it truly faces a conundrum regarding their allocation.

To understand this dilemma, let us examine types of reward.

Representing one type of course is pay, which, as with tangible corporate assets in general, is clearly zero-sum. As a result, we can expect the sort of behavior observed by a former employee of a New Jersey financial entity, in which "after someone closed a multimillion dollar transaction, someone else wanted to shift the credit to his new worker so that he himself could look good."

THE FAILED SEARCH FOR ALTERNATIVES

Because financial assets are clearly zero-sum, there is frequent reliance on other rewards which *seem* to have less limited availability, including promotion and job titles. What we find is that appearances are deceiving; the number of possible responsibilities and reporting relationships are inevitably fixed, since, between two people, there is only one combined set of responsibilities and supervisory prerogatives, regardless of their allocation. Hence, like pay, promotion decidedly represents a zero-sum reward.

Another possibility of an infinitely available reward appears to be presented by recognition and appreciation, including, for example, the ubiquitous "employee of the month" award. However, also like promotion, commendations remain inescapably zero-sum because they are ultimately relative. After all, excellence is defined by "exceptional merit or virtue," and vanishes into meaninglessness without a benchmark corresponding to a more frequent and less exceptional level of performance.

To reiterate, then, recognition and appreciation, like pay and promotion, are zero-sum rewards, and are equally reliable as sources of conflict and invitations to political behavior.

Group Rewards

One popular tool for abating political behavior is the use of group rather than individual rewards; this seems to make sense, since group rewards can be acquired only through cooperation, which certainly seems incompatible with conflict. Thus, it is all the more astounding that group rewards manage to *exacerbate* the very problems they are intended to resolve.

Firstly, group rewards do nothing to alter the zero-sum nature of the various resources that are available for rewards.

Secondly, to acquire these rewards, groups rather than individuals are now counterpoised, which can not only maintain but also rather *amplify* conflict, by expanding the number of combatants as well as the scale of the rewards themselves.

Thirdly, it turns out that interdependence among organizational members, and the difficulty of managing it, may remain unchanged or perhaps be heightened by group rewards.

In groups, the better performers suddenly find that they now depend, perhaps for their very income, upon their willingness to compensate for recalcitrance by other members. To reduce inequity, each group member limits effort, increasing inequity and further discouraging effort by others. A salesman in a nationwide pharmaceutical company depicts this process:

When you have a situation where there are multiple people involved in a sales-type performance, individual performance is diminished by group performance, because you can have one person doing very well, basically milking off the person that's doing all the work and that very quickly will take the motivation from that one good person. And you get four people doing poorly rather than four individual people doing very well. You become lazy; you become complacent. . . .

So if you have three people working, one person could very easily sit by and do nothing and do fine, and still get benefits and still get commissions and stuff based on that. And then that transfers over; all of a sudden you have two, people then three people who are being lazy and then the whole team's being lazy and the whole group suffers as a group and they end up getting fired. It happens quite often in the field.

If individual motivation somehow manages to survive group rewards, poorer performers may discover that their reluctant contribution emerges as a scarce resource usable as a political tool to extract concessions from their more motivated colleagues. Thus, group rewards may do nothing to eliminate political behavior, and in fact may heighten it.

Other Reward Options

Other possibilities include "flex-time," the allocation of customized work hours, which, while certainly useful, remains limited, both in the potential value it offers and by the task of coordinating the competing needs of workmates.

A final, commonsense reward scheme that would seem to mitigate political behavior is the use of stock options to align individual fortunes with organizational fortunes, again promoting cooperation. However, this does nothing to alter the relative value of organizational resources, constraints upon their allocation, or competition for them by employees.

Thus, even from the enlightened practice of employee ownership, political tensions remain not far from the surface. As a result, in addition to the ineffectiveness and inefficiency induced by choices about available rewards, unavoidable constraints on the allocation of rewards inevitably promote political behavior. As we have seen, we find in political behavior rewards for lack of qualification, for organizationally nonproductive goals, and in general for the inexorable destruction of the organization.

REWARDED BEHAVIORS

Political behavior is induced not simply by rewards but also by rewarded behaviors, the other component of reward systems.

In a simpleminded way, political behaviors can be viewed as behaviors that, in and of themselves, represent diversions from the goals of the organization, yet are rewarded by it, clearly violating one standard for reward system effectiveness. However, we are about to see that the problem is far, far deeper than that.

As with decisions in general, decisions about rewarded behaviors tend to rely on familiarity and precedent. This tendency translates into insensitivity to changes in the market that necessitate changes in rewarded behaviors. In the words of a national accounts manager for a pharmaceutical manufacturing company headquartered in North Carolina,

the nutritional sales department was driving the business of the company. It was high volume, something that's always going to be in demand. It's like aspirin; everybody's just going to take aspirin; something that's always going to be there. But at the same time, they didn't sit there and think, "okay, you know we've been doing this; this is great, this is our bread and butter right now, but why don't we look into this other venture, like cosmetics. Maybe we should put a little more time into this line: this could increase our sales, our revenues for next year by thirty to forty percent." They were just very narrow-minded like that.

Moreover, managers tend to reward behavior that is defined against a standard internal both to the position and to the work unit. This makes sense, since an alternative would create an "apples-and-oranges" problem of evaluating internal behavior against an external, incommensurable opposite number, by applying an irrelevant standard.

So yes, an internal reward system is understandable; however, it has several dysfunctional consequences.

A Declaration of Independence

Firstly, internal standards are not likely to depend on performance elsewhere. The reason is that employees want to look good, regardless of external events; hence, they prefer performance criteria that are resistant to a slowdown in other areas. Understandably, then, rewards are not likely to be driven by and coordinated with the needs of customers, internal or external to the organization. The result for individuals is a reward for an inflexible role: identified early on as a source of strategy. Consequences for the work unit include exacerbation of an already high level of occupational self-absorption.

A Declaration of War

Secondly, due to lack of coordination with external parties, rewarded behavior in one area is *extremely* likely to produce conflicts with rewarded behavior in other areas. For example, according to a management consultant working with a large machine-tool manufacturing organization in the upper central Midwest,

manufacturing people were getting hammered all the time for getting stuff out the door on delivery schedules. And if they were behind then the shop floor got backlogged and you'd have pieces of equipment all over the place in various stages of assembly and so forth. So the design people, in wanting to keep the customers happy, would say "yeah, we can accommodate that design" and then they'd ship down an equipment change notice to the manufacturing people. They might have that whole particular assembly already completed and they would have to disassemble it.

I could remember one particular thing—the only way they could, without completely disassembling the machine, get to this one particular part that needed to be changed was to actually cut a hole in the side of the piece of equipment and then through this hole go in and make the necessary changes and then put a plate on it and weld the plate on it. So the piece of equipment going out the door looked . . . terrible; the manufacturing people were upset about it.

So the two departments were always at war with each other, because the manufacturing people would say "damn these engineering and industrial design people, can't they ever just stick with a design" and [the engineers and industrial designers] would always be complaining about the manufacturing people not being able to be flexible to accommodate their needs. And the wars raged.

These wars are certainly serious, but they represent only the symptoms of a still deeper problem.

THE DEMONIC POSSESSION OF THE ORGANIZATION

Wars among work units, of course, clearly result from conflict among work-unit priorities, due in turn to different behaviors rewarded in each.

Marching In Step

Furthermore, resolution of these internecine wars is typically achieved by the superimposition of goals by the more powerful units upon their less powerful counterparts. For example, in spite of their need to be timely, manufacturing had to defer to the priority of flexibility, superimposed by the designers and engineers.

At the beginning of the chapter, the point was made that an effective reward system provides rewards for behavior consistent with the organization's goals. In the first chapter, in turn, we traced the etiology of the organization's goals to the goals foisted by dominant work units upon others. As a result of the current chapter, we can now locate the origins of the organization's goals more precisely *in the goals that are consistent with the behaviors rewarded in more powerful work units.*

Furthermore, as we've seen, these powerful work units often populate positions of organizational leadership, whose occupants are thereupon predisposed to define the corporate mission by applying the goals of their favored, native operating areas, as a result of "occupational chauvinism." Additionally, for these leaders, their occupational chauvinism has been validated, and elevated to the level of "occupational omniscience," by apparent, company-wide reinforcement for it.

The Organization of the Blind

What we now realize, then, is that an organization *appears* to reward behavior consistent with its goals, but only because it defines its goals as a *result* of its reward system, or more specifically, through the reward system of its dominant work units. In an organization, then, *the rewards in effect produce the goals.* Because the goals are dictated by rewards, the two are necessarily consistent.

As a result, the organization perceives no disparity between its goals and those actuating its reward systems, and has no reason to think that its reward system is anything but effective. Thus, in addition to its helplessness in the face of its inevitably zero-sum rewards, the organization is helpless to correct its reward system, or even to recognize it as an instrument of self-destruction.

Because it cannot recognize the danger it faces from its own reward system, the organization cannot recognize what was noted in the first chapter: that its mission is defined by, and thus accommodates, work units whose own goals and behaviors are *not* in the organization's interest.

As previously noted, one result is the direct disenfranchisement of critical, operational areas. Moreover, disenfranchisement also takes place indirectly, through individual demotivation. According to an executive who has worked with various real estate, escrow, and insurance companies, salespeople are focused solely on what makes them money. Operations people aren't concerned with how good or bad they are. They care if the company survives, but not how well it survives or how much money it makes. They're interested in the bare minimum of what it takes to keep their jobs.

Clearly, operations personnel tend to perceive in the reward system little incentive to excel, so they respond accordingly, with minimal performance. This further devalues the operations area, a process already well under way. The cost to the organization is not only loss of influence from, but also demotivation within, the very work units that could otherwise produce the greatest long-term benefits to the organization.

THROUGH THE EYES OF OTHERS

We can now understand the nature, and the sinister import, of the fact that the organization cannot recognize the dysfunctional influence of its dominant work units; the organization cannot do so because it is looking at the world through the *eyes* of these work units. In a scenario reminiscent of a classic horror film, the organization has been possessed by its worst enemies. By applying the standards of its dominant work units, the organization cannot see the divergence of its larger interests from the mission they have imposed on it. In effect, *the organization cannot see itself*. It is marching to destruction without seeing the march, or the direction.

In an earlier example, the entire organization functions as "software police," without analyzing that the rewards for doing so are the short-term revenues that best serve the interest of short-timers in the sales department, and exclude the long-term revenues of developing new customers that would best serve the interests of other departments consigned to the organization for the long haul.

THE CAPTIVE ORGANIZATION

This, then, is the danger posed by the organization's reward system: the organization absolutely requires its effectiveness and is unable to detect its ineffectiveness. Like a virus invading healthy cells, the reward system commandeers entire work units, uses them to advance a hidden agenda, and unbeknownst to the organization, inexorably brings it to ruin. Among all of the forces that destroy an organization, none is deadlier.

In the next chapter, we will pursue our grim mission by recognizing that anybody involved in undermining an organization is in good company: that the effort is not necessarily an individual one. We will see that destroying the organization is, in every sense of the word, a group effort.

PART FOUR

THE PROCESS OF FAILURE

7

Together We Fall

> Many sensible things banished from high life find an asylum among the mob.
>
> —Herman Melville

A graduate student signing on to study organizational behavior at some point, rightly or wrongly, must choose between the microscopic and macroscopic branches of the field. The "micro" branch focuses on individual behavior, and has given us various analyses of work motivation, cognitive styles, perception, and the like.

Attention in this chapter is on the "macro" end of things that incorporates an analysis of the organization as a collective, largely from the sociological and perhaps anthropological and more esoteric perspectives. The danger posed by this view is the misconception that the organization functions as a monolithic entity: that an organization may not have physical existence, but certainly acts in a unitary fashion.

Another misconception made possible on the "macro" level is that the organization may or may not act in a unified fashion, but makes decisions as if it does. Graham Allison coined the term "Rational Actor" to identify this model of organizations, as well as to discredit it, by applying it to describe invalid mutual assumptions of unity by the United States and Soviet Union during the Cuban missile crisis.[65] As we have seen, organizations are riven by conflict, although the appearance of unity may eventually be created through the superimposition of objectives by victorious individuals and work units.

Various metaphors for the organization have been entertained over the years. The one preferred here is the *arena,* in which occupants more or less pursue their own activities and occasionally may speak with one voice, as if they are observing a sporting event and root for the home team.

This is not to deny that the "macro" organization can profoundly affect its members; it can, and does. One effect, similar to the blind hysteria that can sweep through the arena, is that the organization can denude its members of whatever rationality they enjoy as individuals. Thus, in addition to the conceptual danger of the "macro" view to our understanding of organizations is the practical danger posed by the "macro" organization to itself.

The purpose of this chapter is to explore such dangers. Our first stop, and a vital one, is at the issue of culture.

CULTURE

"Culture" has been cited in recent decades to explain behavior not only within ethnic and other demographic groups but also within organizations as well, thanks to the trailblazing work of Terence Deal and Allen Kennedy.[66]

Deal and Kennedy assessed both the strengths and weaknesses of various corporate cultures. Despite their efforts to discuss the phenomenon in a "balanced" fashion, the argument pursued here is that, as in so many instances, strengths coupled with weaknesses do not guarantee a wash: that corporate culture is a *problem* for the organization. Reasons include the facts that culture: (1) is "nonrational," since it tends to "emerge," rather than to develop through conscious efforts to help achieve organizational goals; (2) is not flexible enough to accommodate such goals, much less a change in them; and most importantly, contrary both to theory and to consulting practice; (3) is so embedded in the behavior of individuals that it is virtually invisible, inaccessible, and intractable.

Serving as a revealing example was a merger-and-acquisition in which the acquiring health care organization *ostensibly* attempted an internal cultural change from its bureaucratic inflexibility, more or less through osmosis, by merging with a more informally-managed, innovative counterpart. The result, predictably, was a morass of bureaucratic regulations descending upon the acquired company, innovation that was stifled rather than nurtured, and a "cultural change" that was no change at all.

Serving as a more general example is the frequent futility of efforts to implement Total Quality Management, an enlightened and well-intentioned if, largely as a result of practitioner attitudes, a somewhat faddish approach to management popularized during the 1980s. Above all else, TQM is an intended cultural change, designed to produce fully participative interaction. Where TQM typically comes to naught is its subversion by the *very culture* that desperately requires this particular transformation, precisely due to features that are antithetical to and thus cry out for TQM: because, rather than participative, the old culture is authoritative, unilateral, and centralized.

For example, TQM issues may be discussed on a preliminary basis throughout the organization, but are ultimately resolved at upper levels, where such decisions always have been made, revealing the old culture, its trusted ways of making decisions, and TQM as little more than an elaborate charade. As this example attests, an old culture manages to preserve itself, reasons for which include the alignment of self-interest with existing positions.

Deal and Kennedy's analysis takes a "compositional" view of a single corporate culture within an organization. As we shall see in the chapter on communications, corporate culture can be localized *within*, and represents a divisor *among*, various work units. This interpretation is a "decompositional" view of corporate culture.

THE ORGANIZATIONAL SUPERCULTURE

What engrosses us here is an analysis in the other direction: a generic view of a single organizational culture that cuts across all corporations. This is the "Organizational Superculture" that actuates *all* organizations.

At this point, we belatedly define culture as shared norms and values; norms are standards for behavior, while values are beliefs about what is important and desirable.

Following are the norms and values that define the Organizational Superculture, and the function served by each for the organization in which it appears:

1. *Tradition*, the accrual of value simply due to history. The organization feels qualified to defend its traditions because it alone can claim experience with them and with their benefits: experience that is so unique as to elude translation into language understood by others. Representing an example of organizational tradition is the following "biblical" business forecasting method: "As it was in the Beginning, so it is Now. And so it shall be in the Future, Forever and Ever. Amen."

    Functions of *tradition* include evasion of internal and external criticism, justifying practices that serve certain individual interests at the expense of others. As we have seen, there are many good reasons for this function.

2. *Loyalty* and *commitment*, the organization's full claim on individual membership, which enables the organization to build a myth about its value, in order to defuse dissatisfaction with various misdeeds and escape responsibility for

them. Examples include pressure exerted in the nuclear industry against whistle-blowers, the most prominent of whom was Karen Silkwood who, at the time of her highly suspicious death, threatened to reveal industry practices that endangered society.

3. *Hierarchy*, a respect for authority that stifles analysis and dissent, exemplified by every authoritative structure extant.

4. *Duty*, which is fulfilled by hard work on behalf of the organization. *Duty* helps the organization (*a*) claim employee exertions without the reciprocal responsibility of adequate financial or other rewards, as well as (*b*) deflect the employee's attention from rewards in general to work. Representing an example was the aerospace firm cited in the last chapter that evinced no responsibility to reward the heroic efforts of its employees with any recognition.

5. *Collectivism*, a substitute of focus on shared fortunes for individual ones. *Collectivism* diverts attention from individual, personal needs that might be neglected by the organization. The military provides an example in which such neglect is generally a response to necessity, collectivism is essential, and individual grievances threaten to undermine it.

6. *Compliance*, or behavior according to rules, policies, and procedures. The justification is public order, but the actual reason is that codifying behavior seems to reflect the considerable care and thought devoted by the organization to everything that goes on within it, as we saw with the organization enamored of its internal procedures.

7. *Representation*, through which the member embodies organizational standards for behavior simply by performing it. The justification is the organization's pride in its members, but the actual reason is co-optation: obtaining commitment through behavior that creates a personal stake in identifying with the organization. Examples include the legendary dress code enforced by Xerox, which has the implicit function of purveying conformity.

According to a manager, for example, such norms and values clearly influence employees in the nationwide communications company who, first of all,

feel that the company is trustworthy and will not sacrifice them at the end. Second, employees should be loyal to the company they work for. It is wrong not to support the company's decisions. Third, everyone should be a team player; deviation from the norm is not acceptable. These values are part of the company's culture. . . .

As we can see, these values are part of virtually every company's culture.

THE MYTHOLOGY OF CONSENSUS

Not surprisingly, the Organizational Superculture imposes, through all of these norms and values, pressure to support rather than analyze upper-level decisions. The nationwide communications company was seeking employee support for a contemplated merger with another company. The manager notes that,

as a result [of its culture], many employees may respond to the CEO's call to help convince the shareholder to vote in favor of the merger. By participating in the program, they avoid the feeling of being an "abnormal" member of the group, or labeled as a disloyal person.

Upper-level decisions gain their apparent consensus for several implicit reasons.

Typically presented early on, prior to any debate, they can be presented to address not counterarguments but rather the wide range of issues cited in the decisions themselves. Alternatives, by contrast, tend to be offered in the context of a debate, so, forced into a combative role, they appear to address the upper-level decisions themselves. As a result, the upper-level decisions appear to be public-spirited ones, while alternatives appear, or can be presented, to be political tools, calculated to undermine upper-level decisions and their sources.

Furthermore, assisted by their authoritative sources, upper-level decisions can be made to reflect nothing less than the organization itself. Originating from less well-known and less highly-regarded sources, by contrast, alternatives appear to demonstrate ignorance, if not animus against the organization that borders on betrayal.

Upper-level decisions also enjoy other advantages from their proactive expression: they are the arguments that tend to be fully-considered, fully-realized, and fully-justified. By contrast, any alternatives are forced to appear rudimentary, ill-considered, and ill-formed.

Pressure to support upper-level decisions is an obvious effect of the company's culture. Less obvious is that, reciprocally, apparently unanimous support provides reassurance *for decision makers themselves* by validating *their* decisions. As seen earlier in the case of the charismatic leader, support from others can vouchsafe the decision maker's mythical belief in his or her own acumen. Due to its sources in manipulation or constraint, support from others is equally mythical.

One result of mythical consensus is the illusion of support for, and opportunity to rationalize, pragmatically and particularly ethically controversial decision making. As in the case of taxes and other individual liabilities, therefore, the organization can very effectively relieve its member of responsibility for collective liabilities as well.

Most importantly, decision makers themselves are assured of organizational alignment behind their own decisions, which, as we've seen, tend to run toward self-interest rather than toward the interests of the organization. Anticipating or receiving such support, decision makers tend to throw their weight behind the superculture: but unconsciously, as we've seen in the design of self-serving jobs. Other members in turn readily accede to the unconscious pressure of decision makers.

Unfortunately, there is another interest: that of the organization, which in light of its nonexistence can only look on helplessly at its members marching in lockstep toward its ruin.

In sum, then, the Organizational Superculture serves to galvanize the entire organization behind the narrow interests of its decision makers.

ETHICAL LICENSE

Representing another set of tools for relieving members of responsibility are the various inanimate mechanisms by which organizations are identified, including "systems," "processes," "operations," "procedures," "methods," "structures," and so on. Even members themselves are identified collectively and functionally, rather than individually and personally, through such nomenclature as "personnel," "staff," "management," the "department," and so on. Such terminology is used in *this* discussion for purposes of generality. Its use in organizations is to create an official domain.

There are many purposes for creating an official domain, one of which is to configure a decision-making body while at the same time excising all vestiges of human participation in it. The dehumanized organization has an ineluctable, mechanical volition that is beyond human comprehension and control; within the dehumanized organization, the human being is reduced to the inhuman caparison of the role. Thus, members can defuse their own responsibility for an organization's decisions by retreating not only into their own limited power but also into their own *irrelevance*.

Ethical dispensation of this type was demonstrated by an arguable whitewash by the Presidential Commission "investigating" the 1986 Challenger space disaster. According to my review of the Commission report, in the February 1989 *Academy of Management Executive*,

the tendency to substitute abstractions for individuals was vividly illustrated by the Presidential Commission. . . . The Commission barely noticed the individuals responsible for the disaster, and instead assigned responsibility to:

1. Collectives ("Both Thiokol and Marshall continued to rely on the redundancy of the secondary O-ring long after NASA has officially urged that the seal was nonredundant single-point failure");

2. Inanimate processes ("The initial analysis of the problem did not produce much research"; "Later flight readiness reviews gave a cursory review and often dismissed the recurring erosion as within 'acceptable' or 'allowable' limits"); and

3. Nothing at all ("There was an early acceptance of the phenomenon"; "O-ring erosion was not considered early in the program when it first occurred: NASA levels I and II were not informed of these developments in the flight readiness review process").[67]

Through the language they adopt, then, organizations make ethical and practical transgressions easy to commit and easy to rationalize. According to one observer, organizations often resort to the opposed tactic of concentrating responsibility on a "scapegoat." We find that scapegoating tends to: (1) respond primarily to irreversible and glaring public exposure that demands some remediation, (2) target a plausible culprit with few resources to hide or resist, and (3) deflect public attention from parties with more resources, authority, and, as a result, responsibility. Undetected, unpunished, and unimpeded, the true perpetrators are likely to continue in the same irresponsible but probably more evasive vein.

Due to disownment or diversion of responsibility, then, organizations are built to fail not only in achieving their purposes but also in *recognizing* that failure.

THE INTERNAL IRRESPONSIBILITY OF ORGANIZATIONS

Due primarily to their ethical license, organizations are built to fail also in meeting the goals of society: goals that represent their very reasons for being, according to some observers. The social responsibility of organizations is an issue that pits the "classical" or free-market view, that this responsibility is confined to earning a profit, against the alternative belief that an organization has additional responsibilities. The classical view reflects "casuistry," the particularization of moral standards to an individual context. The alternative view is predicated on the belief in moral unity, which applies the same standards to all contexts.

In medieval times, casuistry justified acts on behalf of the kingdom that were proscribed on behalf of the self. This surcease has now been extended to organizations, under the assumption that Darwinian selection of the most productive of them is possible only if they are allowed to act freely. To achieve this competitive advantage, for instance, corporations might receive the ethical license to engage in predatory pricing: a level of exploitation perhaps viewed as offensive when demonstrated by and among individuals.

We will examine this assumption more fully in Chapter 10. What concerns us here is the fact that casuistry has reared its head not only in behavior *by* but also *within* the organization, among its members. What this means is that interpersonal behavior may be ethically objectionable in other contexts, yet is perfectly acceptable within the organization.

Official Behavior

An important reason is that, within society at large, "business" has been allowed to sanctify the machinations of businesspeople by acquiring a mythical status, not unlike "religion" and "nation." Business is mystified by the *seriousness of purpose* that it both commands and deserves. After all, it is no accident that "let's get down to business" means "let's get serious."

Due to its seriousness, the standards of business are expressed in a norm of *professionalism*. Due also to its seriousness, business is entitled to enact its own laws: or, more precisely, to act as if it is *above* the laws of social interaction.

To give otherwise offensive internal behavior this legal imprimatur, organizations operate under their "official" aegis that extends, to internal behavior, the serious purposes of business. Furthermore, official behavior is depersonalized by assigning it to roles, effectively loosening ethical constraints. However, the depersonalization of behavior is visible only to sociological analysis; to those directly affected by it, this behavior remains experienced in a very personal way, with effects that are also hugely personal and potentially destructive.

Official Misbehavior

As a result, we find behavior that receives wholehearted authorization within organizations that would yet be absolutely unacceptable and unthinkable among individuals in normal discourse. People whose everyday relationships are civil and amicable suddenly find themselves on the receiving end of communiqués, typically in writing, often from groups, from individually anonymous sources, that range from abrupt to outright abusive. The functions served by this communication are legitimized by their official status, representing within the organization its internally "public" interest: as a reprimand, as part of a performance review, or as justification for a personnel decision.

Additionally, since professionalism is expressed in official behavior, and official behavior transpires between roles, responding in kind is perceived as nonprofessional, since it is retaliatory and *personal* rather than task-oriented. Because it is seen as nonprofessional, such a response from victims of official abuse is absolutely foreclosed. In this manner, the absolute authority of the aggressor is rationalized.

Such was the situation confronting an employee in a Southern California entertainment company, whose manager, according to another employee, unbelievably

got in a screaming match with [her]. They were cursing in the middle of the office. I've never heard such language from someone who's supposed to be your superior, regarding this woman's personal banking situation. She thought she had to tell her how to do her banking, and she was cursing at her because of it. She wrote her up because she cursed back.

Moreover, in confronting such abusive behavior, the employee confronts as well the length and breadth of an entire organizational subculture. Because it has escaped previous notice, let us take a hard look at it.

EXECUTION-STYLE MANAGEMENT: THE DEVELOPMENT OF A MANAGEMENT SUBCULTURE

The traditional, benign, and reassuring view of managers is that they function simply to serve their followers. It may seem somewhat surprising to suggest that the behavior of managers is instead determined by, and responds to the needs of, not their direct reports but rather *other managers*. The reason is that management is itself a group that has its interests, formulates its goals, develops its culture, commands its considerable resources, rewards its members, and controls their behavior in order to serve its own interests and achieve its own goals.

The Mystification of Management

The manager first recognizes, as a source of personal power, not membership in a specific work unit but rather the management position itself. For this reason, considerable effort is devoted to maximizing the power offered by this position. One way to accomplish this is to mystify the managerial role, just as organizations mystify business itself: to render it so impervious to the understanding of others that it is: (1) immune to evaluation, (2) assumed to deal with sophisticated issues, and thus (3) reserved for high-level individuals.

One way to mystify the managerial role, in turn, is to invest it with a high level of secretiveness. This may be accomplished through Management by Exception itself, which removes the manager, and the management function, from the mundane, routine activities that are visible and accessible to direct reports, reserving the person and the responsibility for higher-level events. Another, related property of management that serves the same purpose is its deliberate exclusiveness, achieved by apportioning time frugally with subordinates and dramatizing time spent with higher-ups.

Providing an example is the ritual of The Management Meeting. Employees are typically apprised of it in advance, for the explicit purpose of preventing interruption but also for the implicit purpose of publicizing Big Doings in which general participation is forbidden. The importance of the event is magnified by the obvious excitement displayed beforehand by participants, by frequent references to it afterward, and by keeping employees in the dark about its purposes, its deliberations, and its conclusions, other than what they need to know regarding their own function. The selective dissemination of certain information only deepens the mystery surrounding other information, and the management function, in general.

Furthermore, meetings and related forms of interaction help members of the management subculture establish social roles, flex credentials, and exchange professional respect, in order both to receive acceptance and to qualify others as credible sources of such acceptance. In addition, credentials of membership have cachet only in contrast to their absence: i.e., among lower employees. Thus, the management subculture draws its sustenance from the "otherness" and perceived inadequacies of the people its members outrank.

A SOCIETY OF VICTIMS: THE ORIGINS OF AN EMPLOYEE SUBCULTURE

The otherness of lower employees often exists entirely within the minds of upper employees who are convinced of it, often as a result of stereotyping.

Stereotypes about Lower Employees

A "stereotype" is defined as "the assignment of an invalid characteristic to all members of a group."
One reason for stereotyping is to *enable the self*.
Upper management levels are rife with the conviction that lower employees lack the prerequisites to be anything *but* lower employees, including required knowledge, skill, experience, and ambition. Upper management levels are also thickly populated with beneficiaries of promotion for political rather than meritorious behavior, as we have seen. In one sense, then, disqualification of lower employees is thereby a transparent attempt to disown lack of merit.

Another reason to disqualify lower employees is to *assuage guilt* by justifying organizational subjacency as voluntary. One reason for this perception is that, to higher-ups who know about such things, bigger organizational doings are disconnected from the bustling, day-to-day interaction of lower employees who thereby appear to be fully occupied with other concerns, with no apparent interest in matters known, by those involved with them, to be important to the organization.

In general, stereotypes of lower employees serve the same functions they do in society at large: among other functions, they: (1) provide a *cognitive "shorthand"* to parsimoniously explain, all at once, complex, perhaps unrelated events; (2) *express traditional values*, in this case regarding how lower organizational classes are viewed by occupants of upper ones; and (3) *demonize the victim*, relieving those actually responsible for various misfortunes, including, of course, oneself.

As a result, a management consultant notes that, in response to lower employees "who did still voice their concerns, the [upper-level] "Shirts" often saw them as troublemakers and guys who just wanted to stir the pot. They were union guys; they were just trying to make matters worse."

In some cases, organizational and societal stereotypes are confounded. In a manufacturing company in the Los Angeles area, according to an employee,

our labor force is ninety-five percent Hispanic and I know a lot of our executives think that . . . they're not educated.

A lot of them don't speak English, but there's actually quite a few that I've found—and it kind of shocks upper employees—that are actually doctors and lawyers in their own countries; obviously, not here, but they're very knowledgeable people and they have gone through a lot of schooling. . . .

[So] there's like a little world out in what we call The Shop . . . because when tax time comes there's tax guys who do the taxes, and legally, they know what they're doing, there are lawyers to help the divorces, and there's their own little network back there. [Yet] they're on an assembly line, punching a time-clock. . . .

One obvious, long-term result of this superficial, top-down view is a failure to recognize and develop the in-house human resources whose commitment, familiarity, and untapped abilities could otherwise be applied to organizational success. The result is an unrealized opportunity for such success, and, instead, yet another source of organizational demise.

Stereotypes by Lower Employees

Stereotypes also serve self-esteem needs, which may explain their occurrence among lower employees as well as upper employees. According to an employee in the Southern California healthcare industry, for example,

the hourly employees always complain about the salaried employees, that they take long lunches, that they leave early, or that they don't work their entire eight hours because they don't have to. So in my department they complain all the time about the exempt employees.

Individually valid or otherwise, this generalization maintains the myth that diligence, if not the reward for it, is exclusively the province of lower employees, implying that upper rank is *not* a function of merit.

THE CLOSING OF MANAGERIAL RANKS

While the distance between the two cultures may be artifactual, the conflict that results is real enough.

One implication of this distance is the predisposition it provides for upper employees to back each other in disputes with lower employees. For instance, it is certainly easier to eschew sympathy with "union guys" than it is to understand the potentially universal constraints facing them. The result is that any manager at odds with a lower employee can count on knee-jerk support from peers.

As an example, we have an abusive Project Manager in the Southern California special effects and design concepts company mentioned in Chapter 5:

Everyone in the company knew that top management accepted this Project Manager's behavior because they never took any actions to stop his behavior (and yes, they knew about it) . . . He was also a personal friend of the CEO. The end result, the company lost many valuable employees because of "backing up" the Project Manager's behavior.

Of course, lower employees can also count on mutual support; however, this support is impeded by procedures for isolating the lower-level disputant, muted by lack of opportunity to express this support, trivialized by lack of power, and invalidated by lack of qualifications. As a result, any dispute casts the lower-ranking participant as an outlier, with all of the deviance and moral turpitude associated with that role.

Reports an employee regarding her supervisor in an entertainment company in California, for instance,

I had walked in and she was mad at a mistake but I had not made it. But she took it out on me. It was the type of thing where she told her manager and everybody else above her that it was directly related to me and my negligence.

And so they called me in and talked to me and everything and I explained the whole situation. It wasn't anything I worked on, so they were totally confused how I even got involved in the project. And so I told them I didn't; I had no idea what they were talking about. So I walked back to my desk, wrote my resignation, and walked out right then. I didn't even give them two weeks.

The problem for the organization, and a further step toward its demise, is that many conflicts result from well-founded employee concerns and grievances that, due to their burial beneath the heavy cloak of the management subculture, *never see the light of day*. For the entertainment company, the unacknowledged problem was a deranged manager who invited a response that deprived the organization of an employee who in turn was probably far more capable and certainly far less lethal than the manager was. For employees, particularly at lower levels, the problem was, and remains, the stereotypical view of them as incapable of bettering themselves.

THE PYGMALION EFFECT

Stereotypical assumptions about the employee may or may not be individually valid. However, they certainly *seem to become* valid as a result of the response they invite from their victim.

Specifically, an employee assumed to be disqualified for a job is unlikely to be entrusted with tasks that require job qualifications and permit their demonstration and further development. An employee denied the opportunity to demonstrate or develop these qualifications is certainly in no position to invalidate their assumed absence.

Stereotypes that villainize their victims perpetuate themselves in much the same way. A management consultant observed the phenomenon within "classic labor relations stuff, probably in every heavy industry . . . where cultures become adversarial and it became sort of a self-fulfilling prophecy. Management didn't trust the workers; the workers felt mistrusted, so they acted in a way that was consistent with management expectations."

Thus, true or otherwise, assumptions about lower employees certainly seem to *become* true at the very moment they are expressed in behavior. There is a name for this phenomenon. This process is called "expectancy" or the "Pygmalion" effect, named for the legendary Greek who sculpted a statue of a woman that in turn came to life and fulfilled all of his romantic desires.[68]

The Pygmalion effect is a response that is consistent with, supports, and perpetuates the expectations expressed in the behavior that originally invited that response. In groundbreaking research on the issue, subjects serving as "teachers" elicited better performance from a single group of "students" when told to expect good performance than did so-called teachers who were told to expect poor performance.

Pygmalion in the Organization

In general, organizations are tailor-made to produce the Pygmalion effect, due to the importance they attach to, and their ongoing evaluation of, virtually every aspect of individual worth. Individual worth garners the attention of the individual seeking to claim it for the obvious reasons of self-esteem and the personal value to be derived from the organization. Negative evaluation of individual worth can appear to "come true" because it focuses, in self-fulfilling fashion, on two critical dimensions: (1) competence, degrading confidence, commitment, and thus performance, and (2) ethics, eliciting ill-will, and retaliation consistent with ethical shortcomings.

For an example of both, a management consultant working with a West Coast high-tech manufacturer of hard drives observed a female employee who

had a very negative and belligerent attitude. She was very defensive about any kind of feedback. In this organization we were participating in a . . . feedback experience and in fact I think that she knew that she was going to get bad ratings from her teammates, which raised the ante and raised the anxiety level and she was even worse in behavior around the time we were doing this.

And then, when the results came out and I had to sit down with her and give her her feedback she actually threw the feedback report across the table at me and exemplified, demonstrated all the behaviors for which she had received poor ratings. And then, when we had the team session she would not participate. She sat there during the whole meeting while sixteen other members of the organization participated, freely gave each other feedback and all that. She sat there stubbornly with her arms folded across her chest and she would not participate in any of the outdoor activities. She demonstrated again exactly the reason why she got all the kind of scores she got.

Self-fulfilling Negative Feedback

As earlier noted, employees are predisposed to anticipate and perceive negative feedback, since positive feedback, given the ease of delivering it, tends to be dismissed as window dressing. Because it dominates employee attention, negative feedback will dominate ours as well.

Anticipating or perceiving negative feedback, the employee is likely to devote an extraordinary amount of time and effort to monitoring, evaluating, and interpreting any conceivably relevant information about, and from, the evaluator and evaluation process. Clearly, one direct result from all this is distraction for the employee and degradation in performance as a result.

Another method to rectify an actual or imaginary negative evaluation is to minimize exposure to it, through: (1) reluctance to act alone, and reliance upon others for assistance; (2) the assumption of minimal responsibility; (3) preference for "safe," low-risk tasks, over more ambitious (and perhaps more useful) ones; (4) failure to complete a task, in order to delay evaluation; (5) when working with others, not pulling one's weight by opting for all of these alternatives; and (6) avoidance of explicit feedback itself.

All of these responses appear to justify negative feedback (1) because, in one way or another, they degrade performance and (2) they can be interpreted by any interested parties as indicative of low self-evaluation. A low self-evaluation in turn tends to receive a high degree of credibility from others, since it is obviously not contrived for self-aggrandizement and seems imbued with personal insight not available to others.

Consider the following response by an employee in a manufacturing operation to her evaluation, as reported by her manager:

I had to fire this employee because she was doing things. . . . Reviews were coming up like six months later; she knew she kind of had a mid-write-up, so she was kind of anticipating this horrible review, and it just got worse.

The write-up did not do anything good. And the day I fired her she basically said, "I knew this was coming; it's not a surprise; there was nothing I could have done" when it was completely in her hands. It's like the most amazing thing I ever saw.

. . . things like coming in late, leaving early, taking long lunches, going to the doctor, quite often when she'd say, "I should be back in an hour" and she'd be back in three hours, but not call. Kind of weird behavior. . . . I couldn't have every employee doing that. Here and there things happen; you know, life happens, but it was like all the time. Constant. And it just kept getting worse. And then she started bad-mouthing everybody. . . .

Implicit in this behavior is the employee's attempt to *actively* bring about anticipated censure, in order to characterize it as the product of choice, rather than incapacity, the obvious reason for which is self-esteem. Apparently, the personal doubts engendered by the possibility of negative feedback are aversive to the point of unacceptability.

Other efforts to redress negative feedback focus on methods other than performance itself, since performance has been disqualified by feedback (or the expectation of it) as a way to achieve this goal. The employee is therefore left with methods of influence that include various excuses, including external handicaps, the responsibility of others, and performance by others that is at least as poor. It certainly *appears* as if the employee seeks through influence to evade a professional, objective appraisal through substitution of personal, subjective criteria. These machinations in turn certainly suggest that performance itself leaves something to be desired.

Furthermore, through their transparency, these machinations identify the employee not simply as a poor performer but also as too inept to conceal it.

EVALUATION WITHOUT ANALYSIS

Contributing to the Pygmalion effect, of course, is the *evaluator* as well as the target. At bottom, this contribution is made possible by the evaluator's *lack of analysis*.

Representing a nonorganizational example was a group therapy process in which a participant displayed a lighthearted attitude characterized by other participants as compensatory for inner anger, and appeared to oblige this characterization by responding to it with, in fact, increasing irritation. For observers, the reaction was consistent enough with expectations to justify them, while exonerated as the culprit were the expectations themselves (along with their incessantly repeated expression), given the lack of further analysis.

Due to this analytical poverty, then, expectations of evaluators appear to be confirmed. It is this appearance that, in general, constitutes the sum total of the Pygmalion effect.

Representing an organizational example, according to an ex-employee, is a response *to evaluation* that appears to be sufficiently combative to justify the expectations of evaluators. A manager had been under fire for her attitude and rather than change her attitude, her attitude got a lot worse. "I'll show them for challenging me," that sort of thing. . . . "I'm not to have staff come in and dictate what their review should be or how I should behave" and shortly thereafter another employee told her that she didn't appreciate the way she had been behaving and she was saying "I am not going to change. They're just going to have to get used to it." It got worse, and worse, and worse, and worse.

Thanks to the response of the victim, the evaluator now has reason to believe that a negative evaluation shall have found its mark. Evaluators are in effect *training themselves* to deliver a negative evaluation. Again, the subordinate is likely to assume that feedback is negative, and to respond in a way that, with the connivance of the evaluator's analytical shortcomings, *ensures* that it in fact will be negative.

PERFORMANCE ANXIETY

One route for the Pygmalion effect is the painfully familiar "performance anxiety."

In its classic, sexual form, the male who dreads the inability to achieve a penile erection is focused on his erection itself, or, more precisely, on its absence, and certainly on the response of the sex partner to its absence: hardly the stuff of a stimulating, male erotic fantasy, and thus a sexual spoilsport that, in self-fulfilling fashion, validates the original fear.

Performance anxiety reduces performance itself by redirecting the attention urgently required, from performance to performance *evaluation*. Performance evaluation, in turn, receives excessive attention due to excessive fears about its outcome that as a result of that attention are fulfilled, producing widening anxiety as a result.

According to a former legal secretary in Atlanta,

I went in with the attitude that I could just barely, barely meet the standards of the firm. So, there I was, always on edge, and as a result of always being on edge, nervous that I did not perform the job very well.

I messed a lot of things up because my train of thought was always broken by the feelings I was having of nervousness and a lack of self-confidence in performing the job the way it was supposed to be performed. As well, I had continual feelings of agitation which really pointed at the fact that I was angry at myself for not overcoming the nervousness I was feeling. So I got angry at myself a lot for the mistakes that I made, my bosses would get upset, and it seems that the harder I tried the more I messed up because the higher my nervousness level and agitation level were. . . .

In the work situation, performance anxiety affects performance precisely where it should excel: in a career specialization, wherein the performer presumably has the benefits of training, education, background, and choice. Failure under these conditions raises doubts about the ability to perform well under *any* conditions at all, since this is, as it were, the best of all possible worlds.

Thus, without overstating its effects, performance anxiety in the workplace can easily undermine the victim's entire self-concept. Moreover, the high stakes can only magnify the fear. Small wonder, then, that sexual performance anxiety often stems from its occupational analogue ("I had a hard day at the office, dear"), a testimony to the importance of work-related performance, and to anxiety about it.

Moreover, the inability to perform in the workplace is experienced by its victim as a broad-ranging failure not only to execute a task but also to judge, learn, and objectively evaluate the self. The danger is that these ancillary skills, and anxiety about lacking them, generalize to other tasks.

As observed in Chapter 5, the evaluator frequently allows the evaluation of one task to obtrude on others: i.e., the so-called "halo effect" or "halo error." We can see here that the halo effect can influence not only evaluation but also *self-evaluation*. Clearly, on some private level, divorced from rationalization and bravado, where doubts are freely indulged, we are our own worst critics.

Moreover, in indulging these doubts, we have the willing assistance of the organization. The reason becomes apparent when we realize that, in analyzing the vertical dimension of its social structure, an organization is designed to produce not the effective performance of its critical tasks but rather the *very Pygmalion effect that obstructs this performance*. Let us see how.

ORGANIZATIONAL TRANSACTIONS

Back in the 1960s, Thomas Harris developed Transactional Analysis, through which he analyzed human interaction as a transaction between people, each acting out of one among three possible internal identities: the Child, the Parent, and the Adult.[69]

The first two roles were learned in earlier experience: the Child through behavior and the Parent through observation. The Child is the identity that seeks immediate gratification, has low self-esteem as a result of this indulgence, and tries to elevate self-esteem by securing approval. The Parent is that identity that, in response to the child, judges, moralizes, and levies authority. (We can witness the emerging Parent in the comically judgmental, moralistic, and authoritative posturing of young children.)

The Adult, finally, is that identity that addresses reality not through such evocative roles but rather in a problem-centered fashion.

The Adult persona is an *instrumental* device for solving a problem; the Parent role, by contrast, is an *expressive* device for articulating anger and other emotions. By referring to these roles, we may further understand attitudes and behavior covered earlier regarding performance appraisal and reward systems.

At the risk of appearing a bit reductionistic, perhaps, the Parent exercises: (1) the authority of virtue through stage management of various characterological, moral qualities, by evaluating traits, and (2) the right and duty to ventilate anger, through the threat posed by negative reinforcement and the use of punishment. The Adult, by contrast, prefers to focus on problems, by evaluating behaviors, and by correcting or maintaining them through the more thoughtful manipulation of extinction or positive reinforcement (see Appendix 1).

In interpersonal interaction, complementary roles tend to elicit each other: the Parent role is evoked by the Child, and vice versa. The reason is that each was associated in memory, and by habit is now "triggered" with the appearance of the other.

Adult roles also tend to evoke each other, by communicating, and responding to, expectations of a problem-centered response. As an adaptive interface with the real world of real problems, the Adult role is clearly the most productive role for the work organization, or, for that matter, any enterprise.

The Organizational Family

Thus, it is nothing less than cruelly ironic that *organizations are structured to produce the very interactions that are the least productive of all possible relationships.* The supervisory or managerial function is a made-to-order Parental role, in relation to which the employee, again by association and by habit, is consigned to the complementary role of a Child. Reports a director of a financial institution in Los Angeles,

I think one of the weirdest things about being a manager is being referred to as "boss." You take on a parental role because you tell the employees what to do; your experience is broader than your employees'. You dictate what they do. Your employees are responsible for the do-it-work. You're responsible for setting up their day, just like for a child. You set up their values, tell them what's important. If they do something incorrectly, you make them re-do it. It's like scolding. It's weird.

From the vantage point of the supervisor, the Parental role may be weird, but from the perspective of the employee, it can be positively bizarre and destructive. An employee in a California entertainment company reportedly had a controlling type of supervisor. . . . She got into people's personal lives a lot—she was telling you how to run them, what you were doing wrong, what you were doing right. She judged you on that in your work environment. . . .

One time . . . I was doing my work and she comes over to my desk. I had my back to her and the office was full of people and when people talked you kind of ignored them because you don't know who was talking to whom. She was talking to me and I didn't know; my back was to her and I was working on my computer and she hit me on the head. She knocked on my head like, "Hello? Are you there?" So I spun my chair around; I couldn't believe she had hit me.

That was her way of disciplining. Her way of managing was belittling and making you feel like you couldn't handle your personal life so how could you work for her?

Frozen Roles

The behavior of the Parent/Manager can also create the very problems it is intended to resolve, since, for the Child/Employee, attempts at control by the Parent/Manager impede immediate gratification, making its achievement delayed rather than immediate, and more motivating because it is more urgent. The result is the process noted earlier, through which efforts at maintaining control can undermine themselves.

For example, students in a public school are likely to be made restive and resentful by "busywork" clearly designed to control them, and may express their frustration by presenting discipline problems that begin to pose real problems for control. As a result, *Parental control creates the very problem it is intended to solve.*

Because it both seeks and undermines control, the Parental role establishes a permanent need for itself. As a result, the Parental role, and the Child role that responds to and further elicits it, are *never-ending.*

THE DESIGN OF NONPRODUCTIVITY

In general, then, the organization by its very nature is structured to produce nonproductivity. Organizational suicide has many sources that are more hidden and sinister; by contrast, none is more obvious than this one.

Moreover, the happy organizational Family does not end there; the good times roll on with expanded nuclear and extended relationships. Among employees, we find sibling relationships that support, enable, and perpetuate Child responses. In addition, we can easily find sources of support for Parental responses among the "aunts" and "uncles" represented by other managers. Furthermore, there is certainly the possibility that responses observed in one area are imitated in another, giving us every reason to relish the prospect of the organization as one large dysfunctional family, well beyond individual efforts at control and self-control. The organization has taken another quantum step toward its own demise.

Hierarchy is established for coordination and control. We can see that, on behalf of the organization, it fails to achieve control. In the next chapter, in looking "horizontally" across the organization, we will find that the same thing can be said about coordination.

8

Partners in Crime

But when to mischief, mortals bend their will,
How soon they find fit instruments of ill!

—Alexander Pope

Group behavior is taught in management classes not only because it represents an arena for key decisions and in fact for most behavior in organizations but also because, in comparison to individuals, groups have extensive capabilities that can make for better performance. Group resources include a large amount of knowledge, skills, experience, perspectives, information-gathering tools, social controls, physical capabilities, and capacity to generate ideas interactively, through "synergy."

The major problem presented by groups, and another important reason to teach about them, is that if not managed correctly they present evidence not of their impressive capabilities but rather of their own unique, and crippling, dysfunctions. Furthermore, the successful management of groups may be the stuff of college case studies and academic research, but requires a level of enlightenment that in the real world is a rare commodity. What we are about to find is that such dysfunctions penalize not the groups in which they appear so much as they are aimed directly at the heart of the organization itself.

Thus, group behavior is addressed here because, thanks both to their resources and dysfunctions, groups have a considerable capability to lay waste to the organization in which they operate. In sum, group behavior has found a place in this book because it represents another weapon in the arsenal of members against their organization.

CONFLICT "FUNCTIONALITY"

One problem presented by groups is conflict.

And one way to deny that organizations are built to fail is to deny that conflict is bad for them. Yet this is precisely the position taken by some observers, according to whom conflict performs some useful functions for the organization, including the formation of adjudicatory structures and linking mechanisms, and the revelation of power differences among combatants.

On the other hand, as thought-provoking as they may once have been, there is something logically malodorous about all of these functions. All are functional because they *remove* conflict: either because they end conflict itself, for example by clarifying differential power, or because, as structures or procedures, they can prevent conflict by solving the problems that *lead* to it.[70]

If it is functional to eliminate conflict, conflict itself cannot be functional. It is therefore with a clear conscience that we can claim that conflict is destructive.[71]

Conflict among individuals has the obvious disadvantages of reducing (1) focus on the task at hand, (2) morale, (3) collaboration with others, and (4) commitment to a now-fractious workplace. Furthermore, as they do in so many activities, groups are far more capable than individuals of generating and conducting truly destructive conflict. Conflict among groups therefore warrants some attention, as well as some dread.

A key weapon available to the group against other groups is cohesion, due to its utility in creating an integrated response. Parenthetically, group cohesion is another of the processes misapplied as a "function" of conflict because it precludes conflict *within* the group: again, ultimately identifying conflict as anathema rather than as desirable. In addition, cohesion ameliorates external conflict because it harnesses political power and guarantees a quick, bloodless victory, an indication of its potency as a weapon.

GROUPTHINK

Representing a source if not the very definition of group cohesion is consensus within an interacting group which, in turn, is obviously supported by internal conformity, or "groupthink."

Groupthink was introduced as a dynamic for group process by Irving Janis in order to explain the acquiescence of Lyndon Johnson's cabinet to his policy of expanding our involvement in Vietnam. Groupthink accounted for the juxtaposition of their collective support for the war with their private reservations.[72] (On the other hand, another explanation for this disparity is that these former cabinet members were simply lying, for the benefit of a public now clearly disillusioned with the war.)

Groupthink has been more conclusively demonstrated by the social-psychological researcher Solomon Asch, in an experiment wherein 33 percent of group members deferred to the clear perceptual misjudgments of colleagues, a number that plummeted under conditions wherein one colleague broke ranks and gave the correct judgment.[73] Clearly, then, groupthink is sustained by the group member's belief in it. And, like consensus in general, as we have seen, groupthink in organizations, of course, supports authoritative decision making, because group members are pressured to uncritically accept such decisions, rather than critically analyze them.

Groupthink as an Attractor

For members, consensus very often is almost an afterthought; receiving primary attention are the social rewards it makes available. For the group member, these rewards become ends unto themselves, while consensus, as a means to those ends, is sustained by the deliberately limited analysis it tends to invite.

Groupthink by Compulsion

In general, then, while it certainly suggests diminished capacity, groupthink at least implies voluntarism. When this fails, the organization is not above outright intimidation.

In the earlier discussion of "Organizational Incest," we were given an example of a nationwide telecommunications company, whose managers conduct sham "job interviews" to hire in essence a cheering section. In this company, refusal by the new hires to cheer on command incurred consequences not unlike the indoctrination and brainwashing techniques associated with a Soviet-era gulag. According to a manager there,

if there's any one of the employees that is not reacting to this relationship, then they would be encouraged to sort of find another job because they don't fit in this job. . . . You can always put him into a certain training program. There's a feedback process in the company that enables the employee to develop but the quicker way of doing this is to try to swap the employee with another person who is more conforming. That saves a lot of development effort.

Groupthink and Political Freedom

Out in the wild, the lion earns its reputation as the king of beasts in part by focusing on a single prey, forcing other, potential victims to run for their lives, who in turn eschew the option of collectively destroying the vastly outnumbered predator. Similarly, along with the aforementioned official norm of professionalism, groupthink assures collective public inertia that provides the political predator free reign to feast on individual victims in private.

Groupthink, Political Advancement, and the Anatomy of the Power Struggle

The dispensation offered by the group to its internal political gangster underscores that groupthink is the self-sustaining presumption of not simply universal *agreement* but also individual *powerlessness*. Clearly, individuals become powerless by believing that they are: by eschewing the risks of confrontation, but also by foregoing the benefits of increased power.

One frequent result is the political *fait accompli*: a familiar organizational spectacle in which the loser in a power struggle is sacrificed and supplanted by the victor, generally in short order, while the battle is unremarked and certainly not impeded by onlookers. Events proceed as if unruffled, with an almost eerie normality, which to the victor signifies the totality of victory, the completeness of mastery, and the promise of future domination.

For example, in an overseas service corporation, the President of an American subsidiary was deposed virtually overnight with the connivance of a personal enemy on the staff, who resumed his formal post as office manager and as a de facto vice-president, based upon a longstanding friendship with the new president. With no resistance from other staff, the office manager ruled the roost in a newly-found, despotic fashion.

Groupthink and Political Muscle

Back out in the wild, the lion also earns its reputation through unity of purpose with its fellows, in contrast to its helplessly atomized prey. This introduces another function of groupthink.

Groupthink tends to be actively solicited because it affords the cohesion needed to prevail in conflicts with other groups. Given the "nonrationality" of groupthink, one way to view the political process, therefore, is as one in which triumph is achieved, and domination of the organization is attained, by those groups that manage *to behave the most mindlessly*.

However, this mindlessness may not be a randomly-occurring group trait; unfortunately for everybody else, it may occur in groups with the characteristics that permit the greatest clout over the organization.

THE EVOLUTION OF GROUPTHINK

A group is most given to consensus when simplicity describes (1) its interface with the environment, (2) the goals that reflect the narrowness of that interface, and (3) the tasks needed to achieve those goals. Thus, consensus: (1) is made possible by these limited goals, and at the same time (2) permits the internal integration needed to effectively promulgate those goals to the organization as a whole. These conditions favor the unity and influence of staff units, with their relatively simple, short-term goals, over operational areas, with more complex, long-term goals. We therefore have added reason to be concerned that an organization *is steered in exactly the wrong direction by the members who are able to do so.*

In a publishing house, on the all-powerful publications committee,

many times, if one individual brings up a minor negative comment (especially if it is the CEO or Director of Marketing) such as the title is bad or the author's university isn't well known, the entire committee jumps on the bandwagon and begins to tear apart the proposal. This is extremely frustrating to the editor who has made a good pitch for the project and has a good feel for the potential market.

External Sources of Groupthink

It may also be the case that groupthink and group cohesion are most likely due not only to simple tasks and environments but also to the perception by group members of an external threat.

Observers have long noted that internal cohesion is maximized by an external enemy. One example cited by researchers is increased solidarity among Americans during the Iranian hostage crisis of 1979.[74] What this suggests for organizations is that focus is likeliest to be achieved through consensus by groups that are the most battle-ready and aggressive.

We can visualize all sorts of dysfunctional fallout raining down from this: groups that are prepared for political jousting may be least qualified for the fruits of victory because they are ethically unconstrained; compensating for other, significant underqualification; or simply have the most spare time.

The Construction of Groupthink

Furthermore, researchers have long observed that group cohesion can be effected not simply by passively perceiving but rather by actively *constructing* an external enemy.

For its part, history demonstrates that an external threat creates internal cohesion for which other justifications are absent. Dictators, for example, often create, maintain, or exaggerate an external enemy to build internal cohesion in the face of various privations from their rule, including corruption, disenfranchisement, and physical brutality: a tactic used in the face of declining popularity by Egyptian President Gamal Abdel Nasser in 1967 to blockade Israeli access to the Gulf of 'Aqaba.

Furthermore, by provoking the external enemy, a leader can add to the sense of urgency that suspends internal opposition, a tactic that ultimately backfired for Nasser and has been used more recently with mixed success by Muammar Qaddafi in Libya, Saddam Hussein in Iraq, and Slobodan Milosevic in Yugoslavia.

Within organizations, managers can make similar use of external threats.

POLITICAL WAR

For all of these reasons, and as with countries, political brinkmanship within organizations can erupt into full-scale war. For instance, consider the obsessiveness and scope of the following all-out political conflict in a Southern California healthcare company, according to an ex-employee:

The Finance Division was at war with the IS Division.

I think the CFO really wanted to be in charge and wanted to get rid of the CIO. . . .

He and the Director of Finance, the woman I worked for . . . had me do this project where I sorted the salary information from top to bottom and they identified people that they wanted to get rid of. . . . The Finance people are circling people that they didn't want there anymore. It was like they were trying to run the whole company. . . .

I was in Finance but I was kind of friends with some of the IS people, and I had to be really careful about communicating with them, because if the CFO and the Director of Finance saw me communicating with them, that would have been a bad thing.

. . . The Operations team . . . were caught in the middle, because they needed IS capabilities, because Operations totally ran on the systems. So they really needed to work with IS, but at the same time they had to be friendly with the Finance people to get any staffing, to get what they needed, because Finance ran the budget. And Medical was the same way; they needed both sides. So Operations and Medical were caught in between the two that were going at each other. . . .

It was very uncomfortable; it was very stressful.

As with individuals, politics selects for success the most purposeful and, at the same time, the most organizationally divisive and thus the least meritorious groups. As with individuals, due to required countermeasures, groups justify concern that organizations not only nurture but also *amplify* political behavior.

Additionally, this concern may apply even more to groups than to individuals, since the political threat from a collective war-machine is even harder to ignore than from an individual, and is likelier to ramify due to the need for large-scale retaliation and other forms of involvement by other work units, even uncommitted ones, as we've seen. Finally, conflict among work units is invited by their predisposition to view others through their own specialization, and the assumed marginality of other specializations. Intergroup conflict destroys the organization not only by eliminating co-operation but also by empowering the most self-interested, destructive groups.

To produce conflict at this level of intensity, occupational chauvinism is likely to be amplified by stereotyping.

STEREOTYPING OF OTHER WORK UNITS

This is our second visit to the subject; stereotyping was addressed in the last chapter by applying it to the creation of a "vertical" caste system across organizational levels. We revisit and extend it by applying it to a "horizontal" view of other work units, where the purpose extends beyond the perception of superiority to the contrivance of other differences.

Stereotyping and Identity

Stereotyping of other work units may compensate for internal problems: problems like mismanagement, a lack of esprit de corps, goal dissensus, an absence of motivators, or an absence of pride in one's work. The existential philosopher Jean-Paul Sartre argued that prejudice helps define identity; despite a paucity of other distinguishing traits, it could always be said of an elderly cousin of Sartre's friend that "Jules can't abide the English." Explains Sartre:

My friend doesn't recall that they ever said anything else about Cousin Jules. But that was enough. There was a tacit understanding between Jules and his family: They ostentatiously avoided talking about the English in front of him, and that precaution gave him a semblance of existence in the eyes of those about him at the same time that it provided them with the agreeable sensation of participating in a sacred ceremony. Then on occasion after careful deliberation, someone, as if by inadvertence, would throw out an allusion to Great Britain or her dominions. Cousin Jules, pretending to become very angry, would feel himself come to life for a moment, and everybody would be happy."[75]

In a manner similar to that of Cousin Jules, members of a work unit who lack any substantial basis for group identification may readily find it in contrast with, and to some extent through hostility to, other work units.

Parenthetically, and perversely, people often derive satisfaction by sub-scribing to stereotypes about their own respective groups—even negative stereotypes. In addition to identification, other motives include conspira-torial glee from an insider's view and, ironically, solidarity in the face of duress unleashed by *such forces as the stereotype itself*. Unfortunately, the stereotype is no more true as a result of support by its victims, but for outsiders, certainly appears to be.

Stereotyping and Attribution

Admittedly, a stereotype doesn't arise in a vacuum; it emerges in accompaniment to real differences among groups. In the case of ethnic groups, such differences can, of course, be quite dramatic, encompassing dress, language, and customs. The stereotype can be viewed as a generalization of real differences to imagined ones, but the dynamics of it go deeper, into mutual attribution.

In contrast to dramatic differences from other groups, group members clearly comport quite comfortably and share familiarity with each other. This comfort and familiarity tend to breed suspicion by foreigners, since they cannot share or even grasp it; it inevitably produces some degree of secretiveness; and it *seems* to suggest secretiveness for some commonly suspect motive, about the true nature of the group, as well as its collective opinions of outsiders. Thus, it becomes easy to attribute hostility to the group, as well as qualities that shouldn't see the light of day: for example, thievery to Gypsies, organized crime to Italians, and primary allegiance to the Pope by Catholics.

Although less dramatic and dire than the ethnic variety, stereotypes are traded quite briskly for the same reasons among organizational groups. For example, members of a marketing department may see in accountants the stoic mien associated with disdain, while accountants may see marketers as social gadflies, expressing their own prejudice through gossip and rumor.

Homogeneity

By definition, a stereotype stipulates not only remoteness but also some sort of homogeneity, and often appears to be valid because it develops in response to activities of the target group that *appear* to be homogeneous. There are several reasons for this appearance.

Often, homogeneity is a direct result of the stereotype itself. In the Middle Ages, for example, church laws barred Christians from money-lending because it, and the mercenary quality it reflects, were viewed as the province of Jews, whose resultant monopolization of the activity certainly seemed to reflect the selfsame mercenary bent that in Pygmalion fashion justified the laws in the first place. Within organizations, accountants may be barred from activities and roles that require social interest and skills, due to their presumed lack of either, disabling them from demonstrating or developing the capabilities to exploit career opportunities, for example as managers, that would otherwise be available to them.

Homogeneity as a Casualty of Distance

Further contributing to this perceived homogeneity is the group's inaccessibility, and identification only through stereotypical contexts and behaviors. In some cases, this reflects physical remoteness, which itself may be a function of the prejudice that accompanies a stereotype.

For example, whites who remove themselves or are otherwise divorced from normal social interaction may know blacks only through the media as basketball stars and hip-hop artists. In other cases, remoteness is purely perceptual. For example, Asian Indians are certainly extant throughout U.S. society, but may be most often readily identified as convenience-store clerks.

Similarly, accountants appear among us in various capacities, but are most readily recognized and recalled through activities that appear to be regimented, workmanlike, and antisocial.

In all of these cases, a two-dimensional view provides all available information, which nevertheless seems to suffice, because it implies an unbroken sameness that is sufficiently unappealing to evoke no residual curiosity. For marketers, perhaps, there is no need for additional insight into a group as apparently uninteresting as accountants. Hence, available information *constricts itself*.

Pillars of Stereotypes

These stereotypes are maintained by the fact that people cannot help but contrast their unflattering, two-dimensional view of others, whether in remote departments or nations, with the variety of attitudes and behaviors personally experienced, as well as observed among more familiar individuals. Also maintaining these stereotypes are the following, classic perceptual dynamics: (1) an internal system of prompting that allows the salience, observation, and recall of only (*a*) stereotypical behaviors in group members and (*b*) stereotypical members of the group; (2) the aforementioned "perceptual set," or the credibility assigned to information that supports the stereotype, which thus receives inordinate attention or weight; and (3) stereotypical attributions that also have the credibility of previous testimony and at the same time, since they are wholly imaginary, can be easily concocted and assigned to group members.

Thus, an Irishman may be noticed and recalled largely through drinking, by defining his drinking as a drinking "bout," and by contriving drunkenness as his activity at a social gathering. Similarly, engineers can be entirely defined by technical rather than recreational or social interests, while human resource personnel appear to be utterly consumed by bureaucratic compliance with regulations and procedures: speaking of whom, according to a management consultant,

HR people are stereotyped in the sense of "They don't understand the business. We don't know what they do understand but it's not what the rest of us understand." Therefore, they're not going to have a lot of power and influence in the organization. So the people who probably have the most focused education around issues of change and development are sort of shut out. "HR's too important to be left to the HR people."

Stereotyping and Myth-Making

Based as it is on perceptual foreshortening, a stereotype is clearly a myth. The reason for devoting considerable discussion to the subject is that stereotyping represents more than a social oddity; stereotyping figures very prominently in the interaction of organizational members just as, like it or otherwise, it virtually *governs* the interaction of peoples. Proof of its dominance is offered by the continuous insight of discovering similarity with other people, indicating previous assumptions of nonequivalence on some sort of grand, biological scale.

As a myth, the handy feature of stereotyping is that it permits the construction of original, tailor-made assumptions about the stereotyped group.

For example, an associate of the author claimed that in order to save money, Jews invented things like gift-giving and greeting cards, virtual non sequiturs that were somehow permitted because they were linked linguistically, if not logically, to a familiar stereotype. In organizations, stereotypes can be similarly constructed to ennoble their users: thus, to marketers who pride themselves on creativity, the accounting department "has no imagination," while accountants may assign to themselves a hygienic approach to office-keeping by impugning the marketing department as "a bunch of slobs."

Thus, stereotyping becomes an exercise in poetic license, providing a veritable receptacle of descriptors.

THE COSTS OF STEREOTYPES

Stereotyping has other purposes as well, including disownment of responsibility. The result in organizations is a tendency to blame other work units for an internal or shared error and failure to solve it.

In addition to deflection of responsibility, stereotypes incur the costs of the insularity that they justify, conflicts they may create or exacerbate, and mismanagement from which they are intended to deflect attention. They also produce the *grossest* of inefficiency, as observed by a management consultant in a manufacturing operation in the Northeast:

The executive vice-president of operations viewed attorneys as a necessary evil, pain in the neck, really not business oriented, in fact, if anything, they really sucked off business. This was an old-time guy in his late fifties, something like that, who'd been in operations for years and years and years. A cowboy kind of guy. He had been very successful, but didn't have much use for attorneys.

The attorney—the general counsel—on the other hand, had been raised in the northeast, and so this kind of cowboy type guy was anathema to him. The vice-president would come in to work sometimes wearing his cowboy boots. You know, on Beacon Hill, you just don't wear cowboy boots.

And so these stereotypes kept the two of them from ever developing any kind of a rapport and a relationship. They'd pass each other in the hall and they'd barely even see each other.

And the disastrous consequence for the organization was that the operations people (this was in the late eighties) were getting hammered by the Environmental Protection Agency on a number of different sites and areas where they had had plants and where they had buried waste and all of that so the operations people and the general counsel and the attorneys should have had a very close relationship with each other. In fact, neither department did because of the relationship the two senior guys had.

Stereotypes help to bring the organization to ruin directly, by facilitating conflict, and indirectly, by undermining communication and cooperation. Collective destruction is invited by the individual benefits of stereotypes, which naturally take priority for members. For the individual indulging it, a stereotype provides a favorable self-definition, through implicit inclusion in a highly regarded in-group, and through contrast to and exclusion from a discredited out-group. Nonorganizational out-groups include the "black sheep" within families or a persecuted minority within society itself.

IN-GROUPS AND OUT-GROUPS

Reasons for Creating Them

Within organizations, a manager may *deliberately* create and distinguish an in-group and an out-group, reasons for which correspond to the reason often given for stereotyping: in the case of managers, it simply makes their task cognitively simpler, according to business analysts Jean-François Manzoni and Jean-Louis Barsoux.[76]

Another reason for the practice is that it rewards high performers at the minimal cost of excluding them from the out-group, simply through their pride and relief at the honor. A third reason is that it builds cohesion in an in-group adjudged to clearly deserve that status and, because its members are the high performers, promises the most benefits.

A fourth possibility is relief from the responsibility and blame for punishing offenders, by delegating the task to agents within the "in-group." A fifth possibility is, again, to divert attention from mismanagement, through the smoke screen of perhaps imagining or creating, certainly neglecting, and now exploiting a group of poor performers.

Results of Having Them

According to Manzoni and Barsoux, among the consequences of creating an out-group are that its members emotionally drain their bosses, demonstrate to other employees their shared vulnerability, add to others' workload, vicariously contribute to the pain of others, waste colleagues' time on complaints, and retaliate by victimizing their own subordinates.[77] In addition, the organization reaps the inequity of victims, their reduced commitment and loyalty as a result, all of the dysfunctions of the conflict contrived between equally contrived adversarial groups, and, again, diversion of attention from the real issues of management.

Additionally, the ubiquitous Pygmalion effect surfaces in the dynamics of an out-group. As any victim of discrimination can attest, the role of an outcast produces an inventory of responses that are so unappealing to others that they appear to justify the role; these include defensiveness, ingratiation, self-consciousness, and withdrawal, in addition to the many equally odious reactions noted by Manzoni and Barsoux. As is the case with stereotyping in general, a final dysfunctional effect is diversion of attention from the mismanagement purveyed *in the act itself* that is *revealed* by such a blatant manipulation of human vulnerability in the first place.

Thus, group processes go on their merry way, while the organization in which they transpire figuratively trembles from the effects.

"RISKY SHIFT"

Representing a case in point is "risky shift," the tendency for groups to make riskier decisions than individuals.[78] There is some research-based reservation to assigning this dysfunction to all groups at all times, but where it does appear, it spells some serious trouble for the organization.

In general, risky shift is likely to appear when the "shift" is in fact not all that "risky" for participants.

In one organizational scenario, a course of action that normally appears to represent a high risk is likeliest under the desperate conditions when all else has failed, when the margin for error is narrowest, but when a greater risk is presented by doing nothing. For example, an organization will take on debt, of course, when its financial situation is sufficiently poor to minimize the probability of repaying the debt but when any alternative will certainly produce bankruptcy.

In this case, the real problem is posed by the uninformed decision making that has *produced* this crisis and now necessitates a high-risk, low-probability solution. This type of decision is characteristic of early stages from which the organization as a result is unlikely to emerge, late stages that directly precipitate failure, and in all-too-many sad cases, a combination of the two.

Risky shift may also be observed among personnel who are somehow protected from the potential costs of their decisions. We are likely to find these personnel within work units and in positions that enjoy this protection as a result of job mobility: as noted earlier, among staff and upper management.

Thanks to their job mobility, these also happen to be the personnel whose power extends to influence over the corporate mission. Thus, we have redoubled concern that these goals will advance the short-term return and marketability of those advancing them, but will impose the greatest long-term risk and expense upon the organization.

In sum, then, we are likely to see risky shift from areas and individuals that can easily afford it, spreading unchecked throughout an organization that cannot.

THE UNOFFICIAL ORGANIZATION

To this point, the focus has been upon issues among formal groups within the organization. There is another form of interaction contrived by participants to be less formal.

A well-known actress, reacting to a question about her steady supply of boyfriends in the acting field, responded that she wasn't actively seeking the companionship of actors: it was simply that she worked with them, so they were the people she came to know. To a certain degree, and among a wide variety of relationships, powerful interpersonal bonds appear across the entire corporate world.

Sources

There are many reasons for this, perhaps the most obvious of which is that we spend perhaps the majority of our waking hours at work, the time during which we also tend to be physically and mentally "at our best." Over the long haul, work presents an extended opportunity for others to know us as few others might, as it permits the unfolding of our naturally-appearing personal styles, a variety of situations in which to demonstrate them, and opportunities to show them through close interaction.

As a result, work relationships can become at least as important as, no less personal than, and on occasion replacements for, relationships outside of work. Workmates begin to share a private, idiomatic interpretation of the past, view of the present, and anticipation of the future. In sum, workmates develop a shared history, language, and culture.

Arguably, such interpersonal ties may be to the benefit rather than detriment of the organization; for example, and overlooking some obvious dysfunctions, one can easily picture a particularly inspired level of performance among lovers responding to nurturance, approval, or a desire to impress.

Costs

Nevertheless, the organizational benefits of interpersonal relationships tend to be incidental; more typical are dysfunctions, since informal dyads present not only their own agendas but also a higher priority to participants than collective goals. This was demonstrated in the recent dishonorable discharge of a married officer who reneged on a promise to end a romance with an enlisted female: a promise on which his future military career clearly and ultimately depended.

Interpersonal relationships absorb us because they, of course, apply many of our most critical and storied needs. Interpersonal relationships absorb us at work largely in reaction to a manufactured, "official" organization.[79]

Through the de-skilling process, the official organization accounts for only "part" of each member, which is why some sociologists have observed that members behave in a manner consistent with their perception of "partial inclusion" in the organization.[80] Moreover, the part for which the organization accounts represents the member poorly, if at all.

The individual member tends to prefer his or her unique style of behaving and interacting, as a result of familiarity, adaptation to the responses it elicits, or the perception of positive reinforcement. The limited opportunity for such uniqueness in the official organization impels the member, in effect, to create an unofficial one.

For example, according to a director of transportation at a geriatric care facility in Chicago, and in response to her supervisor,

the aspect of my personality that was never called upon by him and was never even acceptable to him was my very outgoing, kind of bubbly personality that my coworkers loved and thrived on but he didn't; he didn't appreciate it. To him, that was a black mark against me, whenever I did show that part of my personality. I think to frustrate him I showed it more and more around him and got the positive response and acceptance from my coworkers in front of him.

Like its official counterpart, the unofficial organization comes replete with its own norms and values, which include favoritism, reciprocity, and personal loyalty. All reflect personal preferences that *deliberately* displace consideration of objective merit. Because of this, personnel decisions tend *not to serve the organization.*

The tragic news for the organization is that it has created the unofficial domain for these decisions, by insisting on an official domain for defining its individual member. The organization has thereby created its own Frankenstein: its own *agent of destruction*.

Furthermore, as we saw in the last chapter, the organization promotes the Parent/Child interactions that serve it most poorly. Based as they are on earlier familial experiences and observations, the organization has become in effect a huge simulated family, with dysfunctional effects also noted in the last chapter. The point here is that, regarding personnel decisions, all organizations are, for all intents and purposes, *nepotistic*, with the dearth of merit-based judgment implied by the term.

We are not done with groups. In the next chapter, we will explore destructive effects from one of their signature behaviors.

9

The Company of Strangers:
Organizational
Communication and the
Lack of It

They have mouths, but they speak not; eyes, but they see not. They
have ears, but they hear not.
                                            —The Book of Psalms

COMMUNICATION AGAINST ITSELF

To cut to the chase, communication problems are revealed only if they are
communicated; since these problems interfere with their communication,
communication problems in effect *conceal themselves*. As a result, an organization besieged by these problems is unlikely to know about them.
Given their importance, an organization afflicted by an undiagnosed communication disorder is *in grave peril*.

One reason for which communication problems conceal themselves is
that people who are directly involved may *themselves* be unaware of that
fact, for some intriguing reasons.

Communication as a Source of Awareness

The common supposition has long been that *thought* precedes any *communication* through which that thought is expressed. That seems to make
sense: one has a thought and then expresses it.

However, an interesting alternative introduced by the linguists Edward
Sapir and Benjamin Whorf is that *communication precedes thought*, by

providing the structure that the thought needs in order to form in the first place.[81] For example, according to people who work with them, hearing-impaired people display learning disorders that reflect (1) an earlier failure to diagnose the hearing problem and, as a result, (2) an absence of verbal communication during a critical maturational period.

Of course, this entire argument does not fully resolve the chicken-and-egg issue that communication may provide grist for the mill of thought, but at the same time it expresses, and therefore must presuppose, a prior thought.

Inability to Recognize Inability

Nonetheless, we might conclude that thought requires *some* degree of prior communication. Accordingly, we may consider that one of the concepts unavailable without communication is "absence of communication" itself; thus, somebody failing to communicate about certain issues may be unaware of that failure.

We may extend the possibility that communication precedes thought to interaction in a group, wherein, after all, communication is intended to take place. Hence, just as a noncommunicating individual would theoretically lack the cognitive equipment needed to develop coherent thoughts, so might a group in which participants are communicating on a subject poorly or not at all.

This raises the possibility that, as is the case with the noncommunicating individual, the thoughts that are beyond the repertoire of a noncommunicating group include the idea that *it lacks communication about certain issues*. If this is the case, then communication problems are likely to elude the very individuals beset by them.

Consider the following events at a lumber dealership in Miami, according to a strategic planner who met with its department heads:

I interviewed the various department heads throughout the chain; there were twelve or fifteen department heads and myself, and we started comparing notes with what I had found from each of them. And the department heads were astonished to find that sitting across the table from each one of them, virtually, was someone who had information that was very, very vital to their own functioning.

For example, they didn't know the price of certain items. They didn't know what it cost. They had no handle on what the selling price should be. They didn't know that certain items were stored that they were running short of, in another part of the chain. They had all these facilities, right at hand, but there had been absolutely no communication.

So, they were in the dark. Each one of them was really groping in the dark, until they had this meeting. And when the meeting broke up, everybody was really congratulating me and each other for having unearthed all this information. And we ended with the agreement that we would have a similar meeting once a month, just so everyone was kept *au courant* with the total functioning of the company.

What they had there were actually three blind men who stumbled onto the elephant and they get these different versions of what the creature was depending on what they were holding. So they all had different perceptions as to what the company was, what it was doing, what it was not doing, what it was able to do, what it was not able to do, and then it all jelled together when they found out that they were all part of the same problem.

One problem, of course, was communication. Department heads had failed to communicate not only about their interdependency, and the resources they possessed to handle it, but also about their ongoing failure to communicate on the subject. As a result, the need for and possession of resources each represented an issue that failed to surface as a point of view.

Research as well as practical experience supports this interpretation of events. To review the conformity experiments by Asch, cited in the last chapter, a third of the subjects conformed to the perceptual misjudgments of all seven role-players, while far fewer subjects conformed when just one of the seven role-players gave the correct judgment.[82] According to Irving Janis, each of Lyndon Johnson's cabinet members privately and silently opposed the Vietnam War.[83]

Clearly, then, there is research support for the conclusion that the sole representation of any perspective precludes any *communication* of that perspective: that a point of view may vanish from sight simply due to lack of support from others. Regarding a particular issue, then, "failure to communicate" disappears from awareness when there is failure to communicate: under, and *only* under, the precise conditions in which it is an issue. To reiterate, then, *communication problems conceal themselves.*

The Epidemic of Silence

Thus, communication problems tend to be concealed from the people displaying them. Furthermore, since knowledge can be disseminated only through communication, another sobering issue for organizations is that ignorance about communication problems will generalize from those initially displaying them to everybody else.

Hence, communication problems, like communication itself, are shared, and can be expected to spread. An important point is that they are shared with and spread to personnel at upper hierarchical levels empowered, through traditional, centralized decision making, to do something about organizational problems, including these selfsame barriers to communication.

STATUS EFFECTS

Clearly, then, communication barriers tend to be hidden from hierarchical levels at which they can be addressed. Representing another barrier to communication about communication is hierarchy itself.

Procedural Sources

Communication barriers due to hierarchy have been called "status effects," or the effect of position on communication,[84] one of which is elimination of upward communication altogether. One reason for this in turn is an absence of any procedure for such communication; for example, there are unlikely to be any procedures for a lower employee to call a meeting with the board of directors.

Furthermore, the hallowed "scalar" principle of administration traditionally confines communication to a pair of levels, such as between a supervisor and direct reports. As a result, any upward message is either delivered to the next level or withheld; if delivered, interpreted as well; perhaps distorted, even willingly; and in effect censored by each participant.

Other Sources

Closely related to procedural constraints are the structural ones connected to organizational design. As a result of burial in the deepest and most remote organizational levels, lower-level employees are probably unable to identify, much less consort with, potential problem solvers. In addition, lower-level employees may lack the informal tools to communicate effectively with potential problem solvers. Finally, lower employees are also faced with perhaps insurmountable *attitudinal* barriers to upward communication.

Earlier, we saw the assumption that they lack, and are thus denied opportunities to demonstrate or develop, qualifications for promotion, including skills, experience, commitment, and ambition. This disqualification tends to limit lower-level communication, by withholding (1) any credibility from it and thus (2) any incentive to provide it. Furthermore, by exclusion from the communication process, employees are further denied the opportunity to demonstrate or develop the qualifications they are assumed to lack. Thus, status effects contribute to the Pygmalion effect that supports the ongoing, perceived disqualification of employees.

To review: thanks to the effect of procedures, structures, resources, and attitudes, employees at lower levels are the direct victims of barriers to communication across levels. On the other hand, employees who at upper levels monopolize the decision-making capacity to do something about communication barriers are isolated from any information about them. Thanks to such barriers, then, *knowledge* of them is confined to their victims, so that communication problems effectively conceal themselves from their solution.

Other Issues

Status effects also interfere with communication about critical issues other than communication itself. One set of issues buried by status effects concerns the organization's production methods, which are best known to lower employees in their capacity as line personnel. Another concealed issue is the external environment, about which lower employees are most knowledgeable in their roles as customer service representatives and buyers, among others.

Observers often explain this phenomenon by noting sardonically that the personnel to whom this otherwise-concealed information is confined are the only ones who actually *work*. A more precise explanation is that these are the personnel responsible for the routine, labor-intensive *interaction* with things and people, on a close and continuous basis, through which otherwise covert problems for the organization can be made to show themselves.

The environment, and the organization's technical competence to address it, clearly represent some of the client-driven, technology-based organization's most critical issues. As a result of status effects, information about these issues is confined to those powerless, and withheld from those empowered, to respond to those issues.

According to the director of transportation at a Chicago geriatric care facility,

someone below me, one of the bus drivers, had mentioned that a particular client was not receiving the transportation service that she had hoped to. She felt that it wasn't providing her everything she thought she would be provided with, and it was presented to my superior by me. But it wasn't something that I had actually witnessed or heard on my own so therefore it was kind of overlooked.

And I watched it and I checked with her and I was watching her on her daily schedule and it was true: she was not getting to go to the places that she wanted to go. And when I presented my superior with the problem, *then* he looked into it, and he changed her schedule.

Until intercession by the director, the problem remained with the bus driver, its solution withheld. In this case, upward communication was foreclosed by unforgiving attitudes. According to a management consultant,

I think that part of what happens in organizations becomes sort of a self-fulfilling prophecy. People in the lower part of the organization view themselves as not having an impact, so therefore they don't offer input. If you don't believe your input's going to be heard (and I really do believe that), in many organizations, it's so drilled into people, so much a part of our behavior, it's an instinctive response. "I'm here; you're up there. It's not my role to feed up." And so, therefore, information doesn't pass.

And I think there's an expectation of people in senior positions that these folks don't have any interest, they don't have the big picture, so therefore they're not going to get involved. It's all part of this role that people assume, that's unwritten, but it's just played out. . . .

PROBLEM-SOLVING AS A NEGLECTED INTEREST

In many cases, lower employees may be most immediately or heavily penalized by the *very problems about which they cannot communicate*. For example, the bus driver's job may be directly jeopardized by sufficient customer disquiet and defections over inadequate transportation service. Hence, both knowledge of a long-term, perhaps critical problem, and interest in solving it, are localized to personnel *unable to do anything about it.*

Interest without Knowledge

In other cases, a potential, constructive problem focus never comes to fruition, because there is no knowledge of the problem to begin with. This is because the organization denies to lower employees the information they need in order even to recognize the very problems by which they may be most threatened, for the following reasons:

Hierarchy is typically designed to increase responsibility for coordination and large-scale, long-term planning in an upward direction. To enable these functions, ascent in the hierarchy is associated with access to information about an increasing scope of (1) employees, (2) events, and (3) purposes: all elements of the "big picture." Having been denied this vantage point, lower-level employees are denied the information often needed to recognize the actual scale and time frame of the otherwise seemingly trivial short-term issues they encounter.

For example, according to a management consultant,

there are many instances where lower-level employees work without any real awareness of what they're doing, where what they're doing fits in. They know their particular job, they know their function but they don't see the picture. No one's ever imparted the bigger picture to them.

A classic example was a turret-lathe operator for an aerospace company, a real craftsman and had the machine parts to really high tolerances, but he had absolutely no idea of what these parts were for. He had no idea of their function. All he'd get is their machine specifications. He had no idea: were they going into a satellite, were they going into a rocket engine? He had no idea: none whatsoever. No one ever bothered to tell him.

I remember having a conversation with the President of an aerospace company one time, and we were talking about the mission and the strategy of the organization and it was proposed during this conversation that that be communicated through the whole organization and he questioned why people lower in the organization might need that, might benefit from it.

Lacking such information, issues that should set off alarm bells among higher-ups, if not panic at lower levels, remain addressed by lower employees in a routine, standardized fashion that alerts no one to their urgency.

In addition, included within the large-scale information withheld from lower employees is information regarding other employees. As a result, a lower employee is unlikely to recognize a problem as one that is shared with other employees: as a problem that is widespread and systemic rather than personal and idiosyncratic.

Hence, what is in fact a large-scale problem is likely to be interpreted as isolated and, in the broad scheme of things, trivial. Furthermore, the perception of the problem as trivial alone discourages communication to other employees that would reveal its true scope, perpetuating rather than addressing the problem.

Apparently, lack of access to the big picture bedevils creative efforts by not-so-low employees as well. In the marketing department of a mortgage broker,

I was working on an Internet loan organization which is a huge, expensive project, requiring a huge amount of infrastructure, a team effort between the techie group, operations, sales, and marketing. In order to make it launch perfectly, it has to be totally automated. From the beginning, we knew it had to run by bells and whistles, that *people* would actually do the automated functions if we couldn't standardize the products. Everyone agreed. Then the CEO quashed the whole idea, revealing a program and an existing product that would in fact automate the whole program and [that] made the whole project unnecessary from the beginning.

Ships Passing in the Night

As part of their responsibilities under a Management by Exception regime, lower employees in particular are implicitly trained not to involve management in their affairs, as we have seen.

Furthermore, job-related problems pose a greater risk to lower employees than to others, since there is neither much room to demote lower employees, nor much skill development needed to transfer them. Lower employees therefore have reason to fear the discovery of their problems.

Accordingly, lower employees have considerable incentive to keep information about problems to themselves and to keep supervisors at arm's length. Hence, just as the "big picture" is monopolized at upper levels, lower-level employees monopolize information at lower levels.

In addition, according to a management consultant,

what I'll often find is that people at the lower levels . . . never mention [problems] because there's a fear that they're going to be seen as stepping out of line, that they're going to be questioning some superior's judgment. There's an assumption on their part oftentimes that the superior sees the same thing and there's a doubting that, even though they suspect something's wrong, they feel like it's wrong, they see that the boss doesn't seem to think anything's wrong, so maybe I'm wrong. But I'm not going to take a chance anyway, telling the boss about the problem I see here. He's not interested in hearing what I have to say.

In conclusion, then, the situation is that the "big picture" is often needed to provide context and meaning to information received at lower levels. Lower-level information in turn is needed to clarify the "big picture." Both sets of information are interdependent, yet never the twain shall meet. Because a paucity of information limits available output, information within organizations *restricts itself*.

EVALUATION OF SUPERVISORS

Also known primarily if not exclusively by lower employees is the quality of their supervisors. This issue is critical to the organization, and information about it is concealed deliberately and *entirely* by status effects.

The Assumption of Bias

The rationalization for doing so is that lower employees are not simply incapable but biased as well, with the credibility of negative feedback compromised by the fact that its role as a grievance is adumbrated by its appearance as some sort of *retaliation* by the aggrieved employee. According to the Chicago director of transportation,

I knew that my boss was performing bad business, within the organization. I knew that he was changing numbers in annual reports, he was taking pay from some people, so that he could give it to himself. He would transfer money out of the organization's account and put it in his own. I went to the board of directors. I told them I wanted to talk to them about illicit behavior on my boss's part. They always found a reason why they couldn't meet with me.

Grievances, of course, are likely to be in an upward direction, since, given the realities of organizational design, they constitute a dispute with a specific decision or a general policy formulated on an upper level. Any such criticism is generally presented and perhaps genuinely intended as consistent with equity and for the greater good.

The Assumption of Self-Interest

On the other hand, the lower employees who represent the likely source of the criticism seem to have the most to gain from self-interest, along with the smallest stake in the organizational interest. Thus, any grievance is assumed to advance the more nefarious purpose of a hidden agenda. Small wonder, then, that internal critics in general, and whistle-blowers in particular, are frequently characterized, and probably perceived as well, not as altruistic but rather as "opportunistic": as nakedly political.

The Assumption of Favor-Seeking

Further compromising its credibility is the lack of an official medium for negative subordinate feedback, which is thereupon shunted to more surreptitious venues designed to transcend hierarchical obstacles, unaccommodating procedures, and personal danger, by exploiting personal connections, special favors, and opportunities for secrecy, respectively. All of these are easily misconstrued as strategies intended to substitute favoritism for objective analysis: as if the lower employee has anywhere else to turn.

Management with Impunity

By contrast, the managerial party to the grievance has the access denied to lower employees, both to colleagues and to higher-ups, to air a perspective in a way that need not appear as an attempt to circumvent established protocol or evade public scrutiny. As a result, the manager's perspective appears to be a disinterested and legitimate one, ingenuously advanced for objective consideration.

Moreover, upper management often share the guilt imputed to their colleague: as suspected by the Chicago director of transportation, perhaps "the board of directors were in on the scam" perpetrated by her boss. For many reasons, then, the lower participant in a dispute consistently encounters a stone wall.

In sum: organizational processes heavily favor the manager in any dispute with an employee. One result is an unobstructed path for mismanagement, with the costs of unqualified if not corrupt leadership, to the organization. Another cost to the organization is through inequity for the lower employee, reducing motivation and commitment.

COMMUNICATION INTERRUPTUS

A third result is the creation of a clear disincentive for upward communication, at the cost of its various benefits. Lost benefits include the resources that can be brought to bear by a group, including a veritable wealth of ideas.

Creative ideas tend to be brought to a standstill by supervisors who fear being outperformed by a lower-ranking and presumably less-qualified source. Even more galling to employees is the frequent propensity of supervisors to harvest and claim pride of authorship over good ideas communicated through them by necessity to upper levels. One obvious cost to the organization is the tendency to credit, overestimate, and exclusively empower a disqualified supervisor, not to mention a crooked one. Another cost of this practice, again, includes a lingering sense of inequity and a probable chill on useful upward communication, since there is little reward and incentive for it.

TO KILL A MESSENGER

Even where such communication is made available, various forces act to sanitize it to the point of disutility.

Very often, the most useful news is bad news, because it concerns a problem that without intervention can persist, expand, or ramify into other, more severe problems. Employees are reluctant to bear ill tidings to supervisors for fear of victimization by the tendency to "kill the messenger," a fear that dates back at least to the source of the expression: a messenger who was executed by Persian King Xerxes for delivering the news of a military defeat at the hands of vastly outnumbered and clearly underrated Greek forces.

There are several specific reasons to fear an *occupationally* fatal consequence of delivering ill tidings to the boss.

One reason is a fear of appearing so knowledgeable about the bad news as to be construed as in some way responsible for it. A related but more elaborate reason is a concern that the manager receiving the news may wonder about the fact that it was previously concealed, about the messenger's role in that concealment, and about the possible incriminating reasons for that role: all of which seem to point an accusing finger at the messenger. Additionally, as someone who seems sufficiently comfortable with the bad news to share it, the messenger may be viewed as somehow benefiting from the bad news, either previously or currently, to the point of responsibility for it. Another possibility is that the messenger may be seen as delivering the news in such a way as to guide an interpretation that misdirects the manager's blame for it elsewhere.

An additional and perhaps well-founded possibility is that the messenger may fear personal reprisal as an attempt by the manager to symbolically restore the appearance of control. Less symbolic and far more pragmatic is the messenger's fear of elimination simply to conceal the bad news from others who don't yet know about it. More generally, there is probably a very good reason to fear the aversive workplace that bad news can produce.

Finally, there is probably a good reason to avoid the consequences of implicitly challenging the supervisor. From the employee's perspective, according to a management consultant, the supervisor "might think I'm challenging him, or questioning his judgment, or her judgment. I'm going to have my head lopped off and I'm not paid enough to get my head lopped off. If they wanted to know, they'd ask me."

As a result, upward communication tends to exclude the very problems that organizational decision makers need to know and solve. Even worse, spurious upward communication, of the sort represented by sanitized bad news, conceals both the absence of real communication and the failure to address the problem; this can lead only to a worsening situation represented by news that is no longer simply "bad" but rather is rapidly becoming downright catastrophic, as well as ever harder to deliver.

CUSTOMER DISSERVICE

Additionally, status effects extend beyond lower employees to embrace customers as well, precluding input from and limiting service to them, for several reasons.

Although there are exceptions, customer service tends to be the exclusive domain of lower employees. As we have seen, these are the employees who are expected to lack competence and dedication. Thanks to the fact that this becomes a self-fulfilling expectation, the organization can rest assured that it has interpolated, between itself and its customers, individuals who have developed little ability or concern to represent it competently. Furthermore, in response to any mistreatment, customers recognize, often to their exasperation, that their only recourse is to take their business elsewhere, which will be noticed only by the very individuals whose offenses indicate that they couldn't care less.

For examples of poor customer service, we needn't go far: we have the quick-thinking employees at a health club in Los Angeles who, when a customer was injured, sprang immediately into action, to deliver to the bleeding victim a legal waiver form, along with a pen to sign it; the customer who called the "customer service" department of his auto insurance company and was amazed to hear the phone ring unanswered 46 times, then got the brainstorm to be transferred to that department by calling the sales department, where the phone was picked up on the (you guessed it) first ring; another customer who called the "claims" department of the same company and, if he hadn't hung up in disgust, would probably still be on hold (this was back in the '80s), perhaps waiting for the company to *form* a claims department; a specialized amplifier repair shop that after four months returned an amplifier to the customer that was not only unrepaired but upon closer examination had been further damaged by repair "experts"; a nationally prominent investment company in New York that catered to its customer by bouncing her checks and refusing to allow her to make withdrawals; and finally, less customer disservice than an insult, and arguably, perhaps, an act of genius rather than neglect, a letter congratulating the customer on being awarded "referral privileges" by his credit card company, which meant the right to solicit new customers as a salesman *without pay*!

Personalized Disservice

As we have seen, lower employees are discouraged on many levels from involving supervisors. Accordingly, customer complaints tend to be treated by customer service personnel as having only local implications, and are handled superficially, by avoiding major altercations, delays, or disgruntlement by other customers.

The result is that customer complaints are treated by customer service personnel symptomatically, rather than diagnostically. Customers tend to be treated stereotypically, as "chronic complainers," "troublemakers," and the like. To mix metaphors, stereotyping of customers serves to create a reservoir of Untouchables beneath the customer service personnel, who would otherwise be the organization's bottom-dwellers. In sum, then, customer input is treated as a low-level problem, by personnel relegated to be low-level employees.

According to a management consultant,

today, all organizations profess to believe in customer service. We rediscovered the customer. You can go into a lot of retail stores, I don't care what they say, that's not the way their employees behave.

For example, in the drug store set . . . they put their managers up in the front of the store so you can see them, but they give them so much paperwork to do that they really don't want to be bothered with customers. So not only are they not paying attention to customers but out there where you can see them not paying attention to customers. Aggravating. But they're doing their job.

Or when the clerks are doing the inventory control by having all these stupid little numbers on things. But . . . you can't get any service as a customer. And the problem isn't their customer; the problem is their control system. So they're doing it at the customer's expense. But that's the job they do.

Somebody asked me "Why are the clerks in the grocery store always rude?" I said, "Well, why wouldn't they be? You create a job where sooner or later most of the people are going to be wearing these things on their hands . . . and they're really evaluated on how quickly and how efficiently and how few mistakes they make. And why should they be friendly to customers?"

Disservice as an Entitlement of Status

As external stakeholders, with no position in the organization, customers in some sense represent the organization's lowest-ranking victims of status effects. Disservice may provide the sole recompense, and source of prestige, to the lower employees perpetrating it.

Of course, customers are also the organization's very lifeblood, as well as its only source of market information. Loss of this information represents a *catastrophic* status effect.

At the risk of sounding both speculative and anthropomorphic, it may be that neglect of customers expresses the organization's collectively low estimation of itself, of the products or services it offers, and therefore of anyone who would purchase what it produces.

Likelier and certainly less speculative is that, while customer service is a sales-related function, its neglect expresses the short-term view of sales that have percolated down the organization. For example, in dealing with a mortgage broker, a home buyer reported that

I got everything preapproved up front, months before. They made certain representations about what the loan was going to be, interest rates, all that type of stuff, and when it comes right down to it, at the last minute, when everything has to be signed, everything changes. Interest rates are higher, there are percentage points that have to be paid up front, and things like that, and you're in a position where you're in a jam where you don't even have time to shop around any more. Either they're completely incompetent, or they do it on purpose, because they get you in a vulnerable position, and you're forced to do something that you don't want to do.

According to my real estate agent, this type of thing is common: it happens all the time.. . . .

A mortgage broker probably feels that its lack of opportunity for repeat short-term business immunizes it from the short-term consequences of this particular abuse. What it overlooks—again, due to the dominance of sales or marketing personnel pursuing short-term goals—is the possibility of reducing long-term sales from the loss of referrals and the like.

Mortgage brokers can be reassured that this set of priorities is shared by just about all organizations. They should be less reassured by the fact that, thanks to these priorities, they also share with other organizations a self-made disaster.

RESISTANCE TO INPUT

Resistance to input from customers in many ways maintains a tradition developed by the organization from its earliest days.

As one important motive, the founder comes to view the organization, and its output, as an extension of the self, defended with a similar level of ego-defensiveness.

Despite identification and other ego-related motives, probably the greatest impediment to input is created by economic reasons for starting a new firm. As we've seen, economic benefits are writ large by the founder's almost exclusive vulnerability to losing them, occupancy of an ownership position for monopolizing them, and imagined insight into how best to reap them.

As a result, the early organization has a built-in resistance to input in the person of its most powerful member, the architect of its vision, and the individual with the greatest influence on other and future members. As we saw, one consequence was the birth of the micromanager; more broadly, we find an organization led by somebody who doesn't listen.

Secondly, it is precisely this early stage that presents the naive organization with its most urgent need for information, and at the same time obstructs such information. Organizations, of course, always need to be informed, and flexible, but perhaps never so much as at their beginning.

Thirdly, such an attitude of omniscience is validated by the acquiescence of members, for whom it resonates with their need to justify their own commitment to the organization. Since the organization has yet to prove itself through performance, commitment by all concerned—founder and other members—is fortified through faith in the myth that the organization is unique and highly qualified.

Organizational Narcissism

To a certain extent, like any individual, each organization *is* in fact unique; it is the only one doing things in its own particular fashion. The problem is that, as in the case of individuals, organizations feel that they cannot be fully understood by others. Thus, members extend this belief in their uniqueness to their belief that they are not only the only ones doing what they do but also the only ones able to *evaluate* what they do.

The result is the following type of leader, observed by a management consultant:

You'd tell him things about what he needed to do and he'd give this enthusiastic "Yeah! Oh, God! By God, we're going to do that!" and then, nothing would happen. Nothing would change. And he would always have some convenient, very plausible excuse as to why things didn't happen.

The fact of the matter is that man was not going to listen to anybody or anything. He had been successful and he was going to continue to be successful doing it his way. It was very, very frustrating because you'd get this big come-on and then nothing would change.

And the company went out of business.

THE PRIVATE VOYAGE OF THE START-UP

As time passes, the organization develops its own history. This reinforces the organization's sense of being unique not only in its methods but also in the accumulated experience needed to fully understand, apply, and evaluate its methods. Outsiders have no frame of reference for evaluation, since there is nothing external against which the organization can be benchmarked. Thus, the organization has become an "apple" in a world of "oranges."

The Exclusion of Outsiders

Feeding this belief in its own uniqueness is the development of language within the organization that appears to become the sole medium for discussion of what it does. To the ears of insiders, the language of outsiders sounds like the imprecise, unsophisticated cliches employed in the absence of knowledge and experience.

To apply a horrific but illustrative example, the language of accusers, confined as it was to such familiar and well-trod legalisms like "mass-murder," sounded superficial and off the mark, if not irrelevant, to the ears of cult murderers in the infamous Manson family, to whom it represented evidence of their own esoteric knowledge of, and ability to solve, the race-war problem to which they referred as "Helter Skelter." By their inability to see their own pathology from outside of it, the Manson family failed to see that they were guilty simply of mass-murder, and nothing more, or less—demonstrating the exclusively inner-directed organization's blindness to its own misdeeds, by failing to apply the benchmarks that come from external input.

Due to the widening gulf between the languages of insiders and outsiders, the organization develops a basis for trivializing any external criticism. Criticism simply cannot be expressed in a manner that will ensure its reception; in the truest sense of the word, criticism lacks a language.

The Isolation of Insiders

As we saw with grievances, criticism by insiders doesn't fare much better. To be understood, internal criticism is couched in an ostensibly common language while its source is probably a lower-level "novice" seen as (1) unfamiliar with the language and (2) using it as some sort of contrived affectation. In essence, then, internal criticism has the ring of abuse.

Furthermore, such an apparent abuse of a common language reinforces the perception that it is applied solely for self-interest: as we saw, a motive that is easily imputed to lower employees who seem to have the most to gain from it, along with minimal stake in the organization. Internally as well as externally, then, criticism remains without a language.

Hierarchy and Isolation

Taking a cue from The Founder's original indulgence in it, managers eventually embrace resistance to internal input as a norm for their own behavior. Additionally, this posture provides some very attractive functions for the manager.

At minimum, leadership has been defined by researchers, and perceived by practitioners, to include the possession and promulgation of a vision.[85] To a certain extent, then, effective leadership implies some proprietorship over purpose, and independence, if not imperviousness, to external input into that purpose.

More forcefully, resistance to this external input helps to: (1) obviate the manager's apparent need for assistance; (2) retain the manager's apparent position of indispensability; and, given that the whole spectacle is interdicted by the perceptions of others, as we've seen, (3) maximize the manager's apparent value to the organization and actual power over others. Furthermore, this posture serves to disqualify any sources of input not only from meeting but even from *understanding* the manager's need for information, fueling the ongoing mystification and value of the managerial function and role. Hence, resistance to input ultimately serves as a political tool, to buttress the manager's qualifications, value, and power.

"Meta-Ignorance"

As we saw earlier in this chapter, silence tends to "spread" from the potential source of communication. The potential target can also perpetuate this silence, through failure to be exposed to, to appreciate, and as a result to seek, the benefits of input.

Communication is a source of knowledge. Without communication, there is not only ignorance, but also *ignorance about one's ignorance*. This is the condition, and the fate, of our noncommunicating organization.

In sum, resistance to input is purely a function of the pretensions, privileges, and aspirations made available by hierarchy. Hierarchy in turn affords the power to turn this malady against the survival of the organization.

Thus, the eventual result of the founder's subjective omniscience is that the organization has been launched on a private voyage, in which external criticism is perceived as an attack and internal criticism is perceived as a mutiny. As a result, the organization is well-equipped to rebut any suggestion that it is not doing what it ought to be doing.

By the time external events have become too deafening to ignore, the problem they present has probably advanced into a crisis, with which the organization can deal only in a familiar way: by looking internally, at methods that have worked in the past. Thus, the increasing urgency of the outside world pushes the organization deeper into itself.

Hierarchy and Culture-clash

Hierarchy can also interfere with communication in other ways as well: for example, by bringing to bear cultural differences. Cultural differences in turn reflect likely hierarchical discontinuities in education, age, ethnicity, and gender, due to population shifts over time and discrimination: variables associated with strong enough differences in norms and values to, in essence, confound each hierarchical position with its own, independent culture.

While a significant obstacle, this one is generally an apparent one and thus easily anticipated and recognized, if not resolved.

Far more insidious is the following, less obvious obstacle presented by culture to communication.

THE GREAT CULTURAL DIVIDE

To back up momentarily, "corporate culture" may be analyzed by applying the generic view of an Organizational Superculture across all organizations, or the compositional view of one type within each organization. Here, we pursue a third possibility: the "decompositional" view that corporate culture is specific to and varies among the organization's work units.

A decompositional view of corporate culture is justified by the variety of norms and values among different work units due to differences in personnel, functions, reward systems, and history.

Each national culture, of course, is associated with its unique language, creating barriers to comprehension that may be difficult to surmount but easy to recognize as a problem, since they are signalled by unfamiliar, alien vernacular. Language barriers become more difficult to recognize as a problem when the same language is used by people from alien cultures, each investing a single word or phrase with a unique meaning that escapes the other party. These differences *begin* to approximate the communication problem facing organizations from its multiple, internal corporate cultures.

The Invisible Divide

In organizations, members typically use the same language, absent the variety of accents and other clear signals of different interpretation. The use of common expressions implies that they have a mutually understood meaning. Thanks to differences in culture, they don't.

This is illustrated by a joke making the rounds of the Internet these days:

One reason the Military has trouble operating jointly is that they don't speak the same language.

For example, if you told Navy personnel to 'secure a building,' they would turn off the lights and lock the doors. Army personnel would occupy the building so no one could enter. Marines would assault the building, capture it, and defend it with supportive fire and close combat. The Air Force, on the other hand, would take out a three-year lease with an option to buy.

Likewise, a management consultant observed that, within a high-tech company on the West Coast,

the engineering organization considers itself to be very light on its feet: very adaptive, very aggressive. There isn't anything they can't do and can't do rapidly.

Yet, despite how quick they are to respond to targets of opportunity, there's still a difficulty between them and the product marketing people who interact with customers in the field and "This is something I'd like to see on this particular piece of equipment." And it's like, "We've got to have this now. We have to have this now." And now, to the engineers, [means] maybe three or four weeks. . . . And they've actually responded in three or four weeks.

There's still a rub between the marketing people and the engineering folks around that.

One reason for this difference, shared by the marketing director in the mortgage banking firm, is that

in the marketing department, a deadline is a real deadline: you have to get advertising in on time, or it's over. In the technology area, the deadlines seem to be movable. They were supposed to have installed Windows '95 by the end of last year—they're just now getting around to the branch offices.

Differences in priority and interpretation generalize across virtually all sectors of the organization, particularly regarding time. Whereas marketers tend to be rewarded for compliance with strict deadlines, engineers and other technicians are rewarded for quality, which consumes time. Sales tends to be rewarded for maximum volume in minimum time, which can conflict with the greater time required for (1) the innovation rewarded in research and development, (2) the accuracy and internal consistency rewarded in accounting and finance, (3) the compliance with procedures rewarded in administration areas, and (4) the compliance with specifications rewarded in manufacturing. The administrative focus on compliance with procedures can grate on the less structured areas of advertising, marketing, and research and development, which require more flexibility. The list is endless. . . .

Because such differences tend to go unrecognized, their effects include misunderstandings, the conflicts that result from misunderstanding, and ultimately the organizational demise that can result from internal conflict.

THE HIDDEN VOICE OF THE ORGANIZATION

The larger problem is that with increasing influence over the corporate mission, more powerful work units in effect win the right to commandeer communication for the entire organization: to speak on behalf of all other units in the organization. Organization theorists refer to this as "the management of meaning": the function of guiding the organization's interpretation of events.[86] Keep in mind that the language remains the same for all units, obscuring differences in meaning.

The result, then, is that any work unit that can impose its purpose on other work units is likely to do so without their knowledge, since any differences among purposes can be concealed by shared terminology. In an earlier example, along with the sales unit coining the term, other units contribute to the software manufacturer's function as "software police," without analyzing the long-term costs that, with the eventual egress of salespeople, they alone will incur.

Furthermore, by managing meaning, work units able to dictate organizational purpose can also dictate the general belief in their *right* to dictate that purpose, by deriving the influence that comes from purveying a high valuation to their own function. As a result, for example, a powerful Legal Department can sustain its powers by promoting a widespread sense of thrall about its capabilities and criticality.

To expand on an earlier point, communication is a way to derive and to provide knowledge. Without communication, there is no knowledge. As a result of dominance by certain units in analyzing the environment, we earlier noted that the organization cannot *see* itself. Now, thanks to communication, we can confirm that the organization cannot *know* itself.

COMMUNICATION ABOUT ITSELF

Toward the end of the chapter, fittingly, is an admission that communication in organizations is not *entirely* defined by what it omits. There is in fact real communication within organizations: communication that accurately expresses what it is intended to express, and in fact, for the recipient, is probably *too* accurate. Therein lies the problem.

"Metacommunication" is the unwieldy term used by theorists on the subject to denote communication *about* communication.[87] Communication is always accompanied by *metacommunication* because it implicitly, through nuances and other mechanisms for subtlety, presents a message about itself, one of which concerns the relationship between its source and its target. Illustratively, "take this paperwork to accounting" presents an explicit instruction, as well as the implicit message that "I have the *right* to tell you to take this to accounting": a message that the source outranks the target.

Reflecting the authoritative management structure that typifies our organizations is ongoing metacommunication across hierarchic levels that consistently apprises "lower" employees of what they lack. At best, this message may be delivered by a frivolous performance review, neglect of praise or other positive feedback, or Parental expectations of Child behavior. Far more readily interpretable, and more readily described as abuse, is the metacommunication contained in the verbal broadsides of managers, observed for example by a university department chairperson "from the head of the facilities department. . . . This subordinate is fearful that he's going to lose his job. . . . He really gets beaten up, verbally. Accused of failing to think ahead, not making good decisions, doing something without getting clearance. . . ."

Any ongoing communication implies acceptance of "metacommunicated" messages, since resistance would be signalled by some sort of conflict. The relationship metacommunicated from supervisors to their charges is typically an authoritative, "top-down" one. Organizational procedure acts to prohibit any resistance to this particular metacommunication. Results for subordinates include the following predictable effects.

Communication and Self-Abasement

People give credence to external evaluation due to the unavailability of an objective, internal one. Research also indicates that people tend to rationalize conditions imposed upon them, in order to salvage self-esteem by presenting these conditions as a choice, their role as a voluntary one, and their position as an empowered one. It follows that lower employees will reassure themselves that they voluntarily accept their subjacency because it fits their abilities. Therefore, one result of metacommunication in organizations is *low self-evaluation by employees*.

Communication and Complacency

The process of rationalization does not end there.

Researchers suggest that people adapt to conditions by investing them with various sources of satisfaction: a process powered by discretion in assigning weight and value to different things. To workers in the Hawthorne plant, for example, the attention of researchers had importance and value far greater than it would have had for the researchers themselves, which is why the latter were surprised by it. We may thus predict that lower employees will find special merit in the limited abilities they assign to themselves as a result of their organizational position: abilities that become a valued part of their identity.

Beyond this ability, the employee has little incentive to develop. Thus, another consequence of organizational metacommunication is *complacency by employees*.

Communication and Dependence

The expression of attitudes by upper employees regarding the Latin American employees we visited earlier in The Shop can now be characterized as a process of metacommunication. Our correspondent there certainly noticed

the way they talk about them. They do a lot to help them; we have teachers come in and teach them: English course taught, math course taught. . . . Sometimes they'll speak about them like, "Well . . . you have to get Spanish-speaking 401K people to explain to them how a 401K is set up." It's kind of like the way they talk to them.

Now, I understand that a majority of them probably don't understand it, but they always forget that there are 20%, if they target those 20% they could explain it to the labor force. They kind of like generalized that they're all, not stupid but just ignorant. You can hear it in the way they speak.

What comes through in "the way they speak" is metacommunication by upper employees about the presumed ignorance of the employees in The Shop. With each other, Shop employees are able to function as the fully capable people they are. Toward management, they cannot do so with any credibility. As a third consequence, then, and demonstrating the gap between capability and circumstance, metacommunication in organizations tends to enforce *dependence by employees*.

Communication is intended to do a lot of things. One thing that it is *not* intended to do is to subtly disenfranchise others. Yet that is the function of downward communication in organizations.

THE COMPANY OF STRANGERS

In conclusion, "communication" is derived from the Latin "communicatus," which literally means "to make common." The purpose of communication in organizations is to create a company in the full sense of shared participation.

The reality is that we have seen much to suggest something very different; barriers to communication, communication that creates its own barriers, and barriers to recognizing barriers. The reality is a process that reflects or exacerbates divisions, rather than bridging them. The reality, then, is indeed the creation of a company, but a company of strangers.

Communication researchers observe that, due to the abstract, inaccessible concepts reflected, issues elude individual awareness in direct proportion to the generality of their effects and resulting scope of their danger. Hence, within our growing list of self-destructive corporate paradoxes, we anticipate that *the organization that is most immediately in trouble is least likely to be aware of it.*

To this point, we have offered a multitude and variety of evidence for organizational self-destruction. It is now time to unveil the most incriminating evidence of all—a veritable smoking gun.

This is the subject of the next chapter.

PART FIVE

THE OUTCOME OF FAILURE

10

The Smoking Gun: Life Inside the Monopoly

To sit in darkness here
Hatching vain empires.

—John Milton

Let us suppose that it's possible to conjure up an organization that allows us to witness the behavior of its members that accurately, without distortion, reflects their true motives and inclinations. Through these motives and inclinations, this organization would tell us the instinctive collective impulses of organizations in general, and tell us specifically whether they are innately built to fail. To be qualified for such a role, the organization would have to act as if it is free of any constraints that would bias the behavior of members.

Lo and behold—it turns out that such an organization exists: an organization that, by its own lights, is the very apotheosis of organizational effectiveness. To understand the nature and origins of this creature, we need to look first at the entire notion of organizational effectiveness, and in particular to the manner in which this organization feels that it has mastered it.

ORGANIZATIONAL EFFECTIVENESS

There are many views of what organizations have to do in order to be effective. Specific measures appear in Appendix 2. In general, up to this point, our focus has been an internal one, on the achievement of organizational goals.

There is another perspective: the belief that organizations achieve their goals by helping society to meet *its* objectives. To many observers, this function is the very raison d'etre of organizations, and fulfilling it is the very definition of organizational effectiveness.

In this chapter, we will raise, and explore, a third possibility: that organizations are able to meet this environmental standard of effectiveness by pursuing self-interest, so that they meet the *external* standard of effectiveness by meeting the *internal* standard we have employed to this point.

As it turns out, this represents a crucial element of a widespread and politically potent view of the organizational role in society. We will find out whether it is a valid view as well.

THE NATURE OF DEMAND

In the estimation of some observers, organizational effectiveness is defined as the ability to meet some pre-existing societal demand for certain products and services. The "environmental determinism" view is that society in effect presents the organization with some implied wish list, and that the organization avoids perishing by meeting its wishes.[88] The companion "population ecology" view is that long-term organizational evolution results from short-term efforts to adapt to the environment, by meeting such pre-existing demand and thereby benefiting society, and by the annihilation of those who fail to adapt.[89]

This entire notion may be challenged by wondering whether there ever was prior demand in the marketplace for pet rocks, Furbies, Cabbage Patch dolls, or hula hoops: or whether the belief in that demand is simply an attempt to take a teleological view of events that in retrospect are, of course, historical, because they are a matter of record, but hardly qualify as inevitable.

In fact, these examples suggest, and some observers have pointed out, that organizations can *create* demand, a belief articulated by proponents of an alternative, "strategic choice" view that assigns initiative not to the environment but rather to organizations themselves. In some cases, society clearly benefits, when the organization creates demand for technologically advanced or otherwise innovative products or services; one example is the convenience offered by an entire overnight delivery industry that was in effect created by Federal Express.

On the other hand, societal benefit becomes somewhat dicier when demand is created only because a product is fashionable, trendy, or larded with status: examples include clothing, cars, and body-piercing implements, respectively. Even less instrumental to society is the creation of demand through advertising.

Least directly instrumental of all, and a societal benefit of last resort, is the stimulus provided by any organizational productivity to the creation of jobs. The logical sterility of locating societal benefit entirely in employment is revealed by the various offenses it often justifies, typically by conscripting current employees and pandering to public altruism in the effort. These offenses include ecological despoliation, pollution, and waste; hidden, long-term health threats; and in the case of the nuclear industry, not-so-hidden public morbidity, along with potential cataclysm on the grandest of scales. Furthermore, as part of some general macroeconomic equation, employment represents the sole justification for making available various products and at the same time such employment becomes necessary to create a market for these products in the first place.

THE "INVISIBLE HAND"

Suspect though they may be, these societal benefits require that organizations providing them remain unbridled by government regulation and instead enjoy a free hand in pursuing self-interest, according to the economist Adam Smith and his disciples. This is the hallowed belief in the "invisible hand," the argument that social responsibility requires individual and organizational self-interest.[90]

According to this school of thought, the organization successfully pursues self-interest only if it is profitable, which means that customers have been willing to pay for its goods and services. By providing products for which customers have paid, the organization has demonstrated the exact level of responsibility required, and thus underwritten, by society.

On the other hand, goes the argument, society will not financially support failure to meet its standards of social responsibility: this is because customers will *not* patronize an organization that pollutes, discriminates, or defrauds.

According to free-marketeers, because society rewards with profits only products that benefit it, and withholds profits from products that do not, government regulation is *not* required to ensure the social responsibility of business. Instead of government regulation, the market should permit unrestricted competition, allowing customers limitless choice that will reward providers of high-quality products with survival and prosperity.

By promoting survival of the fittest, the free market represents an economic analogue to the biological jungle, reflecting the burgeoning influence of Charles Darwin at the time when Adam Smith was developing this argument. As demonstrated by racists and other Social Darwinists, Adam

Smith was neither the first nor the last to pervert the argument to which he evidently imprinted.

COUNTERARGUMENTS

One problem with Smith's argument is the societal benefit fabricated from survival in the economic jungle.

An Overdeveloped Economy

One imagined benefit accrues from the *economic growth* that is made possible by the unrestricted initiative that in turn is permitted only by the free market. One measure of the growth imperative is the uncontested approval it receives in the financial media. Evidence that growth may *not* be the social panacea it is touted to be is provided by: (1) the product obsolescence that ensures it; (2) the consequent need to dispose of obsolete inventory and underutilized assets; (3) the ongoing need to replace obsolete products with successors that are equally disposable, and that are therefore often manufactured with low-cost, nonrenewable natural resources; and thus, (4) unchecked environmental depletion.

Underdeveloped Quality

Those are large-scale, long-term, and to some, obscure costs. On a smaller scale, in the shorter term, and of more narrowly economic concern, *product quality* is theoretically maximized by growth, and by the free market that ensures growth. That's the theory; in reality, it turns out that the completely free market is *inimical* rather than amenable to product quality.

To its advocates, as we saw, the free market maximizes product quality by giving customers the opportunity to select the best options from among a full range of choices. However, choices can be evaluated by customers only with complete information, which in turn is *unlikely* to be provided by the very free market that depends upon it. Absent applicable laws or the threat of litigation, manufacturers are likely to provide product information selectively and deceitfully if at all, particularly regarding such critical and nonobvious effects as injury and disease. Examples of disclosure only under compulsion inundate us from the tobacco, pharmaceutical, food, toy, and other industries.

Without such compulsion, it is in fact likely that *the more critical is the product information, the less likely it is to be furnished*. Complete and accurate product information on which a free market depends is likely to be made available only by government regulations, for example, through "truth in packaging" laws: ironically, in other words, by a *regulated* market, which is something *other* than a free market.

Social Irresponsibility

Advocates also argue that the free market permits customers to punish social irresponsibility by selecting *out* companies guilty of it. As we just saw, however, the public in general has no defense against the unrestricted, covert, and duplicitous product disinformation likely to be provided on the free market.

Furthermore, the free market offers its victims no defense at all for certain *overt* forms of corporate social irresponsibility as well. These are victims who are limited in number, and therefore in their ability to respond to these offenses using such economic countermeasures as consumer boycotts that for their effectiveness require wide participation.

Examples include victims of discrimination, labor abuses, and local pollution: excesses preventable only through governmental intercession. Representing one instructive and potentially tragic case are victims of rare diseases, curable only through "orphan drugs" that, given their low demand, can be developed only with such government incentives as research grants or low-interest loans.

In justifying free-market disposition of these issues, the free-marketeer is forced to ethically justify failure to meet the needs of victims, and based only upon their low priority to nonvictims. In essence, this argument accords a higher weight to the inconvenience of would-be benefactors than to the perhaps mortal danger facing victims: an argument that, in effect, gives a moral imperative to lack of responsibility, and questions the very rationale for "society" itself.

This argument can be justified by assigning to the abstraction of economic freedom a higher weight than to the reality of individual lives: a set of priorities that has made of our corporation a veritable artistic self-parody.

Negative Externalities

An additional problem with the free market is that, rather than a proxy for social responsibility, profits can readily coexist with the specific form of social *irresponsibility* identified as "negative externalities."[91] Negative externalities are costs dumped on noncustomers, who are disqualified from any leverage over offenders by their absence from the market and lack, therefore, of any economic recompense.

Negative externalities claim victims of passively-consumed or "second-hand" cigarette smoke, firearms, pollution, and drunk drivers, including not only accident victims but also all members of society who bear the medical costs of accidents, through increased insurance premiums or taxes to support public hospitals. Since victims are outside the marketplace, a disincentive for negative externalities can come *not* from the free market but rather, again, only from government.

As we've seen to this point, counterarguments to an unrestricted free market address the fact that the product quality that justifies it is possible, but selectively so, with qualifications for the validity of pre-existing demand and for the value of created demand, and with such exceptions as disinformation, treatment of various minorities, and negative externalities.

We now entertain the additional and more serious counterargument that an unrestricted free market ultimately degrades product quality *in all cases*. As we shall see, the target for this counterargument is conclusive enough to represent a virtual straw man.

ENTER THE MONOPOLY

To restate an earlier point, the free market maximizes product quality to the satisfaction of its advocates by giving customers choices among a full range of alternatives. By definition, the range of choice offered by a free market is limited for oligopolies or precluded for monopolies (both of which will henceforth be referenced as "monopolies," since oligopolies tend to act as monopolies by controlling prices, as pointed out by the economist Paul Samuelson).[92] In extreme cases, customer disquiet can be expressed through boycott of an entire industry; however, even that alternative is foreclosed by monopolistic control over the market for such essentials as healthcare, communication, gas, electricity, and water.

The free-marketeer will argue that the monopoly has defeated the competition and deserves to rule the economic jungle by providing the highest quality products that society requires. In reality, at the point of achieving a monopoly status, the firm has already perhaps exploited various *alternatives* to providing quality, most notably predatory pricing, which entails prices well below a level affordable to the competition. Quality tends *not* to be an option due to its costs, which are likely to erode the profit margin already cut to the bone by predatory pricing. *If product quality is exercised as a marketing option, it usually lasts only as briefly as the competition does.*

According to an employee of a nationwide communications company,

there was a time when even the rate of return was determined by the regulatory commission. The phone companies maximized the return by inflating the cost of the service. [Since then] the industry has become more competitive and regulations are more in favor of competition.

The industry is in a price war. Incumbent telephone companies are now finding ways to lower their floor prices so their products and services can be priced more competitively when competing with new entrants. To gain regulatory approval, they now argue that things do not cost as much as they once claimed.

Monopoly Competition

Welcome to the world of monopoly "competition." Having priced rivals from the industry, the monopoly certainly has no further incentive to maximize the product quality that was probably absent even in the face of some competitive pressure. Examples abound: atrocious customer service by government-franchised cable monopolies, generating an ongoing public outcry for their deregulation; during the 1970s, demands by U.S. automakers for import restrictions rather than match their foreign rivals with competitive quality and gas performance; efforts by U.S. clothing manufacturers to secure government import controls against lower-priced Asian cloth importers; and so on. The irony in all these examples is that, in order to sustain themselves, monopolies evidently require the government complicity to which free-marketeers, in defending the role of the monopoly, are explicitly opposed. In general, quality receives support only when the monopoly has reason to fear less compliant government regulation: even in those cases, such support tends to be nodding at best.

The problem is that the economic jungle is, perhaps ironically, *directly analogous to its biological counterpart, and can in fact award survival* within it to its fittest members, but *only if all competitors engage simply in economic activity, and nothing more.*

Welcome to the Jungle

However, the economic jungle is protected from interlopers by defining it to embrace an entire domain of activity that extends *well beyond* economic activity.

As with other behaviors we have been addressing, we are dealing with human beings, and the behavior of human beings is mediated by perception. By following the dictates of free-marketeers, the organization has the same license to manage customer perceptions of product quality that its individual members enjoy to manage the perception that other members depend upon them, producing from both the same spurious bases for acquiring power. For the organization, power over customers is maximized through the *expectation* of high quality coupled with the actual cost-cutting achieved by providing the very opposite.

We are now no longer discussing economic activity; instead, we are now discussing fraud.

The popular delusion and deception is that, absent any restriction over these noneconomic activities, what has been called the "economic" jungle rewards quality; as we have seen, quality under these conditions is not simply incidental from competition but rather is useless for it and in fact is likelier to be an impediment to it. It is now apparent that far likelier products of this particular jungle are the various substitutes for product quality, including advertising, packaging, and public relations. In sum: this is a decidedly *noneconomic* jungle that, not surprisingly, selects inhabitants who are most competitive at *noneconomic* activities.

This, and not the "economic jungle," is the habitat that engenders the monopoly. We now see that the monopoly is likely to emerge from, and certainly results in, something vastly different from the high quality for which it has been credited. The monopoly is therefore both the high-water mark and the death knell for the argument that, left to their own devices, organizations advance society's interest by advancing their own. In fact, we are about to find out that they do *neither*.

LIFE INSIDE THE MONOPOLY

By reaching its position, the monopoly is now able to feel that it can do whatever it wants. What it does to consumers is the stuff of legends; as Peter Drucker ever so gently observed, "An unregulated natural monopoly, as economists and political scientists learned long ago, will inevitably exploit, in addition to being ineffective and inefficient."[93]

In addition, many a monopoly is transformed into a "monopsony," or a sole purchaser, in the labor market. A monopsony is represented in the classic "company town" by the corporation that serves as virtually the sole local employer. By enjoying a buyer's market for labor, the monopsony can virtually dictate the terms of employment.

A monopoly is well-positioned to *become* a monopsony by using its considerable resources to muscle in to many parts of the world, either unchallenged by rivals or able to annihilate them through various trademark techniques, including, as we saw, predatory pricing.

Of course, there are many monopsonies that are not monopolies. However, we focus on the company representing *both*, for an important reason.

On the one hand, it is as a monopoly, with its characteristic surfeit of resources, that the company is *not* economically pressured to short-change its employees, and thereby enjoys complete discretion to be as beneficent as possible in its human resource policies. On the other hand, it is as a monopsony that the company anticipates exemption from any economic penalty for its human resource misdeeds, since there are no competitors able to entice disgruntled employees with better offers.

As we shall soon see, all of this safe-conduct is an illusion, but, in the manner of illusions, the company doesn't realize it. As a result, the company representing *both* a monopoly *and* a monopsony tells us pretty much all we need to know about the style of management in a workplace that has every reason to believe that it enjoys complete (1) discretion to be "good" and (2) dispensation from any penalty for being "bad."

The Best of all Possible Organizational Worlds

This, then, is the moment for which we have all been waiting: to see exactly what will transpire in the organization wherein management feels that it can do exactly what they want to do, in an organization that is exactly what its decision makers want it to be. This is the fulfillment of the organizational potential: a veritable organizational Heaven on Earth. This is where we find an organization that follows the natural predilections of management, wherever they take it. This is the organization that is free to act on the instincts of *all* organizations, as promised at the beginning of the chapter.

What do we find?

For an answer, let us look into the innards of the monopoly-cum-monopsony, into the world of its employees themselves.

The door is now ajar.

Neglect

First of all, we begin with some mild instances of uncaring or neglectful management. For example, we find, according to an employee for a Southern California aerospace oligopoly, a "field lab testing rocket engines. Any time there was a critical test the supervisor went on vacation. This continued for 10 years until he retired."

Then we find, according to a representative for Australian communications employees, "stress from too many calls; excessive call monitoring and inadequate breaks from the phones."[94]

Exploitation

Then things turn a bit uglier. According to representatives of Canadian communications workers,

"a greed-motivated sellout and a callous response to the employee's efforts to gain pay equity" is how the union representing [the company's] workers reacted to the company's decision to abandon its mostly women telephone operators by selling their jobs to an American call center business.

An outraged Communications, Energy and Paperworkers Union President, Fred Pomeroy, noted that [the company] made $852 million in profits and paid its CEO $17 million in 1997. Profits for 1998 will top $900 million.

"Yet they're willing to destroy the livelihoods of 2,500 operators to make a few extra bucks," he said, stressing that these workers are the same women whom [the company] has fought tooth and nail to avoid pay equity obligations.

[The company] announced on January 11 that it plans to sell its operator services division . . . which means that 55 work centers spread throughout Ontario and

Quebec will shrink to five. This will translate into job loss for the majority of operators because they will be unable to relocate. And those who do move will be faced with a huge reduction in their salaries if the company has its way.

"Plans for a full-scale fightback campaign are underway," said Pomeroy. "We will fight this move in every way possible including through the legal process, collective bargaining, the political process, the workplace and in the streets."[95]

Oppression

It gets worse. Regarding an American fast-food oligopoly operating in Great Britain, according to the Greenpeace organization,

What's it like working for [them]? There must be a serious problem: even though 80% of [their] workers are part-time, the annual staff turnover is 60% (in the USA it's 300%). It's not unusual for their restaurant-workers to quit after just four or five weeks. The reasons are not hard to find.

No unions allowed: Workers in catering do badly in terms of pay and conditions. They are at work in the evenings and at weekends, doing long shifts in hot, smelly, noisy environments. Wages are low and chances of promotion minimal.

To improve this through Trade Union negotiation is very difficult: there is no union specifically for these workers, and the ones they could join show little interest in the problems of part-timers (mostly women). A recent survey of workers in burger-restaurants found that 80% said they needed union help over pay and conditions. Another difficulty is that the "kitchen trade" has a high proportion of workers from ethnic minority groups who, with little chance of getting work elsewhere, are wary of being [fired]—as many have been—for attempting union organization.

[The company has] a policy of preventing unionization by getting rid of pro-union workers."[96]

Discrimination

The *Philadelphia Tribune* reports on the results of a civil court case involving allegations that employees were abused by an automotive giant:

Allegations investigated by the EEOC included wage disparities between Black and similarly qualified white employees, disparities in participation in internal training programs, and denying Black employees usage of the [company's] corporate credit cards. Also, Blacks were reportedly required to make long-distance one-day trips within Alabama, while overnight hotel accommodations were provided for whites on similar trips.

These four employees and "Blacks as a class were discriminated against in terms and conditions of employment, wages, training and promotions," stated the EEOC investigative findings dated July 31, 1997. These findings, obtained by the *Tribune*, also criticized "a hostile work environment" existing at the [company] office.[97]

Enslavement

Now things turn downright foul; the clock is about to be turned back about a thousand years. The following letter by the National Labor Committee in Support of Worker and Human Rights to a CEO alleges overseas human rights violations by his entertainment conglomerate:

Evidence consistently emerges of serious human rights violations and sweatshop abuses. The longstanding systematic violations of human and worker rights at factories in China . . . include: excessive forced overtime, up to 16 hours a day, seven days a week, amounting to 112-hour work weeks; pitifully low wages (e.g., 12½ cents an hour); no benefits; even being shortchanged legal overtime premiums and receiving instead only six to eight cents an hour above the base pay for overtime work; workers being housed in primitive, crowded dorms—in one case eight women crammed into a tiny room measuring 5 by 10 feet; workers illegally forced to pay an "entrance fee" to secure their job; and, most importantly, the repression, fear and total denial of worker rights. [Employees] know that if they are even seen discussing factory conditions they can be fired.

Within one factory,

payment of wages . . . are typically held back two to three months, leaving the workers without money and virtually in the position of indentured servants. The workers receive no benefits, despite the fact that under China's labor law, the factories are mandated to provide health insurance and other coverage. . . .

The women are fined up to three days' wages for missing one day's work. . . . Workers are illegally denied their work contract, which would provide them with some security against abuse. No independent union is allowed at the factory.[98]

It is ironic to note that these human rights violations are allegedly committed by a foreign company from a country (i.e., the U.S.) that consistently: (1) indulges the illusion that such practices are exclusively the domain of the host regime and beneath their own repertoire and (2) ignores the fact that those practices, in fact, *fly in the face* of local policy.

Dictatorship

Finally, in another part of the world, in a resolution by the AFL-CIO regarding support for an oppressive overseas military regime, some of the world's biggest oil companies were targeted

for special scorn by the labor body for "providing it (the military regime) with large amounts of desperately needed hard currency" at the same time oil companies are engaged "in severe" downsizing and cost-cutting which has compromised worker and community safety and is resulting in significant loss of high-skill, high-wage jobs in the United States.[99]

Clearly, then, the monopoly penalizes employees as well as customers: from a cost-benefit perspective, even going out of its way to do so. However, it was stated earlier that organizations ultimately serve neither society nor themselves. As a monopoly, how does the organization penalize itself?

It does this, thanks to our real-time and pervasive communication, since the monopoly is not nearly as free from the consequences of its actions as it collectively thinks it is. Customers have demonstrably translated goodwill earned for employment practices into trust for product quality; examples include Levi-Strauss and Saturn. Conversely, the prohibitive costs of ill-will from the same sources have been demonstrated in the cases of a well-known running-shoe manufacturer and the clothing sweatshops owned by a female celebrity.

Costs to Quality

Furthermore, perceived product quality itself is likely to be a *direct* function of human resource practices. "Equity" theory is that workers compare their own rewards to those of peers, in-house as well as on the open market; that in order to redress it, "underreward" inequity will degrade productivity; and that, in cases where output *quantity* is maintained, for example by piece-rate pay or simply as a minimal job requirement, we may expect such degradation to be at the expense of product *quality*.[100]

Not infrequently, such degradation is *intended*, through sabotage, the defining example of which was the destruction of "sabots," the French word for the wooden shoes anchoring railroad tracks, by disgruntled French workers during the railroad strike of 1910.

In sum, then, product quality, and consequent brand loyalty, are a direct measure of an organization's concern for its human resources. All tend to rise together: or, in the case of our monopolies, *fall* together.

ORGANIZATIONAL SELF-ACTUALIZATION

So what can we learn from all of this?

What we have found is that, in an organization that has the wherewithal to be as *good* as it wants to be, we find an organization that is as *bad* as it can be. Furthermore, for the benefit of all organizations, the monopoly demonstrates the full *costs* of its excesses: that, even in this Best of All Possible Organizational Worlds, the seemingly-insuperable monopoly is in fact fully accountable for its human resource practices. Given this, the potential consequences of such practices by other, more vulnerable organizations ought to make them shudder.

For the benefit of our organizational analysis, full-throated managerial interests are placed at a considerable distance from long-term organizational interests through neglect of shorter-term interests: those of customers, by the monopoly, and those of employees, by the monopsonist in the labor markets. Thus, for the argument made throughout this discussion that an organization represents its own worst enemy, that it is inescapably built to fail, the combined monopoly-cum-monopsony represents the *smoking gun*.

GOVERNED BY FAILURE

A few words are deserved about the monopoly that is represented by government organizations.

There is certainly nothing to be added to the bad press earned by public organizations, and to the good time enjoyed by comedians and economists at their expense. Johnny Carson, for example, once marveled that you could send a letter instantaneously from Los Angeles to the Far East—so long as it is addressed to Fresno, California.

There appears to be abundant reason for low expectations about public organizations; after all, like private monopolies, they typically have no competition, so there is no market pressure on them to do well. And they frequently do not disappoint; experiences reported by customers are often in the realm of the surreal.

What might surprise people is the identity of the culprit responsible for the ineffectiveness they assign to public organizations. It turns out that the culprit consists of the people looking for the culprit: the public itself. These are, after all, *public* organizations, vouchsafed by a democratic, fully-participative political process in which the resource support on which they depend for their effectiveness is availed or denied by *the public*.

SELF-LOWERING EXPECTATIONS

We find that such resource support tends to be denied, and such effectiveness is limited, based on the very *expectations* of limited effectiveness and a waste of resources. Thus, the expectations of the public and the performance of their organizations mutually degrade each other in a classic self-fulfilling prophecy.

So yes, public as well as private organizations are created to fail. In the specific case of public organizations, the initializing event is the public's willful indifference and ignorance about its proper role. For example, the public can participate in quality control over public organizations: through the creation of and participation in watchdog committees.

The likely result of withholding support from public enterprise was illustrated by the differing fate of two towns along the Mississippi River during the floods of 1993. Previously, the town of Bettendorf, Iowa, had voted to collect the taxes needed to build a levee for flood protection; the nearby town of Davenport had refused to. As a result, Bettendorf survived the floods with almost no damage; Davenport was almost completely destroyed.[101]

There is no mystery behind government effectiveness; in government, as in anything else, you get what you pay for. With Davenport, we all in fact got *less* than nothing, since, thanks to its purblind citizenry, the town had to be rebuilt at far greater federal expense than would have been the local cost of preventing the damage.

Self-Interest and Lowered Expectations

The poorly-performing public organization is a myth that becomes a fact when the myth is believed. As is the case with much myth-building, one clear motive for it is a self-interested one, most obviously to save tax monies. When myth-building is advocated on behalf of a business organization, an additional motive for it is to weaken the public, governmental organizations charged with regulating business.

Therefore, the belief that the absence of competition engenders organizational inefficiency (1) is supported by the behavior of private monopolies, and at the same time (2) *protects* these enterprises from the consequences of their misdeeds, by rationalizing the weakening of public organizations that can otherwise control them. The result, then, is to eliminate the only obstruction to free rein by private monopoly, and to the capacity of business to be entirely responsible to itself: or, more specifically, to the *individual members* making decisions on its behalf. This is the goal of business, and the reason for which it may succeed in advancing individual interests, but is built to fail in advancing its own, as well as those of society.

We saw earlier that public organizations fail because, in a fit of pique, the public fails to support them. However, this represents the short answer to the question of government inefficiency.

The longer answer is that many public organizations fail because private organizations seek to emasculate them in order to avoid their own failure in the economic marketplace. Remember: monopolies may succeed, but only by limiting rather than by exhausting the marketplace: through disinformation, limited choices, and the like. This requires a public organization willing to forsake its goal of policing private trusts. Thus, a major reason why public organizations are *made* to fail is that private organizations are *built* to fail.

Representing an example of a failed public organization is a state agency, according an admittedly partisan government affairs vice president for a competitor to the pseudonymous "Telecom" Corporation:

Just two weeks ago, the [agency] removed the state's calling boundaries at "Telecom's" request, creating a single calling area despite its staff's conclusion that only the FCC has the authority to remove or change a state's calling boundaries. By removing the local calling boundaries, the [agency] took away "Telecom's" only incentive to open its local market to competition. What may seem like a short-term price break will not become a long-term solution because of the chilling impact it will have on real local and long-distance telephone competition. Obviously, the decision was not in . . . consumers' best interest—the exact interest [agency members] are elected to protect.[102]

THE END OF THE ROAD

It was earlier suggested that the evidence for the free-market argument is discredited to the point of representing a virtual straw man. The straw man is none other than the monopoly itself. The monopoly represents the end of the road for the organization: both the realization and the destruction of its fondest dreams. It demonstrates that, even in this Best of All Possible Organizational Worlds, the organization is built to fail.

ORGANIZATION UNAWARES

The reason, and the point of citing this piece of evidence, is that the monopoly represents the zenith of organization wherewithal, and at the same time the nadir of organizational self-awareness.

The prior reason for its collectively limited self-awareness is that the monopoly more or less takes for granted both its customers and its employees. As we saw, the monopoly tends to "exploit" customers, in the words of Peter Drucker; the best that can be said is that this demeanor is probably inconsistent with the close-to-the-customer posture demanded by the marketplace.

As we also saw, when combined with the monopsony, this organization does pretty much the same to its employees. In addition to those spelled out earlier, consequences of this human resource approach, for employee motivation, commitment, and cooperation, probably do little to ensure that the organization's personnel will be alive to its environment, assuming that it even wants to be.

Thus, we find a studied distance between the monopoly and everything transpiring outside of it, both as a result of its intended goals and unintended methods. The obvious result is unawareness of and nonresponsiveness to environmental change, which can and does happen, even in the seemingly-protected world of the monopoly: overnight, dominant technologies become obsolete; protected industries become unregulated; economic forces can suddenly smile upon new or different products; and competitors can arise in unanticipated forms, from unexpected places. The monopoly can rest assured that it faces any such need for change bereft of any capacity to meet it. To bring the discussion back full circle to its beginning, examples of monopolies digging their own graves by ignoring the environment come to us from the industries citied in Chapter 1, including the railroad and computer software industires, with near misses in the Swiss watch and computer hardware industries.

Of course, the need for change at some point faces all organizations. In contrast to monopolies, other organizations in a competitive environment face this need far more frequently, generally with fewer resources, and at the same time with the same deficiencies dramatized on behalf of them all by the monopoly. In relation to the monopoly, then, most organizations are more vulnerable to their environment, but possess the same myopia that renders them equally helpless to address it.

In the next chapter, we will see exactly how the organization confronts the need for change, and as a result of this myopia, the mockery that represents its response.

11

The Ritual of Change

A mind not to be changed by place or time.
The mind is its own place, and in itself
Can make a heav'n of hell, a hell of heav'n.

—John Milton

Resistance to change is perhaps the most obvious dysfunction of a company facing disaster; when presented with the argument that organizations are built to fail, respondents generally focused on this issue. In the chronicle we are pursuing, resistance to change is but the last gasp of a company facing disaster for other reasons, yet adds to those reasons a disaster in its own right.

FIXATION

We may refer to this resistance as "fixation," a colloquial term meaning "a state of being fixed" (rather than the Freudian term meaning "a preoccupation or obsession").

Fixation by the organization begins with its members, and with their motives for behavior.

Representing an important source of resistance to change are managerial personnel. According to the leadership theorist Warren Bennis, leadership has been defined to include what he called "the management of trust through constancy,"[103] which is demonstrated by staying the course in the face of adversity. By applying this definition, anyone in a leadership position is likely to view change as capitulation and therefore as antithetical to the requirements of leadership. Hence, managers tend to resist change if for no reason other than to demonstrate leadership.

What this means is that change is resisted by the personnel with the greatest influence, if not absolute authority, over the behavior of other personnel. Moreover, change is resisted for a plethora of other reasons as well.

OTHER SOURCES OF FIXATION

In Search of Immortality

People in general may claim to seek development and growth, but their personal goals are, in reality, much different; this is why personal development and growth are generally undertaken as a last resort, usually through compulsion, and then, only at the insistence of external events. People want to achieve not development but rather a comfortable state of self-knowledge, through the experience of completion and permanence. Self-knowledge, in turn, has a high priority for reasons perhaps best explored, in their characteristically resolute look at reality, by Zen Buddhists.[104]

According to Zen thinkers, the "self" contributes to the illusion of permanence and the fantasy of immortality, which, along with material possessions, represent important elements of the attachments to which they refer as *Maya*. Attachment to the self is one reason for the importance assigned to physical things, the dispirited response to the physical indications and limitations of age, and the terror-stricken contemplation of mortality.

Maya is also the reason why people resist any change that affects their ability to know themselves, because it threatens their carefully constructed cocoon of permanence and immortality. Self-knowledge depends on what we do, because what we do is our mirror reflection, a part of the identity that can be observed by the self.

What we do in turn is reflected in what we are: in the *career* we pursue in order to give ourselves a permanent-appearing status, in the *position* we occupy in pursuing a career, and in the *job* we do in occupying our position. Hence, one reason to resist organizational change *directly* addresses our primal motivation, because it threatens to (1) disrupt a job and (2) undermine important elements of personal identity bound up in that job.

Hence, while it might seem otherwise, it is not overstating the case to connect the posture of changelessness to the illusion of permanence and in turn to the very fear of death itself. That gives us some indication of the obstacles facing a change agent.

Self-Inflation

Self-knowledge can also be imbibed in strong doses from the organization itself, since, as an entity that both includes and outlives us, it represents a powerful tool for achieving our own permanence and immortality. Moreover, self-knowledge from organizations can be highly elevating, since they perform feats on a massive scale that both reflect and magnify our individual contributions to them.

Another force for organizational fixation, then, is our strong individual identification with the organization, and resistance to anything that might change it. For this reason, we find that change tends to be resisted most intransigently in "strong" cultures wherein identification with the organization is most pronounced, which must come as an unpleasant surprise to organizational theorists who have been selling strong cultures for the better part of two decades.

Self-Interest Revisited

Organizational fixation, of course, also comes from political forces.

As we have seen repeatedly, members advance their interests by influencing the corporate mission in a direction that accommodates those interests, often to the organization's distress. The organization's mission therefore bears the footprint of members with the power to guide it in their favored direction. To protect their interests, the considerable power of the "dominant coalition" is arrayed against any substantial change. We can therefore conclude that change is likely to be resisted, and resisted *effectively*, because it runs up against the most potent interests in the organization.

However, resistance to change is certainly not confined to the organization's power brokers; lesser endowed members resist change because they have limited: (1) comprehension of its nature, reasons, or dimensions; (2) opportunity to manage it; and (3) resources to survive it. Regarding change, and to paraphrase an observation regarding our learning institutions, conflict is so heated because the stakes are so small.

As a result, resistance to change is likely to extend beyond powerful members to include anybody who could be affected by it. Small wonder, then, that, in our earlier example, the software developer resisted any change in product mix that would reduce if not exclude her mainframe creations.

The Comfort Zone

For all of these reasons, change is resisted until it can no longer be avoided. Ironically, in order to be effective, any substantive change should begin well in advance of experiencing this threshold of pain, before the need for it has become glaringly apparent; otherwise, costs may already be nonrecuperative, and a competitive advantage may be lost forever. Change is effective, then, when it would disrupt conditions *with which everyone is comfortable*, at the point when all concerned *surmise little to recommend it.*

The Abyss

Moreover, change threatens to throw a wrench into an organizational identity that may have had much apparent success to recommend it: by contrast, the substitute offered by a change represents an unknown quantity that has *no* such track record. Thus, preferences, and certainly rationalization, favor the status quo.

Additionally, across a wide range of endeavors, the unknown presents its own unique dread. Reasons include an anticipation of the Worst Case Scenario, due to: (1) its greatest publicity in connection with its victims; (2) the overestimation of its perceived likelihood from the familiarity engendered by dreading it, and thus by dwelling on it; and in contrast to this familiarity, and never having experienced the dreaded event, (3) ignorance about the actual nature and dynamics of the Worst Case Scenario, given which there is an abiding sense of failing to fully protect oneself from it.

Moreover, even dissatisfaction with a current state of affairs has been made livable by the way human beings tend to adapt: through habituation, by assigning low weight to sources of dissatisfaction, and by creating and focusing on compensatory sources of satisfaction. On balance, we find abundant support for the familiar experiential and research finding that people prefer the vagaries of what is known to the infinite, potential aversiveness of what is not. In the face of an urgent need for change, then, we find the organization marking time.

THE CHIMERA OF PLANNED CHANGE

To organizational scientists, "planned change" represents a veritable savior to the organization in distress.[105] Planned change is a generic term for the process of organizational change to which the full knowledge of social science may be applied.

Planned change is certainly informed enough to sound enlightened and considered, and certainly seems to address the issues raised to this point in the discussion; hence, there is more than a hint of sacrilege to taking issue with it. Nevertheless, there remains something a bit oxymoronic about the whole proceeding.

Change is a new way of doing things. Planning, on the other hand, represents the full weight of what is currently available to the task: old ways of doing things, reflecting the same decision makers, configured in the same social and power relationships, expressing ongoing beliefs and values through habitual, patterned methods of communication and other forms of interaction.

What this suggests is that the intended *content* of change can, in all likelihood, be undermined by the *process* of change. In general, people are likely to embrace change as an ideology, but not as a personal imperative: to endorse change without actually changing.

To revisit a previous example, Total Quality Management is intended to invoke full participation by everybody who will be affected by it. However, as we saw, it tends to be implemented, and to be undone, in the authoritative manner that indicates that the organization desperately needs TQM in the first place.

According to a management consultant, this is what happened at a machine-tools manufacturing firm in the Midwest:

When we first arrived on the scene they had a "quality program" process in place where teams would meet and would vocalize and would capture, on flip charts and so forth, their concerns about various projects, status of projects and that sort of thing. The quality guy was really enthused and he did a good job of facilitating meetings and so forth. He would get the message upstairs to what the people on the shop floor called the Suits and the Shirts at the executive end of the building and they would pass all this information up.

But there were no forthcoming changes; it was as if all the messages they had sent with great enthusiasm went into a black hole. So they never saw the equipment on the floor shifted in position; they didn't see new processes and procedures put in place that could be directly tied back to the work that they had done.

Sometimes TQM fails to make it even into its introductory stage. One result was the irony noted by an employee that the "division of a major company that builds rocket engines started a Total Quality Management system and didn't have the funding to have classes explain the system."

The fundamental problem with planned change is that effective planning requires a level of advance notification that, as we saw, is probably unrealistic. At a later point, when the organization is likelier to recognize the need for change, it is also likelier to be in sufficient distress to entrust change only to procedures on which it has historically relied for crisis management: again, on a process that reflects old ways of doing things. As noted earlier, external events push the organization deeper into itself.

What we find, then, is the parody into which the organization's program of planned change has devolved. Unfortunately, this charade is the only weapon with which the organization-in-extremis faces its mortal crisis. As a result, the organization faces its annihilation utterly defenseless.

At this point, change has become a subject for indoctrination rather than a policy supported by genuine commitment. Change has become a ritual.

Our attention is now directed to the many forms in which the ritual of change appears.

APPARENT CHANGE

One expression of this ritual is insufficient or *apparent change*, sources of which include a desire to effect change as some sort of dramatic statement.

Apparent change is often the first act of a new leader, to underscore differences from the old regime and depict the new one as a no-nonsense, energetic administration that obviously deserves its new position: a motive that also applies to a contrarian decision rendered simply to demonstrate job qualifications, as we saw earlier. "When a new leader takes over," observes a management consultant, "it's incumbent on the new leader to change the strategy to differentiate himself or herself from the predecessor. Otherwise, the person's in danger of not having an identity."

Associated as it is with a novel regime or some other basis for an instantaneous impression, change as a dramatic statement is likely to be devoid of knowledge and consideration of ongoing (and probably adaptive) interpersonal work arrangements. Thus, this type of change will probably be greeted coolly by all concerned. Furthermore, like any change, apparent change will step on the toes of current officeholders.

At the same time, declining to appear as entirely self-interested, and probably anxious to score some points with new management, people tend to wholeheartedly embrace the *principle* of change. The result is verbal commitment to change, but no more, producing change that is confined to the proverbial style rather than substance. In the long term, apparent change may close the door on the real thing, because it shall have given real change a bad name, creating, in its sincere adherents, cynicism about the commitment of change agents and about change in general.

This is what happened at the Midwest machine-tools manufacturing firm. According to the management consultant observing it,

it took about six or seven or eight months and pretty soon people stopped going to the meetings and the whole program just came to a grinding halt.

And what was worse is that it was as if everybody on the shop floor turned a blind eye to all the different problems that they saw and believe me there was a whole host of problems that needed to be repaired and fixed. And nobody reported it; it was just dead in the water: absolutely dead in the water—no communication whatsoever.

Similarly, according to a former city manager of a West Coast beach community, city employees are typically reluctant, after repeated executive purges, to commit to a "new" philosophy. This is due to previous experience, based upon which employees recognize the high probability that, like the philosophy it has replaced, the new one is also on borrowed time.

A management consultant describes the blow-by-blow process in the evolution of a jaded workforce within two companies:

The primary reason why these companies haven't been successful is probably because they don't do what they say they're going to do. They don't have either the will or the discipline to stick to the plan that they set out for themselves.

Interestingly enough, in both these cases, that's what turning around a company and saving it from disaster's usually all about. You draft a plan, you commit to the plan, and you stick to the plan. And neither of these organizations have been particularly good at sticking with what they say they're going to do.

So, what ends up happening is, because the change becomes the norm, and nothing sticks, no one can get behind anything because it's like, "Well, we may be doing this this week, but next week we're going to shift, and lurch off, and do something else." And so, as a result, no one gets behind anything, and the initiative, if it has any momentum at all, it loses it rapidly, or it never gains any momentum, so it just sort of peters out, and the organization continues in its downward cycle.

In the long term, then, the organization has been immunized against the change that it will, at some point, desperately need. And the long term will arrive soon enough.

ROUTINE CHANGE

In the meantime, as the organization awaits the inevitable, another common scenario for the ritual of change is the *routine change medium*, through which regularly located and scheduled procedures are presented as change strategies. The suggestion box is an obvious if much-maligned example, providing an avenue for both expressing ideas about change while censuring those that are substantial enough to create disquiet in the corridors of power.

Another example of the routine change medium is the regularly-scheduled office meeting, in which plans for change can grow to mammoth proportions and attendees leave feeling almost breathless at their amount of "progress" in bringing it about.

However, actual events at these meetings fall somewhat short of their depiction by attendees, have absolutely no repercussions whatsoever, and function primarily to counter the stasis, purposelessness, and irrelevance of participants, by meeting their social needs and permitting their shared validation of personal meaning. These purposes are exposed by an excruciatingly protracted preamble to the whole thing; excessively loud laughter throughout at not-terribly-funny "humor"; status reports that turn into windy, self-indulgent soliloquies; an occasional self-congratulation on some bureaucratic "accomplishment" (see Chapter 5); and the abiding sense that the whole enterprise will never end, if in fact it ever started.

The Unofficial Domain

The third form of routine change is an ongoing one: the permanent aspect of organizational life represented by its *unofficial* domain. To revisit our earlier distinction, the *official* domain is an arena in which corporate role behavior is prescribed and enforced: in which an individual disappears as a person and re-emerges as an "employee," fulfilling the role expectations of a position.

The unofficial domain, by contrast, refers to a set of activities that are earmarked and segregated from official activities. The purpose is to permit a ritualized display of individualism and expressiveness, without intruding on the collectivism and instrumentalism enforced in the official domain.

The unofficial domain is represented by the following: (1) social functions at which informality and overweening familiarity are accepted, even encouraged, as a way to counterbalance their expected exclusion during official hours; (2) office inscriptions and nicknames that convey various organizationally countercultural values, including hedonism, sloth, and incompetence: the extent of tolerable limits to humanize an official role devoid of these human frailties; and (3) a brief nod toward personal expressiveness, typically through humor, and often at the beginning of a meeting, to provide the bonding and goodwill needed for the dreary role performance to follow.

The unofficial domain is designed specifically to counterbalance the utter absence of dynamism and unpredictability in the official realm, through the palliative of the controlled sound and fury of real human life, with all of its surprises and serendipity.[106] In this sense, the unofficial domain presents the permanent spectacle of change, to help employees tolerate the organization's official unwillingness to tolerate such change on a more substantive level.

NONROUTINE CHANGE

The fourth and deliberately less common indulgence is the *nonroutine change medium*: an effort to convince participants, through its very departure from routine, that real change has taken place.

An example is provided by the off-site meeting, often patterned on the model of training or "T" groups, which presents opportunities for apparent interactive breakthroughs through exchanges that are purposively frank and honest. Such breakthroughs tend to come at a fast and furious pace, often telegraphed by personal and interpersonal crises, the ubiquitous tears, and a concluding sense of newfound and permanent closeness. Through such novel experiences, participants are convinced that such novelty will descend upon future working relationships.

Typically, it does not; sooner or later, participants awaken to find that the novel surroundings of this event define it as aberrant, consign any apparent change only to this context, and allow participants to resume business as usual at their workaday posts. Some participants are disillusioned by the inexorable reversion to role behavior, by the ephemerality of this melodramatic little exercise, and by the lip service apparently accorded to change in general. Others are thankful to be done with the whole thing, to quit pretending to care about those about whom they in fact care nothing, and to return to reality.

THE CHANGE PROGRAM

A more drastic, thoroughgoing disguise for change is signalled by the *change program,* recent examples of which include Quality Circles, Team Building, and, once again, Total Quality Management, a nomenclature that tends to be deliberately varied so that organizations can demonstrate their ownership over the program and in turn its indigenousness and appropriateness to each.

The Consulting Project

The typical change agent in such a program is the organizational or management consultant. As a credible change agent, the role of the consultant is compromised by dependence on the organization for future contracts. Right off the bat, this, of course, limits any opportunity for substantial change.

Moreover, given their authority, contract managers probably have some responsibility for the problem they present to the consultant: if not for creating it, at least for tolerating it. Due to the consultant's dependence on them, however, exoneration is assured for perhaps the problem's true culprits.

The reason why contract managers both retain and constrain a consultant is to legitimize their perspective in some policy or strategic dispute, by applying an external, "objective," and "expert" solution. According to the witness from whom we heard earlier about the war between the Finance and Information Systems Departments in the healthcare company,

the Finance Division, after I left, had a consultant come in and do a systems analysis to see if they were doing things right. And I heard that the Finance people influenced the consultant to make certain suggestions on getting rid of some of the IS people. And it was just a real mess.

This influence may be subtle. Contract managers may preemptively confine the solution to an acceptable range by (1) introducing the problem in a manner that is defined to accommodate only certain solutions; (2) taking an active role, ensuring that the consultant depends on it for project completion; (3) exploiting this role to arrange sources of innocuous or favorable information; (4) co-opting the consultant by inviting the latter's participation in some privileged procedure, ostensibly to enhance insight into the organization; and (5) assisting and thus managing the process of communicating the consultant's recommendations, either by representing or handpicking the audience for them, and transmitting and thus filtering them to everybody else.

The Change Ceremony

Together with an interface with the external change agent, another element of the change program is the *change ceremony*, a panegyric to change that can assume highly formalized, elaborate, and detailed forms. There may, for example, be special sessions for introducing and justifying the program; "workshops" for collaborative problem solving; and a conclusion for reporting solutions, reaching consensus around them, and committing to them.

The ceremony's purpose is to dramatize proactive intervention in some problem, unambiguous commitment to solving it, and fulfillment of that commitment by taking, or at least sharing, responsibility for it. The purpose of all this drama, in turn, is business as usual. According to a hospital administrator in Southern California,

the way TQM has been circumvented is that the top management appears to embrace TQM: however, it is really *not* embracing TQM. And they have a specific plan—how they would like to proceed with the project or policy, and they select, as part of the group, employees that they feel are leaders among the staff. However, [they] are easily persuaded by the top management.

And, in addition, as they're doing the fact-based decision statistics, they give the group certain statistics or lead the group to believe that only certain statistics would be useful which, they know, would support the case that they would like to proceed with, and thereby not give full disclosure to the statistics, but enough statistics to lead the group toward the chosen path that the top management wants in the first place, thereby manipulating the whole system.

The purpose of implementing TQM may be to ostentatiously demonstrate the seriousness of commitment to quality and customer service, simply to buttress the prestige of change agents. According to an employee in a publishing house,

> I have gone to battle (in my current position as managing editor) to prevent a quality measurement from being put into place because the systems suggested would create more paperwork for everyone and provide the least benefit to employees. The push for the quality measurement system is so that "we can be a model for the company" and "be the first department to put this into place." I say, "Hogwash. Let's create the system that benefits employees best, improving their skills as professionals, and forget the papertrail."

The focus on appearance rather than on performance and satisfaction says all one needs to know about the seriousness of change agents. In this case, the motive for a quality movement was to score points with internal constituents, for individual career enhancement. In other cases, the appearance of quality was featured in a virtual advertising campaign, directed to customers. According to an employee of an auto finance corporation,

> our TQM process is that if we develop a product or a service, we ask very loyal dealers who have no knowledge of the specific product we just developed to support our product and to be sort of a poster child for that product: whether or not it's profitable for the dealer but, in most cases, it actually reduces the expenses for our corporation.
>
> We get these dealers to support the product, indicating that it's their original thought process. We then put their pictures in the automobile news, indicating that they were the true benefactor of this new product or service, and they, in turn, become the spokesperson for the product and solicit other dealers in the area to sign up for it.
>
> The thought process behind doing the Total Quality Management on products and services in the automobile sector is that we believe that the dealer body will look at us as more focused and more centered around their business unit, adding more quality because we are a service industry so we feel that if the perception is we add more quality we, in turn, can charge a higher rate. So if we add more quality to the dealers, whether it's perceived or not, we might be able to charge a higher premium because other lenders in the area won't be giving them that same quality or that same product.

In still other cases, change agents try to impress, not colleagues or customers, but rather *themselves*. Through an active role, change agents persuade themselves that the organization is firmly in command, rather than at the mercy, of events that have probably grown downright ominous under conditions that cry out for change.

MISDIRECTED CHANGE

The underlying purpose of the change ritual, in its various forms, is, of course, to preserve the power arrangements favorable to those controlling it. Another tactic to accomplish this purpose is *misdirected change*.

Of all the buzzwords to evolve in management science, "change" may be the most venerable of all. A buzzword is assumed to represent such a good thing that its use and form are unexamined.

Change is assumed to represent such a good thing that it took highly insightful research to give credence to arguments against it. By offering just that, Donald Klein cautioned that an organizational change may be ill-advised because it may threaten system welfare; undermine individual self-esteem, competence, and autonomy; represent a process that is unwieldy, precipitous, unfeasible, and if any of the above, irreversible as well; and may express the suspect motives of change agents already heavily invested in the project.[107] All of these represent hazards from what we call misdirected change.

As a buzzword, "change" is directed through an internal advertising campaign at employees. Organizational members are treated, often with a shameless lack of originality, to reassurances that "people are our greatest asset" or "our most important resource"; are evolving into "knowledge workers," with increases in performance expectations, if not in pay; and that for them, "leaner" surely means "meaner": a posture certainly directed at the competition, not at them.

DECEPTIVE CHANGE

This last application underscores the use of "change" as a buzzword to sell *deceptive change*, the purpose of which is, in a word, cutbacks. The problem is how to keep participants on board long enough to do their jobs while awaiting their own terminations, often by allaying personal doubts after the termination of coworkers.

To accomplish these objectives, "change" is expropriated, along with its favorable cachet, to characterize threatened or actual layoffs, to promise various benefits and enlist the commitment needed to achieve them. Commitment is gathered by promising the benefits of parsimony, including simplicity, cost reductions, greater profit margins, long-term organizational survival, and security for members.

The hope is that such commitment will supplant the recognition that, in fact, the organization will be a much more aversive and ominous workplace in the days ahead, presenting fewer (and probably overworked) employees, facing an uncertain future in the face of the internal or external crisis that precipitated this chain of events. The only "change" is that, for a workforce willing to go along, things will be getting worse.

BELATED CHANGE

This, then, is the Ritual of Change in its various forms. The one likely instance of substantial change occurs only when change agents discover that their individual, short-term cost exceeds the individual, short-term benefits of resisting it. This occurs only when the organization is in such ruin that the people without the resources to resist have been largely sacrificed, and the change agents are clearly next. This is *belated change*: when change that is commensurate with the threat facing the organization is unavoidable and, at this late date, ineffective as well.

For the organization, this monstrous approach to the need for change is typically the last stage in its failure. This is when the organization has learned in advance the lesson that it needs to do things differently—and ignores it. The reason for the delay is that the underlying problem reflects, and any effective solution threatens, the power arrangements that can be deployed against change.

A management consultant confessed to some difficulty in identifying organizational problems among his current or past clients. The reason is obvious: organizations seeking the help of a consultant tend to be, for the moment at least, healthy organizations, enjoying the benefits of self-scrutiny, internal communication about problems, and openness to external solutions to them.

What we have discovered is the other side to this coin: that *the organization that needs to change most urgently is least likely to do it*. This is why, at the point wherein it faces demise, the organization has no defense. The result is the eventuality predicted throughout this book: the end of the organization.

The last stages of the organization do not represent a gentle, short-lived affair: rather, it is a protracted, self-sustaining, and agonizing process of self-immolation.

The "Cutback Spiral"

Social processes are ongoing processes because they sustain themselves. As in so many other social processes within the organization, we find this to be the case for the "Cutback Spiral" observed by researchers in the dying organization.

After deluding themselves, deceiving other members, and ultimately facing no alternative, the organization jettisons some of its workforce: typically, the least qualified and most expendable. Since the cause of downsizing is insufficient revenue in relation to cost, the organization clearly wants to squeeze additional productivity out of its workers.

It is not clear that downsizing organizations are succeeding. Based on two surveys conducted in 1993 and 1994, the American Management Associates found that roughly *half of the downsizing companies it surveyed showed either no change or a decline in operating profits*: a significant finding, particularly given the poor figures that must have spurred cutbacks in the first place. Employee productivity either remained the same or declined for well over half the respondents.

The reason probably resided in the third set of figures. In the 1993 survey, employee "morale" declined for 84.1 percent of the respondents in the downsized companies, and for 86.0 percent in the 1995 study. By comparison, morale remained constant in the two surveys for 13.4 percent and 12.1 percent, and improved an infinitesimal 2.4 percent and 1.9 percent, respectively.[108]

For many researchers, the problem for the morale of termination survivors can perhaps best be understood by analyzing them as analogues to survivors of other events, like the Holocaust that, while obviously more horrific, produce qualitatively if not quantitatively similar reactions.

Like their Holocaust counterparts, termination survivors experience a complex of emotions that include grief about the loss of coworkers; guilt about not being among them; anger on behalf of victims, coupled with a sense of dependence on authorities for their own fate; fear about that fate; and uncertainty about how best to address that fear. Reflecting this uncertainty, performance vacillates between a frenetic attempt to prove one's worth and equally frenzied efforts to pursue employment options elsewhere.[109]

Of all employees, termination survivors were retained because they are the best-qualified, and thus potentially the most marketable. At some point, termination survivors will probably be sorely tempted to exploit their marketability by exiting the company, thereby reducing the quality of and further denuding the surviving workforce, exacerbating an already tenuous capacity to do its work, reducing revenues still further, necessitating further cutbacks, and so on.

THE END GAME

Through the Cutback Spiral, the organization emerges as somewhat of a tragic figure. In the entire process, there is precious little room for movement by either the organization or its captive crew.

Even the empathic organizations that elect to provide notification and outplacement services sufficiently in advance of layoffs nevertheless pay a stiff price. Particularly given their already vanishing revenues, these companies face unaffordably fast and widespread egress of essential employees, including those who, while not even targeted for layoffs, evidently prefer alternative employment options to the possibility of tempting fate.

On the other hand, the less creditable but understandably more common path of corporate deception is at least as difficult to maintain; when exposed, it reduces morale to an unworkable level in critical times, and eventually produces a backlash of cynicism and loss of commitment. For their part, it is in the employees' interest to know everything, in order to pursue that interest, despite its potential cost to the organization. Because of the cost, it is in the organization's interest to conceal this information and prevent employees from pursuing their *own* interest. The organization and its members are therefore openly, clearly, and ineluctably at cross-purposes, pursuing different and competing agendas.

This was acknowledged by a research team investigating downsizing, according to whom

there is tension between the need for broad input from stakeholders and the cross-functional team and the need for confidentiality during the planning process. Indeed, confidentiality during planning risks undermining the trust and empowerment that managers should try to preserve. . . .

Unfortunately, none of the organizations we studied had completely solved this problem. . . . [110]

Regardless of the path it chooses, the organization is probably now left to a merciless fate. In the next chapter, we will explore how its members manage to avoid recognizing it.

12

The Blind Leading the Blind: Learning How to Fail

To be ignorant of one's ignorance is the malady of the ignorant.
—Amos Bronson Alcott

There has been a lot of attention directed lately to the effect of role models, and the potential benefits of mentors, on the maturational development of young people. In many respects, the same can be said of our impressionable organizations. As is the case with individuals, we are about to see that role models often have a counterproductive if not destructive effect on our organizations.

THE BIRTH OF A SHARED ILLUSION

As we saw earlier, decision makers in organizations and elsewhere have various shorthands to overcome human limitations on making decisions. These shorthands include "heuristics," or rules of thumb, that provide familiar, generally concrete, but not necessarily relevant information, particularly in the absence of other information.

In making decisions about the organization, the founder, CEO, or other key decision maker is heavily influenced by precedent in other organizations, particularly successful-appearing ones. The apparent success of other organizations, and the lessons to be derived from it, provide reassurance against subliminal and well-founded anxieties in the face of an uncertain and treacherous environment.

However, to rely on other organizations is to rely on an optical illusion.

Analogous to what we can expect among them is what occurs in the "Work Hard, Play Hard" sales culture, according to organizational anthropologists Deal and Kennedy. Thanks to "burnout," employees have a short shelf life, departing the organization after a brief tenure, making older salespeople a rarity, and confining the sales force to young people with almost no experience who therefore lack the ability to provide lessons from previous failures. Organizations are somewhat the same; those who vanish take with them the secrets of their demise.

The Complacency of Distance

In addition, demise *seems* to represent the fate not of all organizations but rather the less efficient ones. This is because, for several reasons, organizational demise is viewed not as an inevitable and generalizable process but rather as an atypical one, applicable only to its victims.

One reason, suggested early on in this study, is that the organization experiences a privatized, inaccessible relationship with its craft. This renders the organization both impervious to the ministrations and subjectively immune to the failings of outsiders. We find much the same thing with individual people; in response to the news that someone has suffered a heart attack, for example, our response is that the victim was overweight, or a smoker, or had some other, distancing characteristic.

In like fashion, the causes of a single organizational demise can be particularized to its victim, because demise can always be attributed to unique characteristics. For example, the organization was "heavily leveraged," or "poorly managed," or "not liquid enough."

Moreover, in both individual and organizational cases, destruction is often viewed as the result of deliberate and ill-advised action by the victim, reassuring the rest of us that survival is equally the result of deliberate but better-advised action. In both cases, demise seems to be insulated to the less fortunate if not the more self-destructive among us.

"Neocentrism": The Chauvinism of the Present

Contributing to this is the perception of a quantum, qualitative distance between the knowledge of the present and that of the past. Based upon current knowledge, the past is, of course, perceived as but a subset of the present. Moreover, current knowledge *always* appears to be complete; it is revealed as deficient only as a result of additional knowledge. As the poet Wallace Stevens put it, "All history is modern history."

Therefore, the past is, at any moment, perceived as but a subset of a *complete, fully realized* present. We may call this belief "neocentrism." As a result of neocentrism, we in the present experience omniscience, reducing further any ability to relate to the denizens of the past.

Implications abound, in all walks of life. For our current purposes, one implication is that organizational demise is perceived as a condition only of the past; in the present, it is viewed as correctable. Protected by our own omniscience, demise awaits only those organizations that in effect choose it, through inefficiency.

As Freud observed, people cannot picture their own demise. To a certain extent, the same is true of organizations.

FALSE PROPHECY

Thus, as inefficient contemporaries or even the vanquished competition, departed organizations are not simply rendered mute by their demise but rather seem to validate the sagacity of survivors. Reinforcing the belief that survival equates to wisdom is the role of other surviving organizations as "teachers," a role that appears to be justified because they appear to have learned The Secret to Success but, in fact, have not yet had enough time to fully do themselves in.

As a result, according to a management consultant, a major source of corporate strategy is

copycattism. X-Y-Z company out there has really been a success producing widgets with an extra widget on the right side. That's what everybody wants. "Look how successful they've been. We've got to do that too." That's the way strategies are formed, mostly through copycat stuff.

And the way organizational arrangements are formed now, if they're formed in any kind of way that's different from the particular needs of people, go out and do a benchmarking study of other organizations in our industry; see how they do things. And if we are different from the way that others do them, particularly if others are doing them in a cheaper way, we must be wrong. So we've got to change to conform to the way they're doing things, without looking at a particular aspect of an organizational arrangement that we have in place now and how it fits our strategy. The notion is: if they're doing it cheaper, it must be better.

And often that comes out of a sense of inferiority; we've got to be like them when we grow up, like one of the big guys.

"Copycattism" *seems* like receptivity rather than resistance to input, but, in reality, equates to the latter, since, as the consultant indicates, copycattism prohibits introspection, representing only a superficial, uninformed effort to adopt the trappings of others' apparent success.

Of course, other organizations contribute to their mystique by doing their mightiest to be perceived as successful, if only to secure the patronage and loyalty of investors, customers, and employees. Organizational psychoanalysts might infer, as another motive, the need to reassure the self against the well-justified fear of nonbeing. Thus, the case made by other organizations is persuasive because it is meant to be, conveyed as it is through advertising, public relations, and other controlled media, and buttressed by their own sources of self-delusion.

ORGANIZATIONAL AMNESIA

Contributing to this self-delusion is the fact that the organization represents its own audience for the information it provides regarding its success or failure.

Like individuals, and in part because individual members are responsible, organizations learn about their own success and failure through perception and memory. As in the case of individuals, both processes are heavily biased to impart the experience of success.

Individual Misperception

Through perception, individuals display the self-serving bias: the tendency to claim credit for success and disown responsibility for failure. In individuals, this bias is driven by self-esteem; in organizations, it is drawn from individual self-interest as well as self-esteem, since decision makers have a stake in appearing creditable for success, competent at their role, and well-positioned in performing that role. According to an ex-employee, regarding her manager, "Kristin,"

anytime something went well she would say to the VP, "We accomplished this" or "We accomplished that." "We were able to get this done." If something blew up, it was " 'Henry' didn't do this" and " 'Carol' didn't do that" and "I told 'Cynthia' " . . . There was always someone to blame. But she never gave the people that got the job done credit. It was always "We." And she had absolutely nothing to do with it. . . . Taking credit for anything good, but sure pointing the finger if anything was bad.

Ongoing perception eventually provides a reference for memory, although a clearly unreliable one. If individual perception is unreliable, individual memory is doubly so, given that it is based on selective, retrospective impressions of an already selective information-gathering process. And compared to individual memory, moreover, *organizational* perception and memory are even less reliable, since they transcend individuals, rely on word of mouth, and are tractable to many sources of misinterpretation or manipulation.

Organizational Misinformation-Gathering

The organization's ostensible and ultimate purpose of gathering information is of course to maximize organizational effectiveness; however, as we have seen, the organization instead gathers information through, and to the benefit of, its more powerful members. Due to its legitimacy, then, "organizational effectiveness" is thereupon pressed into service as a device cited by these individuals in order to justify their individual purposes. This is because, as we have seen, individual interest is typically cloaked in the guise of organizational responsibility. Rising to the task are various measures of organizational effectiveness.

These measures come in various shapes and sizes, but despite their *appearance* of objectivity, they tend to share the *reality* of ambiguity, an opportunity for *flexible interpretation*, and thus an unending utility for *delusion* and *deception*. As a result, measures of organizational effectiveness can legitimize any among a wide variety of individual purposes, including organizationally destructive ones.

To appreciate their capacity for mischief, the reader is referred to Appendix 2, in which these measures of organizational effectiveness are summarized and evaluated.

Organizational Misinformation-Processing

Such as it is, and in order to fully evaluate the organizational utility of individual action, information "gathered" by the organization is processed through quality control systems: the methods for evaluating compliance with internal standards.

Despite the nominal inroads of Total Quality Management, with its collectivization of responsibility for quality, one precondition for *objectively* controlling quality is to separate responsibility for achieving it from the authority to evaluate it. Consider the odds of effective quality control in the following arrangement, reported by the marketing director of a mortgage brokerage firm in Southern California:

The sales organization paid their people, who are responsible for monitoring quality control, based on gross sales. That's what their bonuses are paid on. That means that when we pull loans in, that the same people, who are responsible for making sure that those loans are good and they don't go bad later on and end up costing us a fortune, are being paid based on how many loans we bring in. It eliminates the check.

According to a former Creative Director, there was the case of a part owner of an advertising agency that I worked for where all creative effort had to be filtered through him before it was presented to a client. This man, unfortunately, had a tremendous ego. And in the advertising business in general, there's something called "pride of authorship" and there's a lot of jockeying to get one's efforts to fruition.

He had the final say on everything that was acceptable to presentation to clients. ... Anything he came up with was automatically approved; there was nobody to pass judgment on it except himself.

There were a number of occasions when I had to go out to an account with something that he had created, where the account really thought that I was demented for having even presented it.

There was one case where this agency owner had three or four or five big rocks on his desk; they were slightly larger than the size of a baseball. And somehow, he decided that that would become the theme of a campaign: those rocks. He said, "Robert," that's the campaign: right there." And I said, "Where?" And he said, "In those rocks." I said, "I don't get it." He said, "Believe me: it's there. Just present it to them."

I presented it to them with every intention of making it acceptable to them, and they doubled over with laughter. . . .

However, nobody was laughing at some of the owner's other accomplishments:

Inasmuch as he was an owner, there was nobody who could disapprove of where he spent money. He ran up personal expenses that were charged to the business. And this rubbed a lot of people the wrong way, because part of our income was a profit-sharing plan: a pension plan. And part of what he was spending—and it ran into hundreds and thousands of dollars a year—and what he was spending, of course, ultimately came out of our pocket.

But he would charge long-distance calls to Puerto Rico where he was pursuing a young lady. And he made these calls at great length every day. He had an addition built on his house which was purportedly a studio in which he would prepare advertising work.

So these were expenses charged to the business that went to him personally. And it was only possible because there was no one who had oversight on these expenditures.

Contrary to the public arena for conducting governmental affairs, most private organizations conduct their affairs behind closed doors, effectively immune from oversight by stockholders or other interested parties. As a result of this immunity, the power over a function is sufficiently absolute to evolve into authority for *controlling that function*. Results include the abuses we have just observed.

While this violates any commonsensical notions of effective control, effective control is the last thing on the minds of personnel who have managed to catapult themselves into positions of governance: a conclusion consistent with our accumulated evidence for their actual interests, which tend to run to the short term and individual rather than long term and organizational.

Thus, the control system devised by many an organization may be charitably described as ineffective. The less charitable term for this arrangement is corruption.

Organizational Memory Loss

Any element of reality untarnished by individual perception and memory, or by organizational perception, is unlikely to make it unscathed through the collective memory of the organization.

On the national scale, by analogy, Americans have gloried in heroes whose mythical status plainly doesn't square with often more lurid or prosaic facts: examples include the largely self-made character of Buffalo Bill, the exaggerated John Henry, and the nonexistent Paul Bunyan. On the one hand, such mythology can be blamed for various misdeeds, including the willful neglect of earlier atrocities against Native Americans, which may continue to undermine their standing in ongoing legal disputes. On the other hand, American hero worship may contribute to a self-image of independence and intrepidness that may stand the American soldier in good stead in combat overseas, assuming that he or she belongs there. Hence, this mythmaking may or may not be destructive.

The same conclusion may apply to *organizational* amnesia.

Memories Coming True

On the one hand, any effective performance may, before it occurs, require an initial bit of delusion, through faith in the absence of any evidence that supports it. As the Houston Rockets basketball forward Scottie Pippen characterized his attitude, after a strikingly poor performance in a prior game, "I *forced myself to feel good* [emphasis added]. I knew I had to come out aggressive . . . I knew I had to lay it on the line." Parenthetically, results in the following game were vastly improved.

Similarly, the contents of organizational memory, while apocryphal, may provide the sort of mythology that can help individual motivation. In a Southern California–based pharmaceutical company, for example,

the "heroes" stories are that the two scientists who discovered each of the drugs that became their first two major products that established them as a successful international company were both cases where it began to appear to top management that the lines of research were not going to go anyplace and that they were wasting their money doing this stuff, because they were not going to find a product. And according to these stories, both of these two people were told to stop and they didn't. They kept on doing the work, secretly.

And then they made the discoveries that made these commercial drugs. Then they were heroes, because they stuck to their own thing. What if it's not true?

Grim Reality

The problem is that trafficking in myths is clearly the opposite of objective analysis, and can invite disaster.

Organizational memory tends to be biased in a positive direction by the following: (1) by the exclusive availability of data from the information-gathering that serves the purposes of the powers-that-be, as we have just seen; (2) by the loss or "mortality" of, and unavailability of testimony from, victims of the very untoward events that, if properly recalled, would balance if not dominate this memory; (3) by the larger-than-life, heroic versions of human beings that can survive in memory; and (4) by the tendency to romanticize the past, in contrast to (and perhaps, by replacing constructive actions with nostalgia, accountable for) the current privations that justify a fond, backward gaze.

Moreover, this positive spin represents the very purpose of current leaders who seek to build faith in the organization and support for their leadership of it, who can do so through a leader's ability to "manage meaning" for the organization.

Amnesia in Action

For many reasons, then, organizational memory tends to be fictive and "feel-good" and, as the sole intermediary with reality, provides information for decisions that, as a result, are based not on *reality* but rather on fanciful *visions* of reality. For example, according to a former real estate agent and manager, possible consequences regarding the late founder of her company include the fact that

the bottom line is that he was one of the worst businessmen I've known in my life. What he did do was, by sheer will and presence, make it easy to carry on in the perception that he was such an identifiable character. When he walked in to a room, the room rocked. It made all the employees feel bigger, that they belonged to something bigger than they were: even though, when he died, we were so seriously in the red that we would have folded if he hadn't died, and used the insurance money to pay the debts.

The upshot was that the late real estate company owner's "wife and her friend came in, cut the costs, got rid of the limousine, did all the obvious business things. Everybody hated them for it, but within four years they put the company in the black and sold it."

Here, the company was rescued by people who *refused* to subscribe to romantic organizational memories of its founder.

In the following setting, there was no rational, revisionist interpretation of the past, although there was also no local competition to exact a price. According to a department head, a university president

was in the school of business when this place literally closed the doors for financial reasons. So they got rid of the then-President.

[The successor] had a business background; he had been an executive with Sears. So he knew how organizations operate more than the incumbent did. So he inspired enough confidence in some donors and some other people they kept the doors open and the place has gone on to thrive.

Today, as people look back on his Presidency and that near-disaster—the crisis that almost put the university out of existence—they tend to see him as almost saint-like. On the other hand, I was here in the later years of his administration and I know what didn't happen and what he couldn't do to move to the next step. Yes, he averted disaster but he didn't also have the skills to deal with the changing environment, the changing competition, the students . . . but institutionally, we remember him as far more than what he was at the time.

Regarding broader issues,

if you talk to faculty, they always remember selectively what was good about the curriculum versus what's bad about the current curriculum . . . they remember when this department or that department was particularly strong for reasons that they probably manufactured today but weren't true at the time.

A management consultant and academic dean describes an individual process analogous to the organizational one:

I was sitting around over a weekend, sometime after my father died, with my two brothers. I spent some time with one brother and then some time with the other brother. And so we were all telling stories about Dad.

And the person that was portrayed in these stories was three totally different people. And I'm sitting here thinking to myself, "The stuff that my brother Jeff says he remembers could not be true if the stuff that I remember is true." And after a while I didn't know, because we put that spin on even when he was alive.

You know, each had our own relationship and saw him reinforcing a value in some things about us that we liked about ourselves and wanted to have reinforced. Then, we said "Well he must be like that too." So we sort of created memories of this guy that are probably not true, or exaggerated at least.

Apparently, the same thing happens in organizations.

As we saw, along with its older members, the Work Hard, Play Hard corporate culture loses its organizational memory, according to Deal and Kennedy.[111] However, we are starting to appreciate the fact that organizational memory is highly overrated altogether. In its ostensible efforts to learn the lessons of the past, and in its actual attempts to receive validation from the past, the organization tends to remember *the wrong things*.

In sum, then, the organization tends not only to *perceive the wrong things as they occur* but also *to recall the wrong things in retrospect*. Furthermore, by continuing to perceive the wrong things, the organization builds spurious memories well into the future. The result is that the organization anticipates its future with the rosiest-colored of possible glasses.

We therefore find an organization availed of almost limitless tools to fool itself into reassurance of its indestructibility, and tolerance for individual acts of mayhem, due to: (1) its own survival to this point; (2) its capacity to select, interpret, and project information; and (3) the same capacity enjoyed by organizational contemporaries representing points of reference.

MANAGEMENT FADS

Thanks to the didactic value read into its surviving soul mates, the organization has proven to be highly susceptible to management fads. The reason for such fads, of course, is that there is a consistent need for them, due to their inevitable invalidation, given the continuous propensity of previous adherents to expire.

As a result, we are treated to an endless parade of the Right Way To Manage, including Taylor's Scientific Management, Barnard's Functions of the Executive, Fayol's Fourteen Principles of Administration, the Human Relations School, Gantt Charts, Just-in-Time, Leader Match, Path-Goal Leadership, Situational Leadership, Transformational Leadership, Management by Objectives, Management by Walking Around, Management of Meaning, the One-Minute Manager, Open-Book Management, the Matrix Organization, the Learning Organization, the *Un*learning Organization, Quality, Quality Circles, Total Quality Management, Team-Building, Theory Y, Theory Z, and probably the only approach with any staying power: the contextual or "Contingency" approach, which means simply that for any management style, as is recommended by the situational ethicist or the 1960s pop song, its day will come.

Due to their novelty and as-yet-unproven lack of worth, management fads represent yet another device to focus on management while ignoring the real management issue it faces. The real issue refers to the fundamental forces destroying the organization without its collective awareness.

HUBRIS

The common link among various management practices, inbred as well as imported, and a reason for their downfall, is "hubris," which is defined by Webster's Dictionary as "wanton insolence or arrogance resulting from excessive pride or from passion." Hubris is revealed in the unwillingness to admit that one is wrong.

In addition to all of the other dysfunctional practices for which they are structured, organizations are perfectly designed to nurture this quality of hubris. More than anything else, personnel are evaluated for Being Right, since Being Right represents the various qualities for which the employee is evaluated, including competence, reliability, diligence, thoroughness, and so on. (Interestingly, one is likely to observe a feigned appearance of understanding or knowledge from people who sense a risk to, and feel a need to defend, their intellectual honor. By contrast, one is far likelier to observe an admission of misunderstanding or ignorance by people with a clearly high intellectual self-evaluation.)

Efforts to forestall the appearance of Being Wrong include some of the most catastrophic decision errors in the organization's repertoire.

Intransigence

One simple and direct possibility is intransigence. And one tip-off of the threat to which intransigence is a response is its expression with an exaggerated depth of feeling which, in and of itself, is designed to impart respect for any argument that justifies it.

Ancillary Decisions

A more elaborate option for expressing intransigence is to make supplemental decisions that presuppose the validity of an initial, and controversial, decision.

For example, rather than simply defend the choice of market segments, a marketing specialist may target complementary goods to the same group. One reason is to assuage internal doubts: one can feel especially committed to a primary decision if it has ramified to other decisions. Moreover, attention displaced to alternative decisions masks any doubts about the original one and localizes any such doubts to them. An additional reason for this conspicuous display of commitment is, of course, to convince others.

"Nonrational Escalation of Commitment"

A related method to close the books on a decision has been called "nonrational escalation of commitment," through which a decision is steadfastly maintained beyond the point at which it is cost effective to do so. The reason is to "recoup sunk costs," a focus on potential loss that, in and of itself, according to researchers, produces the risk-seeking posture represented in turn by this selfsame nonrational escalation of commitment: a risky enterprise indeed.

The classic example is the Vietnam War, escalated at each point to justify mounting prior carnage. Other, organizational examples include every instance of "throwing good money after bad."

The Expanding Web of Hubris

Common to all methods for expressing hubris is the fact that failure to admit an error becomes a self-perpetuating process. In addition to the original decision of which it represents a defense, failure to acknowledge that decision as an error is now *itself* a decision that cannot be abdicated without jeopardizing the appearance of one's apparent competence, in *ever-deepening* amounts.

Hubris as a Leadership Trait

We may anticipate the strongest reluctance to admit error by the organization's leaders, from whom Being Right is both a qualification and a responsibility for the role. Additionally, leadership has been defined to include indomitability: the aforementioned leadership trait identified as "the management of trust through constancy." As is the case with "character," explored earlier, "constancy" is demonstrated by commitment in the face of evidence and arguments against it. Therefore, due to the huge personal and occupational stake in the position, we have good reason to fear a high level of hubris from the organization's most empowered decision makers.

Hubris for the Rest of Us

Finally, hubris is within the repertoire of everyone, given a universal need for self-esteem.

Hubris perhaps can best be understood through analogy.

Hubris represents the advancement of self-esteem through methods analogous to the advancement of self-interest by individuals and groups within the organization. Both motives are advanced surreptitiously, by claiming some form of "objectivity": in other words, objective *correctness* by the individual pursuing self-esteem, and objective organizational *responsibility* and *effectiveness* by organizational members pursuing self-interest.

The reason for all of this nefariousness is that exposure of both motives would fatally undermine their fulfillment: (1) by identifying each as an end unto itself and (2) by revealing as a contrivance, and by thus denying, the external validation required by each: respectively, the individual *capability* to be correct, and support *from other individuals and groups* within the organization, as we saw in Chapter 2.

Hence, like intraorganizational self-interest, hubris must be advanced by *appearing to be legitimate.* Thus, hubris is expressed through behaviors that produce outcomes that in turn seem to reflect objective consideration but, in fact, simply reflect the motive to Be Right. These self-validating behaviors include the following:

1. A decision about what constitutes evidence, based on subjective rules of logical argumentation.
2. A search for, selection of, and efforts to shape, confirmatory evidence, reflecting the discretionary nature of perception and memory.
3. The neglect and perceived unavailability of disconfirmatory evidence, again given the discretionary nature of perception and memory.
4. Having been thoroughly sanitized, the support by all available evidence for the decision that has already been made.

Hence, at all levels, the organizational interest is undermined by individual interest, and eroded by deception and by *self*-deception.

CONCLUSION

We have now boiled down the entire process of organizational failure to its individual source. It is no longer an abstraction, and the subject for speculation. It is the product of identifiable, individual behaviors.

We have one more task to perform in analyzing the phenomenon. We must convince any doubters that organizational self-destruction is a bad thing. As we will see in the next chapter, there are such doubters, but there is also an avalanche of evidence to convince them otherwise.

Our attention is now directed to the specific and massive costs of organizational failure.

13

The Agony of Defeat: The Hidden Costs of Organizational Failure

> As always, victory finds a hundred fathers but defeat is an orphan.
> —Count Galeazzo Ciano

Right off the bat, and to reiterate a point that concluded the last chapter, it should be acknowledged that there is no universal belief in the ultimate costs of organizational failure; to the contrary, some observers view organizational demise as a welcome contributor to the product quality that society can expect of successful competitors. This is an expression of our much-discussed population ecology view, that successful competitors shall have benefited from the selection of those most "fit" to give society what it wants.

This argument is a potent and thus popular one. Unfortunately, it is also an invalid argument, one reason for which is that it is based on the erroneous assumption that both the economic "ecosystem" and its biological analogue can support only the exact number of competitors that survive. In reality, both ecosystems display variable fecundity, ranging in the biological case from the desert to the more fertile rain forest, and in the economic case from the monopoly to the more fertile "perfect competition": thanks in part to the resourcefulness of competitors, displayed for example in independent films compared to traditional, "Hollywood" fare.

Another reason to doubt the population ecology argument is that "economic" competition is in fact not all that economic: as a result, retarding or degrading product quality, as we saw in Chapter 10. There are other reasons as well.

NONACHIEVEMENT OF ORGANIZATIONAL AND STOCKHOLDER GOALS

The most obvious victims of the fact that organizations are built to fail are, of course, organizations themselves. By definition, their failure means that they cannot achieve their purposes, however implicit such purposes are.

However, we need to reiterate that organizations do not exist; only their members do. Hence, we need to assign the costs of their failure to living creatures.

One group of real victims consists of shareholders who, probably and justifiably, feel they have been hoodwinked into a bad investment by organizational promise. However, costs extend to other members, including employees.

NONLEARNING BY EMPLOYEES

One set of costs to employees is exacted in their knowledge and learning about constructive participation in, and management of, organizations themselves, for the following reasons.

It is possible for people to learn from their past contribution to organizational failure; in fact, a pivotal recommendation in the next chapter is to exploit such lessons for the future. On the other hand, accomplishing this requires the capacities to: (1) acknowledge one's role in failure, (2) analyze it with enough depth and honesty to understand it, and (3) change in a way that reflects that understanding—a rare set of virtues indeed.

Failure on an organizational scale certainly suggests that lessons were not learned in time to stave it off. More than likely, the event is experienced as such an unmitigated, personal defeat, not to mention a public one, that subsequent energy is likely to be devoted, not to learning from it, but rather in an egoistic effort to avoid embarrassment for it, escape blame for it, and assign responsibility elsewhere. This effort may be facilitated by the complexity of organizational failure, subjective ways of viewing it, and shared responsibility for it, so that some responsibility can plausibly be disowned.

To disown responsibility, furthermore, subsequent behavior may well be ossified to the point of defiantly asserting lack of any culpability. Rather than teach its architects, then, organizational failure may be preserved, and perpetuated, by maintaining the very methods responsible for it, to wreak havoc another day.

Consider the following events, reported by a management consultant, that unfolded for a West Coast computer equipment vendor to Intel:

Quality started to take a big hit and Intel had to send teams in to help out and things just started in a downward spiral. . . .

A new guy was brought in from the outside. But the new guy is not terribly focused. He knows what he wants, but he has had a very difficult time making it happen.

So the material guy is blaming somebody for his problems, and the quality guy's blaming people for problems, they're all in turn blaming next-hire headquarters they say send arrows over the encampment wall into the organization, and the manufacturing guys [are] blaming the quality guys because [they say] the quality teams are not well trained, and the quality guys say about the manufacturing guys "All he wants to do is fix problems; not prevent problems," and the IS guy remains pretty distant, quiet on the sidelines, the financial CFO blames everybody but can't seem to get reports out because the IS system is antiquated.

We've made some progress in getting them to see themselves, but it was truly a classic case of everybody blaming everybody else and no one standing up and saying "Hey, I bear responsibility for this. It's my behaviors that need to change in order for this organization to turn around." As a result, the team is . . . basically going into self-destruct.

The business result of all of that has been that Intel has other companies that have filled the breach, their profit margins are down, and Intel is now telling them that they'd better get on the stick because there's now other people out there. . . .

Contributing to the off-loading of responsibility for failure is our ubiquitous self-serving bias: the tendency to claim credit for success and to disown blame for failure.

NONDEVELOPMENT AND NONREWARD FOR EMPLOYEES

Employees and ex-employees show other costs, in addition to nonlearning. Their experience in the failed organization may well represent a squandered opportunity to learn, and to be rewarded for applying, personal and interpersonal skills. The loss is particularly pronounced and wasteful among the unjustified victims of organizational failure: the capable employees who were shortchanged and deserved better. Individual consequences include future loss of value from failure to receive their due in this organization.

NONPRODUCTIVITY

Losses for other members of the organization include the missing value otherwise contributed by this squandered individual; for members of other organizations, losses include a now unavailable track record that would otherwise earmark this individual as a good risk.

Losses to any organization can be trivialized by the population ecology argument that the loss to one is a gain for another: the argument raised at the beginning of the chapter. It was acknowledged as a persuasive argument, but ultimately depicted as an invalid one. The reason is that it ignores several points.

Firstly, organizational turnover in and of itself incurs some nonrecuperative costs for customers and other members of society, including: (1) most directly, the financial costs of unemployment benefits and welfare; (2) less directly, the possible social costs of poverty, crime, substance abuse, physical and psychological abuse among family members, and other social dysfunctions; and (3) more remotely, the financial costs of defraying these social costs, including the outlay for law enforcement, the judicial and penal systems, insurance, and public hospitalization.

One might argue from a macroeconomic perspective that society does not lose from all this: that the resulting increase in public, legal, and medical employment may offset the loss in the private employment it is intended to manage. In reply, it must be pointed out that there is no guarantee that such public employment is equivalent to or as efficient as the lost private employment that necessitated it.

NONCOMPETITIVENESS

Secondly, in addition to the "noneconomic" competition covered earlier, there are other reasons to doubt that organizational slack will be taken up by providers of replacement goods and services. Demise could have been attributable not to failed product development but rather to mismanagement of various other internal functions, including human resources, finances, and accounting, producing workforce demoralization, misguided investment strategies, or inept control systems, respectively. As a result, the field could in fact be left wide open to more efficient providers of lower-quality, higher-cost goods and services.

Thirdly, we revive an argument made in the introduction that successful competitors may simply be the best of a bad lot. For customers in general, the forces that produced organizational failure continue unabated among surviving competitors.

Fourthly, organizational failure may well hasten the noncompetiveness and ultimate monopolization of an entire industry, from which short-term costs will certainly be felt in product and service quality, as we know from Chapter 10.

The Epidemic of Failure

Due to interdependence among organizations, failure within one can present a contagion for others.

For example, a university graduate program could not secure its badly-needed accreditation, due to the inability of the accrediting agency to secure its *own* accreditation. For the university, results included a graduate program spinning out of control, presenting various forces that promised, in self-fulfilling fashion, to undermine qualifications for future accreditation, including internal conflict, personal stress, collective distraction from the primary educational task, and egress of the capable personnel able to find jobs elsewhere.

The larger cost of a decline in quality is to national competitiveness in the global marketplace, and as a result to domestic quality of life. Specific effects include, again, the social consequences explored earlier, along with the economic costs of cleaning the whole thing up.

Free-marketeers would argue that the competitive slack will be taken up by other countries. Alternatively, there could be simply a universal dearth of quality in goods and services. Most likely, perhaps, is the expanding, interactive contagion of an economic downturn, such as was observed in the mid-1990s in Asia.

NONSUPPORT FOR VITAL SERVICES

When products or services are vital, costs can be to health if not to life itself. When the organization is a governmental one, costs are not only to a vital service but also to the credibility and vitality of our public institutions needed to sustain that service, without which both are further eroded by loss of public trust, as we have seen. With government agencies, there are generally no competitors, and thus no opportunity for any improvement in quality.

THE CONCEPTUAL DEGRADATION OF QUALITY

In general, a decline in the quality of goods and services due to the noncompetitiveness of providers degrades the very benchmarks for evaluating their quality, and thus *erodes the very conception and definition of quality itself*. The reason is that experience guides expectations, so that, as with other learning points, the concept of quality depends upon previous observation of it.

Goods and Services

We find that many decisions about product design and development are determined by organizational failure: either by its preambles in doomed organizations, or among its consequences in surviving organizations, in an industry with reduced competitiveness as a result of it. For example, failure by a key decision maker to take a risk at a major recording label confines the range of highly visible products to the output of recording artists with a proven track record and minimal creativity.

Degraded notions of quality are exemplified across various industries, by "films" that may earn the highest of praise from audiences and self-appointed critics alike, yet are individually nothing more than a high-tech photo opportunity for established stars, a pyrotechnic exercise in special effects, and an ostentatious foray into some contrived "plot"; by supermarket "food" that, in effect, represents a replica of the real article, substituting adulteration and cosmetic manipulation for nutrition and taste; by macrobrewed "beer" that has the unmistakably homogenized, insipid taste of efficiency and mass production; by one-time "service" stations that now eschew or charge a ransom for automotive service; by seemingly convenient and apparently technically advanced but, in fact, increasingly flimsy plastic appliances; and so on. The general result is a diminution of quality without customer awareness of it, save for the nostalgia of aging and, to the realities of marketers, decreasingly relevant people who know that, at one time, things were different, and better.

Public Policy

The effect of providers on customer perceptions and expectations of product quality underscores the fact that, in general, organizations have a profound effect on the way in which people think and act. The effect extends well beyond goods and services to choices and actions regarding public policy.

Thus, we see that quality of output can be degraded not only by commercial organizations but also by government agencies, political parties, political action groups, labor unions, educational systems, individual schools and colleges, business and other associations, and so on. We also have reason to suspect that public as well as private organizations can degrade our very definition of quality, due to the precursors and consequences of organizational failure.

For example, groupthink in a political party may produce a candidate for office that, however deficient, determines the debate and limits the choices in an election, and degrades the perception and expectations of quality in future elections. Risky shift in a political action group can radicalize the debate on a public issue, as well as its outcome. Concealment of a problem within a government agency may eventually cost so much money that the public withdraws its support for a critical social service. Curriculum decisions by faculty purely to retaliate against a political rival can profoundly affect the knowledge and learning of students.

Products That Affect Public Outcomes

Furthermore, there is no denying the social effects of the goods and services that we purchase. As we saw with "negative externalities," a free market can deflect its costs onto noncustomers; thus, the competitive failure of some organizations serves not the product quality of successful rivals but rather, simply, a degradation in the quality of life for us all. For example, one would be hard put to advance a population ecology argument to justify the competitive failure of book publishers, in parts of our cities, with the competitive success enjoyed by manufacturers of drug paraphernalia, guns, and bullets.

Social Attitudes

The influence of organizations may be a premeditated, deliberate affair, for example through political influence, advertising, or product choices or design. The influence of organizations may also be an adventitious event, growing by osmosis among people who spend the bulk of their lives in organizations. As a result, for example, the authoritativeness that pervades and degrades organizations may be expressed in class hatred outside of it. In either case, the failure of organizations is a failure that consumes all of us.

NONSUPPORT FOR ORGANIZATIONS

As a result of their failure, one cost is to our expectations of organizations themselves. Organizations have been created quite literally in order to accomplish superhuman things. It would be reassuring to associate them with, and remember them for, those accomplishments. To the contrary, our association with and recall of them are often for the behavior of human beings at its worst, and their treatment of peers at its most degrading. In this sense, self-destruction degrades not only the individual organization it visits but also the very concept of organization itself.

NONSUPPORT FOR COOPERATION IN GENERAL

Perhaps the greatest cost of organizational failure is to the mutual behavior, relationships, and expectations of people themselves. It is through organizations that members perceive and get to know each other. Due to the effects of organizations, and on what people mutually perceive, members tend to know the very worst about each other. We can expect a further increase in the already considerable store of cynicism about human beings in general, about what we can expect from them, and about what we are prepared to give them in advance of fulfilling our expectations. The cost, then, is to both mutual trust and cooperation.

As if we needed to be told, then, we now have some excellent reasons to dread, and avoid, organizational failure.

A CHANGE OF FOCUS

The thrust of the discussion to this point is that this failure is inevitable, and inescapable. On the other hand, we have also accumulated considerable knowledge about its sources and likely outcomes. In addition to these points, we now know something about organizational failure that has been inaccessible to its victims. *We now know to expect it.*

As is learned by the prey regarding the predator, anticipation can lead to avoidance. We find that one of the tools for avoiding failure is failure itself. We find that failure has much to teach. We have already seen that it can teach the learner how to fail. We are about to see that, if we only learn how to better learn from it, we can learn how to avoid it. Through failure, the organization can learn how to succeed.

That is the subject of the next, and penultimate, chapter.

We are now in a new and hopeful mode. In the next chapter, let us begin to direct our attention to it.

PART SIX

BEYOND FAILURE

14

Learning from Failure: Saving Organizations from Themselves

> For the things we have to learn before we can do them, we learn by doing them.
>
> —Aristotle

In the next and final chapter, we will discover that there is a long-term evolutionary solution to the fact that organizations are built to fail. Evolution involves the development of new forms, which is the result of either adaptation to the environment through change by current forms or their expurgation and replacement, or "selection," of forms that do adapt.

Obviously, intellectually stimulating though it may be as an issue, the annihilation of current organizational forms, and the evolution of replacements, represent luxuries that the present manager can ill afford. For this reason, attention in this chapter is on saving the organization from itself, using solutions within the paradigm of current organizational forms.

A TWELVE-STEP PLAN

As we saw in the last chapter, of all the reasons presented to this point for organizational failure, perhaps the most elusive and ironic is the fact that members do not *know* that organizations are built to fail. As a result, members tend to feel that there is no cost to indulgence in individual self-interest, or even worse, that the organization somehow benefits from it.

As we have seen, reasons for such imagined benefit include "occupational chauvinism," the belief that one's position is so essential that its benefits redound to the organization. Other examples include the belief in organizational benefit from conflict, from political behaviors for waging conflict, and from the self-interest reflected by both. All such paeans to self-interest themselves are self-interested, as ill-disguised, elaborate rationalizations.

If organizations fail because members are unaware that they do, theoretically, and paradoxically, the opposite also applies: the anticipation of organizational failure is a precondition for its own refutation. In other words, organizational failure is made avoidable only by believing in its inevitability.

We have now entered a new phase of the discussion. Our topic is organizational success. We have now been given enough reasons to anticipate the difficulty of achieving it. We can now use our awareness of these reasons as a tool for overcoming them.

Attention is now directed to twelve principles, or steps, for achieving organizational success.

Commitment

The first principle requires a discussion with the self. The issue addressed in this discussion concerns the degree of personal commitment to the survival and prosperity of the organization. Is this a goal to which one is willing to subordinate individual self-interest, at least in the short term? Is the organization likely enough to survive and prosper to be worth the effort? *Should* the organization survive and prosper? Or is it even the right organization to be doing the job it is trying to do? Are the additional resources it is likely to create greater than the resources it will require?

Responsibility

If the answer to all of these questions is affirmative, attention is directed to the second principle, which is to take full responsibility for what happens to the organization. This might sound self-evidently reasonable, but it isn't: among managers and administrators, there is a well-documented tendency to externalize responsibility.

As we saw with Management by Exception, disownment of responsibility for employees has even achieved such legitimacy as to be associated with an entire philosophy. The same is true of organization-wide events; "environmental determinism" assigns initiative over organizational action not to the organization but rather to the environment, conformity with which is essential for adaptation and defines the extent of individual initiative.

Hence, the organization cedes its initiative to the market, to the tactics of the competition, to technological development, and to the other elements of the macroenvironment, or society at large. It is precisely the imagined expurgation of human initiative from responsibility for organizations that justifies skepticism about human collusion in their failure.

Purpose

The third principle is both an obvious and at the same time neglected element: that of *purpose*. An organization's purpose *should be* to meet an identifiable market need, and its panoply of structures, systems, and methods, *should be* consistent with that purpose. According to a management researcher, the CEO of a national airline

wanted [his airline] to become the world's best airline for business travelers. Forget any other market segment. So that was a change from the prior strategy. And he said, "I don't know all the ways to do that, but when you people out in the line are interacting with our business customer and have to meet their needs, this is the rule I want you to follow: we want to be the best at providing the service that's important to these people.

If it's important to them, we're going to do it. If it's not important to them, I don't care what everybody else does, we're not going to do it. We're not going to waste money on it."

So he got rid of his market research department. He said "we don't need to pay forty people to find out what our customers think. Let's ask them."

And the beauty of it was, people understood this strategy: "OK, I can understand that. And then, in my job, I can make these decisions that will let me serve the customer better. If I'm free to do that, if I'm empowered to do that, OK, fine."

As noted earlier, the literature on organizations fairly marvels at the counterintuitive sequence of tasks in organizations; one observer rapturously enthused over the insight that, contrary to what one would expect, purposes emerge from actions, and that as a result "organizations run backwards."

There is much to be said in favor of action as an indicator of purpose and a source of self-knowledge: that we need to act in order to know our subliminal purposes. On the other hand, this insight is a luxury of observing only organizations that have survived.

For the untold number of victims, action without purpose proved to be a present with no future. Thus, what is counterintuitive for researchers and the veritable underpinning of an epiphany is ultimately experienced by practitioners as counterproductive, and as important elements of failure.

Distance

In practice, of course, averting organizational failure is a daunting task, since the problem must be solved by its very source, including the personnel involved, the structure of their relationships, and their patterns of interaction within that structure. For all of these reasons, it can be well argued that resistance to organizational failure is itself doomed to fail.

The fourth principle is based on the recognition that decision personnel will not be disinterested observers but are rather *personally and interpersonally involved in their efforts*. Accordingly, these personnel can be expected to have a personal rather than purely organizational interest in the outcome of their efforts. Practitioners refer to this problem as "getting too close to the situation" to effectively address it; to communication researchers, this problem has been summarized as the recognition that "nothing inside a frame can state, or even *ask*, anything *about* that frame."[112]

The solution, then, clearly requires the involvement of personnel who are *not* involved in the problem. These personnel may include either a temporary consultant or somebody engaged on a more permanent, problem-solving basis.

Failure Analysis

The next two principles are to some degree the point of this entire discussion.

The fifth principle is to *anticipate* failure: to recognize that, ultimately, events may be unplanned and that control can go awry. The sixth principle is to *understand* failure: to recognize that it represents a complex, evolving, and protracted rather than simple, instantaneous, and direct process. Both require the ongoing self-scrutiny of "failure analysis," to recognize on a continuing basis that things may not go as planned.

The remaining principles are for the purpose of applying these two.

Learning from Failure

The seventh principle is *learning from failure*, a pivotal lesson in relation to the others, and thus the title of this chapter.

In a previous journal article entitled "Parenthetic Learning," this writer argued that learning, at its most profound, results from failure, and entails a recognition of the boundaries or limits that surround previous learning: hence its "parenthesis." (It is the lack of such a parenthesis that makes current knowledge seem complete, as we saw in Chapter 12.)

Through Parenthetic Learning, previous omniscience is now strictly qualified to a previous contingency, which constitutes the new learning that adapts to a new situation.[113]

There are many reasons why the direct experience of failure can be a powerful teacher.

As we saw in Chapter 12 and, more generally throughout the discussion, organizational demise begins with littler failures: in things like neglected performance appraisal or the expectation of poor performance. Acknowledgement of failed methods, processes, and systems can mitigate the more dire necessity to acknowledge a failed organization.

In general, the direct experience of failure can certainly impart important lessons about its aversive consequences and motivate its future avoidance. On the other hand, the experience also teaches that there is life after failure, and that it is possible to recover from it, motivating serious attention to the lessons that may take place from recovery.

However, there is a danger.

In his systematic presentation of a "trait" approach to the analysis of leadership, Warren Bennis introduced an important lesson to be learned from the Flying Wallendas, the famous family of trapeze artists. Karl Wallenda, the family patriarch, never considered the possibility of falling from the high wire until only a few weeks before he in fact fell to his death in Puerto Rico at the age of 73. According to Karl's wife, falling was somehow brought about by thinking about it.

Similarly, according to Bennis, effective leaders never consider the possibility of failure, a leadership trait he identified as the "Wallenda factor."[114] In addition to never envisioning failure in the first place is the fact that effective leaders are not derailed by experiencing what *others* regard as failure.

To this may be added the caveat that perhaps the same may be said of all effective performers, intraorganizational and otherwise. For example, in our discussion of the "Pygmalion Effect," we analyzed precisely how failure may emerge from expectation of it.

Here, then, is the danger: On the one hand, it seems as if the approach ultimately advocated here is preoccupation with failure, vigilance to it, and willingness to acknowledge it. On the other hand, it is recognized that such a fixation on failure can help to bring it about. *How do we reconcile these two perspectives?*

That question may be answered in a series of events presented in the recent media. According to *Entrepreneur Magazine*, one of the most instructive lessons on business was the failure of GO Corporation, whose owner, Jerry Kaplan, was called "failure's poster child" by *Rolling Stone* magazine. From his celebrated failure, Kaplan learned of the need to create "a separation between the concepts of personal fortunes and corporate fortunes."[115] Failure does not necessarily invalidate the creative product ideas underlying a business, and does not preclude their success in another enterprise.

Focus on Behavior

Kaplan may have also learned a lesson contained in the eighth principle, which reconciles our conflict between failure as a necessary, constructive focus and failure as a self-fulfilling prophecy: that *failure deserves our at-*

tention without requiring us to be consumed and defined by it. Failure is *not* a personal trait; therefore, it does not signify some wide-ranging disqualification. Failure simply describes a behavior, and nothing more.

The distinction is critical, and generally overlooked. When viewed as a personal trait, failure tends to be strenuously denied because it undermines both the self-interest advanced by competence and the self-esteem that requires a reason to feel good about the self. When viewed as a behavior, on the other hand, failure can do what a behavior can do: it can change.

For this reason, parents obtained more improvement from their learning-disabled children by referencing not what the child *is* but rather what the child *does*. And within organizations, as earlier noted, research and practice demonstrate that, in contrast to trait-based performance feedback, behavior-based feedback elicits a constructive remedy, rather than an ego-defensive response.

Hence, the approach recommended here is to treat failure not as a personal encumbrance and as an element of identity but only as a behavior, a problem, and thus a problem amenable to a different behavior.

Furthermore, failure itself may provide some cachet. Failure attests to the verve and the will of the person risking it. It is also a handicap that elevates the magnitude of subsequent success. As a result, capability is measured by the depth of the failure overcome. At the risk of overstatement, failure can be viewed as a virtual calling card that announces the indomitability of one's spirit.

Self-Scrutiny

Following this theme is the ninth principle: the correction of failure as widely as possible, by *incorporating error-correction as an element of a universal job description.* All employees should be evaluated on self-scrutiny: for honestly justifying what they have done, and for changing what they cannot honestly justify. An analogous method applied in the budget-formulation process is "zero-based" budgeting, wherein every allocation must be justified. The management application suggested here requires the same exhaustive justification for procedures employed by all personnel.

Disproof

Incorporated in principle nine is the tenth principle: a concerted effort to search for *disconfirmatory* rather than *confirmatory* information. Scientific progress and management practice alike consistently validate developments not through information that supports them but rather through their survival of disproof, which requires an exhaustive search and rigorous test of disconfirmatory information. Organizations must learn to do the same, particularly given their personal price from failure. Various proposals have been offered to institutionalize a search for disconfirmatory information by organizations, including the creation of a "devil's advocate" position and role; an adversarial, "legal" model of decision making; and the liberal use of nominal, the more remote "Delphi," and brainstorming techniques to generate new and potentially apostate ideas.

Triangulation

The eleventh principle is a search for disconfirmatory information through triangulation, or the use of multiple, independent effectiveness measures to guard against the tendency to select only the most favorable. By surviving the test of triangulation, the experience of success can be claimed with some confidence in its validity.

Change

The twelfth principle is *openness to change, consistent vigilance to the need for it, and the willingness to embrace it when necessary with the energy it requires.*

A former CEO and current business consultant underscores the need for change in his "favorite business story":

Many, many years ago, before the 45-second shot clock [in college basketball] . . . Bobby Knight was coaching his team.

They weren't doing very well.

They went into the locker room at half-time 20 points down. Bobby did what he was supposed to do: the conventional wisdom. He fired these guys up to a fever pitch. They came out on the court breathing fire and brimstone, spitting bullets— hustle, hustle, hustle, just like you're supposed to do. And they started to close the gap; they got it lower, smaller, smaller.

But they weren't getting it low enough, fast enough. There were only three minutes left in the game; they closed the gap from 20 points to 12 points. What did Bobby Knight do?

He went into a four-corner stall. The long and the short of it is, he wins the game in overtime. The reporters rush into the locker room. They say "Bobby, whatever possessed you? You were the one down 12 points with only three minutes to go. Why did you go into the four-corner stall?"

And Bobby Knight, slowing his mental processes down to that of the average sports reporter simply replied "What we were doing *wasn't working.*"

And that's the most important business story. Because whenever I look at companies that have gotten themselves into trouble, and I can't get them out, they are failing to recognize that what they are doing isn't working and doing more of it isn't going to solve the problem. Quantity and speed are not going to change things. You have to do something fundamentally different.

And the essence of the Bobby Knight story is when it's a really deep crisis, you can even do crazy things and you won't be in any worse shape. Maybe they'll give you a chance.

And that's my favorite business story. And I would say I can't think of a problem I've been called in to solve that didn't have aspects of the people not recognizing that what they were doing wasn't working and it's time to shift strategies. I can't think of one.

The final lesson for the organization facing its mortality, then, is to *change what it's doing*. As we saw earlier, change presents every opportunity to simulate rather than actuate. To be effective, and mindful of its difficulty, change *must be the real thing*.

The foregoing twelve principles represent the components of a "survival guide" for organizations. They are offered with the recognition that practitioners need practical solutions for a problem we have determined to be both endemic and critical: the fact that organizations are otherwise built to fail.

However, practitioners also have a great interest in the long-term, historical developments through which organizations address the problem that they are built to fail, since this will affect the practitioner role considerably. For, as we are about to see, this problem may be solving itself, on its own.

Attention is directed to this intriguing possibility in the next, and final, chapter.

15

The End of Organization as We Know It: Survival in the Postorganizational World

On no other stage are the scenes shifted with a swiftness so like magic as on the great stage of history when once the hour strikes.
— Edward Bellamy

Although this discussion concerns organizations in general, attention has been directed to highly specific types. In particular, attention has been upon current organizations, including commercial and public organizations, in response to the anticipated likelihood that readers place priority upon the practical, short-term issues they are likely to face.

In this chapter, while our concern is ultimately a practical one, it will expand to include the long-term issues that must be considered in more fully expressing that concern. Hence, in this chapter, the camera focus will widen, to embrace the larger units of time that include the distant past as well as the future. To see where organizations are going, we must see where they have been.

To do so, we will present a very brief history of organizations. For those readers who are interested in social and system science, or theory in general, a grand, unifying explanation for organizational failure is presented in the epilogue, safely away from more exclusively practical readers.

A VERY CONDENSED HISTORY OF ORGANIZATIONS

Human history has been divided retrospectively into several stages of cultural development that, however simpleminded and crude they appear to be, serve us well in helping us to understand both the nature of and reasons for the procession of organizational forms that have emerged within them.

The Clan Organization

The earliest stage of distinctly human types has been commonly identified as the "hunting and gathering" stage devoted, as the name suggests, to acquiring food by hunting animals and gathering fruits and vegetables in the wild. According to Bill McKelvey, the organizational historian and taxonomist, this stage began with the advent of tools, at around 500,000 B.C.[116] Organization at this time embraced an entire family or tribe, typically a nomadic one forced into that role by migration of prey or seasonal changes in fruits or vegetables, with a division of labor based upon both these short-term opportunities and the roles culturally assigned to gender and family position. Hence, each family or tribe represented a fully appointed organization with a complete division of labor.

In response to the caprices of nature and the vicissitudes of its own needs, the fundamental purpose or "mission" of this organization may be characterized as *improvisation*. Given the familial or otherwise close relationships of members, we identify this organization as a "clan" type.

The Military Organization

Also among hunters and gatherers we find the military organization, developed from the clan organization in order to wage conflict with other clans over scarce foodstuffs and other resources. The purpose of the military organization was *hegemony*, presenting a division of labor that necessarily spanned an entire tribe to provide the numbers needed to defeat opponents. The assignment of responsibility was both permanent, based upon gender and age, and opportunistic, depending upon the scarcity of food and the presence of opponents.

The Agrarian Organization

The next, "farming" or "agricultural" stage of human history: (1) began at around 6,000 B.C., according to McKelvey;[117] (2) reflected improved techniques to furnish a predictable supply of food and an enduring form of shelter; and for these purposes (3) was distinguished by the development of towns, to provide both a permanent home and a large enough supply of labor to cultivate crops year-round.

The clan organization, which was adequate for the limited scale and time frame needed to satisfy the equally limited needs and appetites of its members, was wholly inadequate to address the larger and longer tasks needed to sow, maintain, and reap crops. The organization at this stage called for a division of labor in which the responsibilities of all residents changed in a predictable sequence across the year, based upon recurrent crop cultivation needs, with specializations based on age and again on gender. This organization may be identified as the agrarian type; its purpose was clearly *reliability*.

The Industrial Organization

This brings us rather quickly to modern times. The next stage of history, and according to many observers the one from which we are only now just emerging, is the industrial stage, the beginning of which has been established precisely by McKelvey at 1770 A.D., with the invention (or more precisely, the perfection) of the steam engine.[118] As the steam engine demonstrates, this stage was initiated by mass-production technology that made available enough goods and services to (1) outstrip current uses and (2) instead permit exchange for other products on a scale that would provide variety and future utility. To make this exchange possible, it was mediated by an economic system in which goods are directly exchanged for currency, which is then exchanged for other goods when they are needed.

To maximize the net revenues received in the exchange, costs must be minimized, producing the high priority on *efficiency* in the industrial organization. Since this form of organization represents the subject of this book, we will spend some time introducing it, and the issues it presents.

Whereas the agrarian division of labor had to match the sequential emergence of agricultural tasks, the industrial organization created a sufficiently permanent environment to maintain enough control over its tasks to realize the cost savings of permanent specialization for their performance. These savings come from eliminating expenditures of time and other resources to changing responsibilities and relationships; development of a high level of expertise for rapid, effective, and error-free output; and, as we saw earlier, creation of economies of both scope and scale, the former by allowing flexibility in coordinating personnel, and the latter by mass-producing not only output but also the very components of the organizational systems responsible for that output. Organizational systems were mass-produced by duplicating jobs, the expertise to train and manage them, and the equipment, supplies, and physical plant required by each.

On the other hand, as we have seen, specialization has also been referred to as "de-skilling," which limits utility to others, value to the organization, and as a result reward *by* the organization to the employee. At the same time, specialization represents a resource that can overcome these constraints, and maximize the power of the employee, but only at organizational cost: by maximizing the dependence of other employees; minimizing their value; minimizing along with it their motivation, commitment, and productivity; creating conflict with them; reducing their efficiency; and in the bargain undermining organizational performance.

Thus, specialization promises individual productivity, interpersonal coordination, collective efficiency, and organizational effectiveness, but delivers something quite different. Despite such poor performance, an industrial organization can enjoy a very long life, by growing to the point of creating self-supporting societal myths, for example, the independence promoted by the automobile industry, and self-sustaining legal protection, for example, the prevention of minimum-wage, child-labor, and antitrust legislation.

In short, the industrial organization can survive in perpetuity by controlling its output, as a monopoly. Additionally, such monopolies typically have had the brawn to achieve monopsonistic control over labor and other inputs.

The Commercial Organization: An Industrial Structure in a Postindustrial World

Thus, it stands to reason that the luck of the industrial organization ran out precisely with the development of the means to combat trusts, through the modern emergence of political democracy. People have had a difficult time reconciling their democratic rights as citizens with the forfeiture of those rights as employees and customers. The economic result of political democracy was a commercial environment, vouchsafed by laws protecting employees and consumers against monopolistic excess and characterized by competition for labor and customers.

For organizations, the result has largely been their failure to adapt to this changed environment. What has emerged is a commercial subtype of the industrial organization that, despite cosmetic changes in nomenclature and strategy, remains doomed to fail in short order by vestiges of its parent type: principally, by the characteristic reliance of the industrial organization on specialization, and by the familiar, traditional supporting cast in organizational systems.

Organizations throughout history have been built to fail, for reasons that will be integrated in the epilogue but remain unique to each: these include the physical environment for the agrarian type, coupled with competition for clans, particularly for the military organization. However, our argument that organizations are built to fail is specifically justified by the commercial organization's reliance on an industrial structure in a postindustrial environment.

It is this argument, and recent evidence, that suggests that this organizational type is on the cusp of an evolutionary stride.

THE NEXT STAGE OF HISTORY

To understand the context for this development, we need to recognize that political freedom is in many senses of the word the antithesis of organization itself. Interestingly, an important objective of organization is "coordination," the German word for which is *Gleichschaltung*, the process for extirpating dissent in the early days of the Third Reich. Interesting, as well, is the fact that modern democracy began at almost the exact instant as the Industrial Revolution: respectively, in 1776, with the American Revolution, and in 1770, with the invention of the steam engine, as we saw.

It appears that modern democracy and industrial organization have been on both a race and a collision course since their almost simultaneous inception. The race initially went in favor of the industrial organization, which developed rapidly, due to competition that was limited in power and easily dispatched. Meanwhile, the democratic tortoise has been closing in on the industrial hare, but slowly, because, in contrast to the industrial organization, democracy has emerged specifically to supplant the most powerful political interests ever developed, including monarchy, authoritarian rule, and dictatorship. The reason to develop these points is that the impact of democracy is only now starting to be fully felt by organizations, producing a response that is just beginning to come into view.

However, some caveats are in order before presenting this response.

Firstly, we discover in examining their history that new forms of organization do not preclude older ones; even at this late date, along with industrial organizations, we still have fishing villages, a "clan" of sorts; other clans among nomadic tribes, for example, the Bedouins; certainly military societies; and exclusively agrarian towns.

Secondly, organizational forms tend to emerge gradually, so that older forms may dominate for a while; despite their singularly rapid development, for example, industrial organizations were for a long time, and in parts of the world remain, far outnumbered by the volume and total membership of agrarian organizations.

THE NEXT FORM OF ENTERPRISE

These issues are raised because, despite the lingering dominance of familiar forms, there are intriguing indications of a nascent form of enterprise, developed to adapt to a new environment that threatens not only the dominance of the commercial organization but in fact the *dominance of business enterprise by organizations in general*. The new form of enterprise has a new purpose, to replace previous organizational purposes of improvisation, hegemony, reliability, and efficiency.

This new type of enterprise is arising in an environment that has been called the Postindustrial or "Information Age," reflecting the fact that organizational inputs and outputs are increasingly represented not by physical materials but rather by information.

Physical items do, of course, provide information; a car can connote wealth, for example. However, to more fully distinguish the two, physical material is bound to a single medium while information ranges freely across various media. For example, a set of statistics can be depicted with equivalent value by e-mail, fax, phone conversation, American Sign Language, or a newspaper article.

In an increasing number of ways, the information environment poses a threat to organizations that, from their perspective, looks positively sinister, even at this point without being fully understood. For example, recording companies are facing the possibility of obsolescence (and, according to those committed to art over profit, not a minute too soon) from independent production and on-line distribution of recordings. Companies long accustomed to managing their reputation through advertising and other forms of controlled communication are suddenly confronting dissident voices on the Internet that are at least as loud, certainly less inhibited, and due to their independence probably more credible than their own. For various product categories, competition on the Web presents clearly superior innovativeness, quality, and efficiency; familiar examples include electronic mail, including mass-mailing capability; greeting cards; up-to-the-minute printed news; and maps; to name but a very few. Where previously able to monopolistically control their output through the industrial type, organizations now suddenly find themselves with almost no such control at all.

On the one hand, what *seems* to be signalled by these developments is nothing more than a realignment of our economic structure to favor new industries; examples include, of course, the personal computer industry itself, along with peripherals; other digital hardware, such as camcorders, CD recorders, and DVD players; and software, encompassing such programming services as Web design and various products, many of which are performing previous hardware functions: for example virtual, software music synthesizers replacing hardware keyboards. Nevertheless, while certainly drastic, this economic realignment is not an unprecedented one; relative to their times, the development of telephone and air travel technologies were no less impactive than the digital variety.

What begins to capture our eye, however, is the socioeconomic impact of this realignment, and the threat posed by a loss of control not only over outputs but also over *inputs*: and not only by organizations within a waning economic structure but also through the use of organizations as a *medium* for a new structure.

THE PROVERBIAL INFORMATION AGE

As in the case of outputs, inputs increasingly represent information, including legal advice; actuarial data; Web page design; and how to manage, account, invest, and in general, do the entire business itself. None of this sounds radically new, which underscores how far we have come from the industrial age in such a short time. However, there is something portentous about the economic character of information.

For one thing, information input has value to many different users, particularly given the ease with which it can be diversified among and customized for each. Additionally, information input is available instantaneously, or nearly so; is portable; and can be readily updated, so while its specific content is rapidly obsolescent, its generic form is not.

For example, while stock prices change, the format and utility of instantaneous, on-line stock quotes do not. Moreover, in contrast to hardware, users have far less ability to maintain the proprietary nature of information, since it can be disseminated as soon as it is created.

Also, information represents ideas, rather than their expression, due to its independence of any single medium. Thus, like ideas themselves, and in contrast to their expression, information cannot be copyrighted. Hardware technology can, of course, be easily and readily protected, both by the length of time needed to duplicate it and by the availability of patent protection.

To sum up the points so far, the organization is increasingly dependent on input that is beyond organizational control, from providers who are also beyond such control, since it is in their economic interest to remain external, independent, and accessible to the many users dependent on them.

THE INFORMATION USER

In this relationship, the design of the user organization is of the network type, in which various organizational tasks are outsourced; these are typically separable from the core, design and manufacturing technology. This type admittedly presents such disadvantages as uncertainty of supply and thus the high unit cost of experts, and only the crudest form of control, through nonrenewal of the contract.

Nevertheless, the increasing popularity of this organizational type is due to such overwhelming advantages as the use of labor only as required, the availability of expertise, the dispensation of upper management to focus on strategy and core competency, and, of course, the absence of any responsibility for benefits. To achieve these advantages, organizations redesign themselves to transform themselves, in effect, into clients that help to create demand for information providers.

THE INFORMATION PROVIDER

Far more significant for our purposes, however, is the nature of the providers themselves.

Many providers remain organizations; however, there are indications that an increasing and ultimately dominant number of them are sole proprietorships. Sole ownership is, of course, not unusual for the start-up firm that inhabits the "embryonic" industry represented by many information technologies; what is unusual is that, given the limited resources required for an information provider, many of them are likely to *remain* sole proprietorships, radically and effectively transforming the very medium for conducting business. And while history is replete with examples of self-employed people as artisans, craftspeople, and artists, we are witnessing an unprecedented shift of key functions from organizations to individuals.

The Scope of the Phenomenon

As sole proprietorships rather than corporations, these enterprises are not independently taxable, and therefore provide no data to the Internal Revenue Service through which their number can be made known; thus, their number can only be estimated. The number of information-providing sole proprietorships can perhaps best be *inferred* by estimating the number of home-based businesses. This would exclude the more traditional sole proprietorships found in business zones, for example, "Mom and Pop" retail operations, such as liquor stores, as well as service providers with an elaborate physical plant, such as dry-cleaning establishments. This would also exclude some business-zoned information providers as well, including both larger enterprises and sole proprietorships, such as tax consultants, thus yielding probably an underestimate of information-providing sole proprietorships.

In sum, then, the estimated number of home-based businesses provides us in turn with an estimated and probably *underestimated* number of the sole proprietorships among information providers that represent the cutting edge of a potentially dominant form of business enterprise.

INTO THE FUTURE

What we find among estimated numbers of home-based businesses is positively startling. As early as 1990, a survey by Pratt Associates of Dallas revealed that 15 million of the nation's 123 million workers work at home.[119] Since then, the Longevity Network, Ltd., has estimated that the frequency of a new home-based business start-up is every eleven seconds, for a total of 8,000 start-ups per day, so that at some time in the near future some 44 percent of households will have a home-based business.[120] Some estimates are higher; according to Dr. Greg Clary, agricultural economist for the Texas Agricultural Extension Service, "Some economists predict that half of the work force will work at home or have some sort of alternative working arrangement by the turn of the century."[121] Network Marketing estimates growth in the $427 billion home-based business sector as a direct consequence of the loss of 3,000 jobs per day to corporate downsizing.[122] As a result, business today is increasingly conducted by a "hidden economy" of very small, very private enterprises.[123]

All home-based businesses may or may not be the sole source of income for a household; in particular, the "alternative working arrangement" mentioned by Dr. Clary refers to telecommuters working nonindependently for an employing organization.

Nevertheless, something is dramatically afoot these days in organizational America; whether through a sole proprietorship or the service of telecommuters, the response to the Information Age is clearly a drastic alternative to the "tightly-coupled," internal interdependence producing the organization's typical array of competing self-interests. Moreover, something is afoot throughout the business world that bodes poorly for the hegemony of organizations in general.

The relationship of the organization to its remote employee is, or is approaching, that of a client to an independent contractor. The relationship of an organization to its independent information provider is, of course, most *assuredly* that of a customer rather than employer, through a consulting rather than employment contract, on an episodic or sequential rather than full-time basis. The implications of this relationship are manifold and profound.

External providers have minimal input into, and dependence for their careers on, a single organization; therefore, they have virtually no need or opportunity to manipulate organizational purpose and methods to satisfy their self-interest. For their part, organizations can achieve efficiency by using providers only as needed, rather than by "de-skilling" them for full-time specialization at low cost. Hence, both user and provider are assuming responsibility to self, but with consequences that are reshaping the future of business enterprise.

THE END OF ORGANIZATION AS WE KNOW IT

One important implication is that critical forces for organizational failure are relieved by a working relationship that may be described as a partnership or joint venture, rather than an employment relationship; the point is that it is a relationship that is *not organizational*. Another implication is that an increasingly important participant in this relationship is also *not organizational*. In sum, we are beginning to see the *end of organization as the sole medium for conducting business.*

The new form of enterprise to succeed the commercial organization is the contractual relationship. Rather than efficiency, the purpose is to provide *freedom*, for both user and provider.

For the user, the freedom furnished by this relationship is to select the type of information needed to meet rapidly changing environmental needs, when it is needed, from a source qualified, by successful competition on the open market, to provide it, without the financial liability for a full-time employee. For the provider, the freedom availed by this arrangement permits the discretion to service multiple clients at prices that reflect market forces. For the client, the high cost per unit of time is offset by use on an as-needed basis at the same time that it maximizes the income of the provider with multiple clients.

Clearly, then, organizational functions are being off-loaded to individuals, so that on some scale and in the aggregate and long term, organizations are being replaced by individuals.

It is, of course, as premature to predict the end of organizations as it was to foretell the end of fishing villages. It is far more reasonable to suggest a conclusion to the hegemony of both organizations and fishing villages over the conduct of business and fishing, respectively. The reason for this shift in the conduct of business is that efforts by individual information providers and information users, trying to maximize opportunity and limit their mutual dependence, help to create a mutual need for freedom.

Furthermore, results are likely to extend beyond the short-term, since we are witnessing the formation not only of new enterprises but also of attitudes that *support* those enterprises. We are witnessing the development of the expectation that business can feasibly be conducted by individuals, and of self-concepts that qualify individuals to fill these newfound roles.

LESSONS TO BE LEARNED

There are practical points for both parties to consider. For the client organization, control over the provider is of paramount concern; as an independent operation, the provider is, of course, immune from performance appraisal and reward contingencies. Additionally, loyalty by the provider is easily undermined by contact with competitors, and by the availability of incentives to share proprietary information with them.

For the provider, the key issue is to develop marketable skills in an environment that is rapidly creating and sharply differentiating between the status of and rewards for the roles of consultant and "temp." In addition, providers have to assume the burdens of insurance, and financial and retirement planning, that, along with other key functions, are willingly off-loaded by organizations.

This, then, is a short list of practical lessons that can be derived from the structural shift of business enterprise, from organizational to more independent forms.

For the purposes of this study, however, some broader lessons apply. Free enterprise is evolving in a way that provides not only freedom but also the subtly different quality of independence, which is the opposite of dependence. The organization is no longer dependent on internal members to provide its external output, and is no longer obliged to pay the costs of human resource management at a level that would secure their cooperation by meeting their many needs. The individual is no longer dependent on the organization for the satisfaction of those needs. Hence, each contributes to an environment in which dependence presents exorbitant costs and independence offers unprecedented benefits. For both, dependence limits discretion while independence provides flexibility.

Therefore, new forms of enterprise are evolving as living forms always do: due to the fact that, in the new environment, old forms will not survive. From this, we can derive a broad lesson that is a welcome respite from the purpose for which this book was originally written.

CORPORATE FAILURE AND HUMAN ADAPTABILITY

When our journey began, our purpose in embarking on it was to recognize that, and understand why, organizations are built to fail. That much has not and will not have changed. The reason, in a nutshell, can be found in the needs of the individuals who comprise the organization, and the incompatibility of those needs with those of the organization itself.

Hence, by using organizational needs as a point of reference, we have been made to depict individual needs as destructive. However, we should remain mindful of the destructive effect of those needs only upon an effort to homogenize, usurp, and control them. It is when we look at the individuals behind those needs that we begin to appreciate the importance of those needs, individual adaptability in meeting them, and creativity and improvisation in order to adapt effectively.

As a result, we derive a picture vastly different from the pessimistic view with which we began our study of organizations, by diverting our gaze from organizations to the individuals of whom they have consisted and, from an era in which organizations failed to meet their own needs and those of members, to one in which each is responsible for itself. There will certainly come new times, with presently unimaginable constraints and opportunities, in which emerging forms of enterprise will themselves be tested, perhaps fail, and have to evolve. According to Michael Pirrault, President of Advanced Teamware, Inc., of Thousand Oaks, California,

there's one thing that I've learned in life that the earth, and all the matters involved in the earth, all operate on cycles. Seasons follow seasons; the seasons of a person's life: people are born, they have middle age, they die. What goes around tends to come around, particularly in the earth, not just in the individual.

Take a look at the history of workers. You had an individual who became a carpenter, or a cobbler, or whatever. And then came the world of barter, so that a cobbler could take his shoes and barter [them] for wheat, or for whatever. And then money was introduced because it facilitated the whole process of bartering and all of that and then three or four carpenters or cobblers got together and said, "You know, if we get together in some sort of a guild here we could produce more shoes together" and then that demanded that there be better organization, and thus developed organizations, and from organizations there were private businesses, came corporations. . . .

And now what we're seeing is because of the Internet and knowledge workers, the ability has now come, because of communications, telecommunications, that people can work anywhere and can work together as teams and so forth, and now we're seeing *the spread of the independent cottage industry again.*

That's also quite inefficient, and people in fact long to work with others because they do miss the human contact. So some kind of an organization will evolve for these knowledge workers. I'm not sure what form that will be but it will take some form of some—I guess, when I reflect on it, it will be some sort of like almost a Bedouin encampment, that will move, and it will flow, and it will go where it has to go in order to survive. It will be a very flexible, very fluid kind of organization with a loose structure, with a leader who is not so much a leader in the hierarchic sense of a leader but a leader who is able to bring people together, to coalesce. That will demand all kinds of new skills in terms of the people on the teams and the people who manage those teams. I think there will always be a demand for somebody to manage or somehow make these events happen. . . . [124]

FROM THE JAWS OF DEFEAT

That's for the future. For now, we have a rare opportunity to witness the process of adaptation, moving at a very high rate of speed. We have an opportunity to witness the creation of a wholly new business enterprise.

What this form of enterprise teaches us is that existence is not destiny: that things can be made to change, and improve. What we have learned from an enterprise that successfully evolves from an organizational form is something that, apparently, human beings have known all along. What we have learned is that human beings, with all of their foibles, can yet be relied upon to change and adapt, without fanfare and commotion, when the situation calls for it.

Human adaptability was the quality that came singing through the events that followed the Northridge earthquake of January 17, 1994. Within minutes and hours of the brief but horrendous 6.8 jolt, people had already "assumed the form," doing what it took to get done what needed doing. They were quietly lined up at lumberyards and hardware stores, hammering splintered parts of their lives back together.

We are seeing that the human race can adapt as readily to socioeconomic change as to seismic change.

It is this feature of adaptability that has made the human race the extraordinarily successful species that it is. It is this feature that has continually converted threats to survival into opportunities to excel. It is this feature that has made failure to survive, for some, lessons for survival for others.

So, yes, organizations are built to fail. However, this obstacle is ultimately viewed not in a spirit of resignation but rather as a lesson and as a challenge, by human beings determined to do whatever it takes in order to procure what they need to survive.

As a result of their efforts, we will have yet another occasion to marvel at the adaptability of our species. We will have another opportunity to recognize the basis for our evolutionary success. And we will be inspired to recognize that, in the hands of this adaptable species, what was once built to fail can instead be made, and destined, to succeed.

Epilogue—Entropy in Human Systems: A Grand Theory of Organizational Self-Destruction

> There is no structural organization of society which can bring about the coming of the Kingdom of God on earth, since all systems can be perverted by the selfishness of man.
>
> —William Temple

Physical scientists have long been drawn to the possibility of developing a grand, unifying theory, to bridge otherwise contrived gaps among artificially discrete disciplines. The effort has been moderately successful; according to the physicist Gordon Kane, commonalities have been recognized among, and theory has been developed that unify, astronomical and terrestrial motion; heat and sound; different sources of energy, including kinetic, gravitational, frictional, chemical, and mass; electricity and magnetism; light and optics; the development of different life forms; organic and inorganic chemicals; space and time; mass and energy; physics and chemistry; and astronomy and physics. However, the effort to develop a unified theory to explain all forces and all matter eluded Einstein for his entire life, along with the rest of us.[125]

By contrast, in explaining organizations, and particularly their proclivity to destroy themselves, the development of a grand theory is facilitated by the fact that our unit of analysis remains the single one of human behavior. For that reason, a single theory of organizational self-destruction is feasible.

The development of this theory requires a process of "induction," or generalizing from the particular issues we have been discussing. Presentation of it is relegated to this epilogue, to reserve it for those with a taste for theory and a preference for unifying explanations, while keeping it safely away from readers with more specific, practical, and applied concerns.

UNDERLYING ASSUMPTIONS

A theory tends to begin with untestable, taken-for-granted assumptions. For example, astronomical and geological theories rest upon the "uniformitarian" assumption that matter acts the same across space and time. A key underlying assumption in our theory is that an organization represents a *system*.

A "system" is defined as "a configuration of interdependent and self-maintaining events that are interrelated in a manner first observed among living organisms."[126] In living organisms, individual organs are so highly interdependent that failure in one is likely to have profound effects on others. For example, heart failure is likely to have a considerable effect on the lungs. Because of this strong interdependence, failure in almost any organ is likely to ramify to other organs and thereby spell failure for the entire organism.

Similarly, in organizations, failure in one department is likely to undermine others. For instance, the failure of strategic planners will withhold the funding needed by financial planners to do their job.

The reason for employing the assumption that an organization represents a system is that it helps us understand why organizations are built to fail. This understanding is cultivated through the analogy of organizations with other systems.

Analogies

A brief caveat about analogies is in order here. Analogies do not guarantee correspondence of their characteristics across analogues; to the contrary, analogues are arresting precisely because they are dissimilar. As observed in *Newsweek* of October 3, 1988, "a metaphor is always wrong. It is likely to be most persuasive when it is most wrong. It is this quality— 'metaphor as mistake' in [novelist Walker] Percy's words—that makes literature so intoxicating."[127] It is because they are so dissimilar, for example, that we are startled, and enlightened, by the revelation that "love is like a rose" or "life is like a river."

As analogies, systems may be open to such questions. What puts us on solid ground in applying this particular analogy is that systems are defined specifically to include only properties that describe each of their individual representatives: internal interdependence, dependence on input, and creation of output. Any other system topics are beyond this discussion, because they are beyond the scope of systems themselves.

For this reason, we will press on with our efforts to understand human enterprises as systems.

THE FAILURE OF LIVING SYSTEMS

For their part, one reason why living organisms are doomed to fail is that internal organs age and eventually cannot function properly. Another reason for demise is that organs fall victim to disease.

A third reason, and one very critical to organizations, reflects the fact that a living organism is an "open" system because it depends entirely on input from the environment. Of course, other organisms are also open systems, so all of them compete for input.

Ironically, if the organism, as a type, is ecologically successful, one result is the presence of direct competitors for input. The result of competition is conflict for essential resources, and either injury or privation as a result of this conflict is a third source of demise.

THE FAILURE OF HUMAN SYSTEMS

Human systems face demise from analogous sources.

Collectively, each "ages," and performs with reduced effectiveness and efficiency, because, as individual analogues to physical organs, members themselves have been selected, trained, or develop interests to perform functions that eventually degrade. Individual functions degrade because they become: (1) ineffective due to individual constraints, from direct physical debilitation or functionally, from adaptation, habituation, or "burnout"; (2) inefficient, due to costs from neglect of interpersonal relationships (e.g., a Parent/Child interaction) or larger, collective processes (e.g., office systems that fail to keep pace with needs); or (3) obsolete in the face of a changed environment. Representing another source of demise, and an analogy to biological disease, is reduced system effectiveness due to conflict by members over resources (e.g., job assignments, pay, and the like) needed by each to pursue self-interest.

Previous observers have noted the inevitability of this conflict, due to the division of labor required to perform the different tasks for which an organization forms in the first place. As we have seen, this division of labor inevitably produces differences in reward systems, culture, and interests across hierarchical levels, among others, from which such conflict emanates. Additionally, organizations certainly fail from such conflict: *directly*, from neglected human resource tasks and resistance to input, and *indirectly*, as we have been given ample reason to infer. Thus, as our First Law of

Organizational Failure, *organizations fail due to conflict among the very functions that justify them.*

As is the case with the physical organism, human systems depend entirely on input from an external environment. This input can be reduced by limits on internal capabilities from all of these organizational analogues to internal aging, injury, or disease, or by conflict with other organizations.

ENTROPY

According to physicists, an open system that loses its external input is described as a *closed system*; a closed system, in turn, heads inevitably into a condition identified as "entropy." Entropy has been defined by Isaac Asimov as "a measure of the evenness with which energy is distributed."[128] Asimov goes on to describe entropy as a loss of *order*,

a quality characterized by a differentiation of the parts of a system: a separating of things into categories; a filing of cards in alphabetical order; a listing of things in terms of increasing quantities. To spread things out with perfect evenness is to disregard these differentiations. A particular category of objects is evenly spread out among all the other categories, and that is maximum disorder.[129]

Entropy is a state that can apply to the type of human system we call the "organization." We have defined an organization as "a configuration of purposeful responsibilities assigned to, and relationships among, its members." One outcome of these relationships and responsibilities is the organization's division of labor.

Interestingly, Asimov's conception of "order," as a feature integral to systems, corresponds to the division of labor that in turn defines the organization. Like any system, a closed organization is built to fail because it loses the *order* that has defined it in its open state.

Entropy in Human Systems

There is reason to believe that organizations operate in or can move *very easily* to a closed state that will ensure the development of entropy.

As we have seen, human systems can, by analogy, age, fall ill, or fall victim to conflict, internal as well as external. These sources of demise can affect all forms of organization, throughout history, as we saw in the final chapter. The clan, military, or agrarian organization can fall prey to internal ineffectiveness or external attack; the industrial organization can be, and has been, done in by the hostile political environment it creates: an instance of a dialectical "antithesis," or counterforce.

However, the focus here is on the commercial organization, the bane of which is external competition that exacerbates the forces identified here as organizational analogues to aging or illness, reducing the organization's own competitiveness. In system terms, competition limits the organization's ability to exchange output (e.g., a product or service) for (e.g., monetary) inputs needed to support other (e.g., human resource) inputs directly applied to produce output. Rivals can limit the exchange of output for financial inputs by attracting customers, and can limit other (e.g., human) input by attracting employees from the (e.g., financial) input that customers have provided to them. Rivals compete for human resources by meeting their needs, with financial input from the output they exchange by doing the same for customers. It all looks like a self-maintaining process because that, in fact, is what it is.

THE MOBILITY OF MEMBERS AMONG HUMAN SYSTEMS

For their part, employees join the commercial organization to satisfy many needs, the most important of which is an economic need. To satisfy other needs or better satisfy the economic need, individuals have a choice of other organizations, to which they may belong simultaneously or sequentially.

Due to these choices, members have leverage over their organization.

For an example of multiple, "simultaneous" memberships, failure to meet social needs at work may be rectified by membership in a bowling league, which seems to work for some people. For an example of multiple, "sequential" memberships, people can simply change jobs. Due to competition for customers, the organization's ability to acquire financial inputs is limited, which limits its human resources and therefore its ability to even *produce* the outputs needed in turn to acquire financial inputs.

Society as a Commercial Organization

There seem to be exceptions; mobility across systems may be prevented in cases of complete control over human inputs, for example, in earlier clan and agrarian organizations and historically in Japan, wherein norms of collective identity are so strong that they support retention of lifelong members through an exchange of lifelong security.

However, in these cases, the completeness of such control forces us to apply the concept of "organization" to society, at large, from which such control is exercised. It is when we view such societies as systems that we indeed, once again, find familiar features of the commercial organization, including competition for disposal of outputs and for financial inputs, but with other societies; coordinated purchases of input from, and availability of output to, other societies; and thus, as in the case of organizations, more or less unified consequences for commercial survival.

In Japan, for example, the 1980s saw generalized prosperity the 1990s witnessed more dire features on an equally monolithic scale. The generalization of prosperity or recession across other societies, including our own, reflects the fact that their economic systems are, as the name implies but to a lesser degree, *systems*.

HUMAN SYSTEM DEPENDENCE ON MEMBERS

Returning to the more familiar, microscopic version of the commercial organization, we find that personnel, thanks to their mobility, depend less on the external input received by the commercial organization than do physical organs on input into their host organism. Thus, the organization is built to fail because it requires its external input more than its members do.

For example, employees participating in a profit-sharing plan may be satisfied with a level of revenues that generates a steady, income-enhancing dividend stream. On the other hand, the industry may be in a growth stage that offers the corporation an opportunity to establish brand loyalty in exchange for investment in product development. Despite its long-term benefits to the organization, this strategy imposes costs that are opposed by employee shareholders because they would cut into dividends.

Individual members may also require a different *kind* of input than the kind needed by their organization. For example, as so often is the case, a new manager may seek to maximize short-term profit margins, and enhance his or her job prospects, by slashing costs through massive workforce reductions and cutting research and development to the bone, enhancing revenues by divesting equipment and selling off inventory. Results may benefit the manager's career mobility, but cripple the organization's long-term profitability.

As a result, the challenge facing organizations is to align their need for external input with the corresponding needs of their individual members. It may be possible to accomplish this, but only temporarily.

As we saw earlier, a company attempted this by offering its employees both recognition and a financial bonus for help in winning the Malcolm Baldridge Award for quality; this would satisfy the individual need for achievement and financial security along with the organizational need for the efficiency that would increase profitability and goodwill that can be brokered into brand loyalty by customers. The result was downsizing, due to a work design that was so efficient that it made its designers superfluous. In general, the consistent alignment of needs by the organization and its members requires an unlikely level of sophistication, planning, perhaps altruism, and outright coincidence.

To sum up, then, organizations need external input, and depend upon their members to acquire it, yet are limited by competition for: (1) customers that provide it and (2) human resources that can acquire it. The commercial organization's competitiveness for human resources in turn is limited by their many needs, and by their choices among organizations to satisfy those needs. Thus, while the organization can survive only as an open system, it is forced to operate under conditions that continually approximate or duplicate the closed system, due to limited or unavailable input.

To reiterate: closed systems head inevitably into entropy. Thus, the organizations that represent human systems are *built to fail*. The result is our Second Law of Organizational Failure: *organizations fail because they depend upon members more than members depend upon them.*

Entropy in a closed physical system (e.g., a car) is the result of each component "obeying" the physical laws that apply to matter, producing, for instance, inertia. In a human system, correspondingly, entropy is the result of people "obeying" the dictates of individual needs, for example, through conflict with other members or membership in other systems.

THE PROCESS OF FAILURE

The number of ways in which a human system can fail corresponds to the number of human systems; however, an effort to understand failure in such systems *in general* requires some equally generalizable laws. To formulate them, we need to identify some concepts that apply to all human systems. The primary concept concerns the events that are described by, and thus comprise, a human system.

Social Processes

Members meet their needs by generating self-supportive *social processes*. A social process is an interaction in which the behavior of each participant over time both responds to, and elicits behavior from, the other participant. Thus, a social process tends to become specific to a particular pair or group of individuals.

We can all relate to the fact that each of us tends to feel, and to act, differently toward various people. In fact, our experience of positive feelings toward others may really be the positive feelings we have about *ourselves* in interacting with them. As La Rochefoucauld observed, "We always like those who admire us, [while] we do not always like those whom we admire." (On closer scrutiny, taken on their own merits, these people may have much less to recommend them than we think, which may be why we are so often disappointed in them. But that is the subject for another discussion . . .)

Social Patterns

Another property of a social process is that it is patterned, eventually developing into a self-fulfilling prophecy in which behaviors are mutually elicited by both participants. It is this property of repetition that gives a characteristic quality to a social process, by making it noticeable and definable in the first place; otherwise, it defers to ephemeral, incidental, and not-very-noticeable behaviors. Examples include the cultural, communication, and other interactive processes explored earlier.

It is also this characteristic quality that allows behavior toward one individual to assume a certain tenor that influences our feelings about ourselves in the presence of the other. In the language of social psychology, it is this feature of social processes through which each of us assumes a certain *role*, illustrated by the ongoing Parent or Child persona adopted over time in an interaction.

Social Costs to Organizations

Social processes may work to the benefit of the human system in which they transpire. However, there is ample reason to suspect otherwise. As we noted in the particular cases of culture and the informal organization, social processes tend to be *emergent*, developing without planning.

Like the individual behaviors of which they consist, the purposes of social processes are the individual purposes of participants; any consistency with the larger goals of the entire human system is purely coincidental. Moreover, as seen earlier, the social processes of one organization may include people exchanging output with inputs of other organizations. For all of these reasons, social processes tend to produce not benefits but rather costs for the human system in which they take place: by requiring, diverting, and consuming time and other resources.

The Dynamics of Failure

Analysis of the specific costs of a social process for its larger social context can benefit from some recent, radical, and yet well-supported insights into the dynamics of natural processes in general.

Not so long ago, it was widely assumed that a process can be initiated or altered by events that were best described as incremental, moving gradually and in the same direction as their eventual state. For example, it was widely assumed that an ice age or epoch developed as the result of various forces that gradually "cooled" the Earth.

More recently, it has been recognized that processes can be set in motion or altered, on a very small scale, by events that are seemingly remote and on definitive dimensions even opposite to the eventual state of the process but actually interactive with other contributory events in a way that increasingly approximates that state. This has been called the "Butterfly Effect"—in the extreme, according to chaos-theory historian James Gleick, "the notion that a butterfly stirring the air today in Peking can transform storm systems next month in New York."[130]

As a more concrete and empirically-verifiable example, recent research indicates that an ice age results not simply from gradual cooling but rather from a change in the angle of the Earth's rotation, which directly induces greater exposure to the Sun's rays, global warming, and evaporation of water. At upper atmospheric levels, the vapor cools and condenses into snow, adding to the size of ice caps that reflect a greater proportion of the Sun's rays, cooling the Earth, enhancing condensation into snow at lower altitudes, adding to the ice caps, and so on. Note that a critical seminal event in the development of an ice age is global *warming*, the implications of which for global cooling are certainly nonobvious.

Note also that the amount of global warming may seem negligible. Thus, there seems to be a nonlinear relationship between the modest level of a precipitating event and its dramatic outcome. This nonlinearity has given impetus to the "chaos" theory that effects may be nonpredictable from causes.

Whether effects are unpredictable or simply are incompletely understood is the subject for another discussion. The point here is that some causes are nonobvious if not unobservable until they produce their effects, and that this certainly applies to social processes. Moreover, because of their nonobvious or unobservable causes, social processes can elude the vigilance of personnel responsible for their productivity to the organization, inducing costs or ultimately failure.

Representing an example is group reward, which has been heavily marketed at various times as a tool for inducing group collaboration and effectiveness. In recent times, group reward has received the credit extended to Japanese management for creating and exploiting group identification.

As we have seen, unfortunately, in addition to collaboration, group reward also justifies delegation of decisions about individual issues to the group, justifying, in turn, management neglect and encouraging the following complex of events: (1) dependence by less skilled employees and recalcitrance by less motivated ones; (2) for both reasons, a greater workload for more skilled and motivated employees; (3) their perception of inequity in relation to peers in this group, in other groups, or on the open market; (4) to reduce this inequity, failure by better performers to perform; (5) given the noninvolvement of management, failure on upper levels to address this problem; (6) group nonproductivity; and as a result, (7) termination of the group. Therefore, despite noble intentions, this particular social process is, in the final analysis, a ruinous one.

To recapitulate, then, social processes tend to undermine human systems because, like the behaviors of which they consist, they address the individual needs of participants, and have unintended, undetected, and ultimately dysfunctional consequences for the larger system, including the diversion of output from it. Because the system exists only through its members, their needs are the only ones pursued. Results include the system's reduced ability to acquire its needed inputs through its members, and our Third Law of Organizational Failure: *organizations fail because their needs are represented only through, conflict with, and are undermined by, the needs of members.*

As a result of this disability, human systems are closed systems, closed systems are ultimately entropic systems, entropic systems fail, and the organizations that reflect human systems are thereby *built to fail.*

UNIVERSAL ENTROPY: "HEAT DEATH"

Ultimately, to expand our analysis to the breaking point, the entire universe is a closed system, because, regardless of its inconceivable dimensions, it remains finite, and depends on energy generated within it. As a result, physicists predict that the universe will fall prey to entropy in, say, a couple of dozen billion years, an event referred to as the "heat death" of the universe. Thus, there is nothing idiosyncratic about the fate we have assigned to organizations; like everything else around them, they are built to fail.

The difference is that the failure of our organizations will presage the heat death of the universe by several billion years. Because of its greater urgency, therefore, and admittedly applying a short-term perspective, we have focused our attention on the problem facing our organizations.

Thus, the good news for organizations is that they are in good company. The bad news is that they will not be around to enjoy it for very long.

Appendix 1: A Primer on Reinforcement Contingencies

To understand reward systems, it is crucial to learn their components. Probably the most important component is "reinforcement," the consequence by which a behavior is deliberately followed in order to shape future behaviors.

Reinforcement can be further clarified by looking at two dimensions.[131]

REINFORCEMENT PARADIGM

The first dimension is *reinforcement paradigm,* which is the type of consequence assigned to behavior. Probably the most familiar of these is *positive reinforcement,* which increases the likelihood or frequency of a behavior by following it with a consequence desirable to the individual performing it. Representing an organizational example is any pay increment to a salary for a job well done, including both a temporary bonus and a permanent pay raise, that enhances future performance.

Negative reinforcement, by contrast, produces the same increase by withholding an undesirable consequence. For example, punctuality may be increased through withholding a pay cut threatened for the continuation of lateness.

Punishment, the threat of which makes negative reinforcement work, is given by following a behavior with a consequence undesirable to the individual performing it, reducing the behavior's likelihood or frequency. The pay cut for continued lateness in the previous example provides an example.

Extinction, finally, produces the same decrease in behavior through withholding a desirable consequence for it: i.e., by eliminating its ongoing positive reinforcement. For example, lateness may be curbed by staggering lunch hours, preventing coworkers from accompanying each other and reducing the likelihood for the reward of meeting social needs that perpetuate lateness and intrude into work hours.

In addition to these paradigms are more esoteric arrangements. One that is designed to produce behavior beyond a current repertoire is *successive approximation* or *"shaping,"* through which reinforcement is given for some portion of a target behavior and then withheld until behavior more closely approximates the target, whereupon the process is repeated, until the target itself is attained. *"Modeling"* or *vicarious reinforcement* or *punishment* is an attempt to alter one individual's behavior through consequences to the behavior of another individual, for example, through public praise or punishment, respectively.

REINFORCEMENT SCHEDULE

Another dimension is *reinforcement schedule*, through which reinforcement or punishment is dispensed according to various time arrangements. These include the following schedules, each with its associated occurrence of reinforcement or punishment: *continuous*, after every behavior; *fixed interval*, after a nonvarying period of time; *variable interval*, after a variable and random-appearing period of time; *fixed ratio*, after a nonvarying number of behaviors; and *variable ratio*, after a variable and random-appearing number of behaviors.

As a rule, continuous and fixed schedules may produce rapid *onset* of behavior, since they are reliable sources of reinforcement or punishment. However, variable schedules produce the most *durable* behaviors, since the individual performing them is accustomed to long and indeterminate periods without reinforcement or punishment. By contrast, due to expectation of consequences at specific times or after a specific number of behaviors, continuous and fixed ratio schedules produce rapid extinction in the absence of anticipated reinforcement or punishment. Additionally, a fixed interval schedule produces an uneven response rate: responses that, due to unchanging expectations of imminent consequences, are highest just before reinforcement or punishment.

Appendix 2: Measures of Organizational Effectiveness

FINANCIAL RATIOS

Among the more objective-appearing measures of organizational effectiveness are financial ratios. These measures can depict a firm's leverage and liquidity; of interest to an analysis of organizational effectiveness are ratios that can provide information about the efficiency of asset use.

A ratio that is frequently cited as a source of this information is the calculation of either sales relative to average total assets or earnings before interest and taxes, minus taxes (i.e., respectively, the sale-to-total-assets and return-on-total-assets ratios). However popular, these calculations could lead to overestimated efficiency if there is minimal current investment in the firm, so that assets tend to be old and heavily depreciated. For this reason, corporations may rely on the ratio of sales to net *working* capital; in this case, however, efficiency, and particularly improvement in it, may still be overestimated when current, "working" expenditures are reduced (e.g., with cutbacks).

A ratio that appears to closely approximate the bottom line is net profit margin, or earnings before interest and taxes, less taxes, relative to sales. Like other ratios, however, this one can help to exaggerate efficiency, in this case simply due to low volume and high prices, the latter of which maximizes profit margin in the case of minimal per-unit cost. Another intended measure of efficiency is inventory turnover, which is the ratio between cost of goods sold and average inventory; on the other hand, a large ratio may reflect not a high level of efficiency but rather short production runs or otherwise insufficient inventories. Finally, the average collection period, or average receivables relative to average daily sales, may measure efficiency, or simply reflect a highly restrictive credit policy.

In sum, then, due to their quantitativeness and clear referents, financial ratios appear to represent the very soul of objectivity. In reality, however, they are highly susceptible to interpretation and, through the variety of information they provide, they are available to support almost any of the organization's beliefs about itself. (For a full discussion of financial ratios and their interpretation, the reader is referred to *Principles of Corporate Finance* by Richard Brealey and Stewart Myers, published by McGraw-Hill.)[132]

In addition to their illusory finality is the fact that financial ratios represent a short-term measure; there are other, equally ambiguous, measures of longer-term performance.

As seen earlier, for example, measures of growth capture an organizational goal that is certainly long-cherished, but also ill-advised. Growth is widely assumed to equate to profitability, but it does not. Also, as noted earlier, growth has subliminal appeal to the egos of managers, who would prefer to be the head of a mammoth undertaking rather than a small and seemingly inconsequential one.

MARKET SHARE

There would seem to be more intuitive value to market share as a measure of profitability, including both its absolute and incremental value, but this too may be unjustified; market share may simply denote an absence of customer choices, and fails to account for inefficiency, so that profits may be subsumed by overwhelming costs. United States automakers during the 1970s and 1980s provide an instructive example.

QUALITY

Measures of quality have recently received favorable attention from practitioners and academics alike as a measure of corporate performance. On the other hand, quality is often measured through customer satisfaction, according to which "quality" emerges in a form that is at best limited in scope (e.g., impulse buying), and on occasion the exact opposite of its traditional denotation; examples include disposable goods, fast foods, tabloid TV shows, and anything offered by the World Wrestling Federation. Customer satisfaction may be measured through two opposed but at the same time flawed methods: (1) new business, which may reflect an absence of choice or a previously small client base or (2) repeat business, which may also be explained by an absence of choice, combined with product defects or obsolescence, planned or otherwise.

Customer satisfaction may also be measured through interviews or sur-veys, which sacrifice "hard" but ambiguous data for "softer" but more directed data. On the other hand, these methods raise a host of research issues, including, but not limited to, biases introduced by: (1) the selection or self-selection of a respondent sample that does not represent the universe of customers; (2) a procedure that provides opportunities for responses that are casual and nonbinding, polite or "socially desirable," or theoretical and disconnected to behavior; (3) questions that fail to capture or exhaust their intended underlying concepts; and (4) responses that fail to capture the underlying feelings of respondents. Similar problems beset interviews and surveys intended to measure organizational effectiveness through brand loyalty, recognition, and reputation.

EMPLOYEE SATISFACTION AND SAFETY

Low turnover, absenteeism, and lateness, along with other measures of employee job satisfaction, may appear to be useful for limiting long-term human resource costs; however, contrary to the wishful thinking of aspiring efficiency experts-cum-humanists, job satisfaction has: (1) little to do with productivity (and in fact the two may be inversely related, due to possible satisfaction from an opportunity to do as little as possible) and (2) even less to do with profitability (which in fact may reflect human resource cost-cutting that might reduce job satisfaction). Morale suffers from the same weaknesses, with an added dollop of imprecision and abstractness. Reduced accident frequency is certainly defensible from an altruistic perspective and efficient in the long term, but offers a highly restricted view of organiza-tional performance.

MISCELLANEOUS MEASURES

From these measures, the fall into the realm of definitional ambiguity becomes a precipitous plummet. One view is that organizational effective-ness simply represents the attainment of organizational goals; this raises limitless questions about the nature, origins, and utility of the goals, them-selves: they may be constructed, interpreted, or altered to permit their at-tainment, to resist their attainment and justify alternatives, and in either case reflect the narrow political interest of their sources, a subject with which we are by now very familiar. Organizational effectiveness has also been associated with a plethora of internal measures that probably have more to do with means than with ends, have an odor of managerial ide-ology about them and, in general, seem to smack of greater interest to academics writing about organizations than to people responsible for their success. These measures include cohesion, flexibility, adaptation, goal in-ternalization and consensus, role and norm congruence, managerial task and interpersonal skills, information management, stability, managerial participativeness, goal attainment by members, and an emphasis upon training, development, and achievement.

COMBINED MEASURES

In sum, then, measures of organizational effectiveness suffer from uncertainty, ambiguity, subjectivity, and narrowness.

To overcome these deficiencies, some people suggest combining several measures. One such approach is the use of an overall, composite measure, which may invite an interpretation of effectiveness consistent with most of its component measures but fail to address insistent problems raised by a few.

For example, a high level of profitability may be suggested by a bulk of measures in use but may be confuted by a few financial ratios that account for a high level of debt.

A systems approach justifies a combination of multiple internal measures, by applying the recognition that they are interdependent, but, as in the case of individual internal measures, it treats them as an end rather than a means to an end. Finally, an ecological approach appears to be the most exhaustive and directive, since it considers the identity, interests, and importance of various stakeholders, but ultimately it reduces to consideration only of short-term, individual political power without long-term concern for the organization. (For a reference source for many of these issues, the reader is referred to *Macroorganizational Behavior* by Robert Miles, published by Scott, Foresman, and Company.)[133]

Notes

1. James C. Collins and Jerry I. Porras, *Built to Last: Successful Habits of Visionary Companies* (New York: HarperCollins, 1994).

2. John Case, *The Dark Side: The State of Small Business* (Washington, DC: Government Printing Office, 1996).

3. The Business Team, "The Safe Way to Go Into Business" in *Business for Sale* (San Jose, CA: BTI Group, 1997), http://www.business-team.com/opinion.htm.

4. Douglas Gray, "Reasons for Success and Failure in a Home-Based Business," *Canada Computer Paper, Inc.* (November 1996 issue), http://www. canadacomputes.com.

5. "*U.S. Small Business Administration Report,*" cited in *Small Business Resources* (North Oaks, MN: DRI Consulting Publications, 1996), http://www. dric.com.

6. *The SOHO Guidebook: Starting Your Business*, CCH Business Owner's Toolkit (Rolling Meadows, IL: Digitalwork, 1996), http://www.toolkit.cch.com/ text/pol_0000.asp.

7. Timothy Bates, *Firms Started As Franchises Have Lower Survival Rates Than Independent Small Business Start-Ups.* (U.S. Government Publication, May 1994), http://www.smallbiz.findlaw.com/text/pol_3020.stm.

8. Case, *The Dark Side*.

9. Ibid.

10. Edward Gibbon, *The History of the Decline and Fall of the Roman Empire* (New York: Viking Penguin, 1983).

11. *Why Family Businesses Fail: Survey Results* (Storrs, CT: University of Connecticut Family Business Center, 1996).

12. "*U.S. Small Business Administration Report.*"

13. Paul A. Lewis, *Small Business: Preventing Failure—Promoting Success*

(Wichita, KS: The Wichita State University Small Business Development Center Publication, 1995).

14. James G. March and Herbert A. Simon, *Organizations* (New York: John Wiley and Sons, 1958).

15. Karl Weick, *The Social Psychology of Organizing* (Reading, MA: Addison-Wesley, 1969).

16. Douglas MacGregor, *The Human Side of Enterprise* (New York: McGraw-Hill, 1960).

17. Emile Durkheim, *The Division of Labor in Society* (Glencoe, IL: Free Press, 1949).

18. William H. White, Jr., *The Organization Man* (New York: Simon and Schuster, 1956).

19. John Kenneth Galbraith, *The New Industrial State* (Boston: Houghton Mifflin, 1970).

20. Ken Benson, ed., *Organizational Analysis: Critique and Innovation* (Beverly Hills, CA: Sage Publications, 1977).

21. Pamela R. Haunschild and Anne S. Miner, "Modes of Interorganizational Imitation: The Effects of Outcome Salience and Uncertainty," *Administrative Science Quarterly* 42, no. 3 (September 1997): 472–500.

22. J. French, Jr. and B. Raven, "The Bases of Social Power," in *Studies in Social Power*, ed. D. Cartwright (Ann Arbor, MI: Institute for Social Research, University of Michigan, 1959).

23. Gibson Burrell and Gareth Morgan, *Sociological Paradigms and Organizational Analysis* (London: Heinemann, 1979), 41–117.

24. Leon Festinger, *A Theory of Cognitive Dissonance* (Stanford, CA: Stanford University Press, 1957).

25. Solomon E. Asch, "Opinions and Social Pressures," *Scientific American* 193 (1955): 31–35.

26. James Thompson, *Organizations in Action* (New York: McGraw-Hill, 1967), 106.

27. March and Simon, *Organizations*, 9.

28. James Gleick, *Chaos: Making a New Science* (New York: Viking Penguin, 1987).

29. Max H. Bazerman, *Judgment in Managerial Decision Making* (New York: John Wiley and Sons, 1986).

30. D. T. Miller and M. Ross, "Self-serving Biases in the Attribution of Causality: Fact or Fiction?" *Psychological Bulletin*, 82 (1975): 213–225.

31. Peter Drucker, *Management: Tasks, Responsibilities, Practices* (New York: Harper and Row, 1973), 17.

32. Laurence Peter and Raymond Hull, *The Peter Principle* (New York: William Morrow and Company, 1960).

33. Max Weber, *The Theory of Social and Economic Organization* (New York: Free Press, 1947).

34. Charles Perrow, *Complex Organizations: A Critical Essay* (Glenview, IL: Scott Foresman, 1972).

35. Fred Luthans, "Successful vs. Effective Real Managers," *Academy of Management Executive*, 2, no. 2 (1988): 127–130.

36. Sigmund S. Freud, *An Outline of Psychoanalysis*, Vol. 23 (London: Hogarth Press, 1935).

37. Jonathan I. Klein, "The Myth of the Corporate Political Jungle: Politicization as a Political Strategy," *The Journal of Management Studies* 25, no. 1 (January 1988): 1–12.

38. Steven Kerr and Jonathan I. Klein, "Increasing Employee Motivation and Effectiveness," *The Journal for the National Society of Fund-Raising Executives* (Fall 1984): 22–25.

39. Arthur H. Bell, "Gut-feelings Be Damned," *Across the Board* 36, no. 8 (September 1999): 57–62.

40. E. T. Penrose, *The Theory of the Growth of the Firm* (London: Macmillan, 1958).

41. R. Morris, *The Economic Theory of Managerial Capitalism* (London: Macmillan, 1964).

42. Shirley Terreberry, "The Evolution of Organizational Environments," *Administrative Science Quarterly* 12 (1968): 590–613.

43. Michael J. Driver, Kenneth P. Brousseau, and Phillip L. Hunsaker, *The Dynamic Decision Maker: Five Decision Styles for Executive and Business Success* (San Francisco: Jossey-Bass, 1994).

44. George Webley, "Against All Odds: The Truth About Demos," *Sound on Sound* (May 1998): 166.

45. H. Braverman, *Labor and Monopoly Capital* (New York: Monthly Review Press, 1974).

46. The Manitoba (Canada) Nurses Union, *Facts for the Front Lines* (1999).

47. Ibid.

48. Ibid.

49. Ibid.

50. Ibid.

51. B. B. Seligman, *Most Notorious Victory: Man in an Age of Automation* (New York: Free Press, 1966).

52. Robert Leeper, "A Study of a Neglected Portion of the Field of Learning: The Development of Sensory Organization," *Journal of Genetic Psychology* (March 1935).

53. Merle J. Moskowitz and Arthur R. Orgel, *General Psychology* (Boston: Houghton Mifflin, 1969).

54. Solomon E. Asch, "Forming Impressions of Personalities," *Journal of Abnormal and Social Psychology* (July 1946): 258–290.

55. Byron A. Grove and Willar A. Kerr, "Specific Evidence on Origin of Halo Effect in Measurement of Employee Morale," *Journal of Social Psychology* (August 1951): 165–170.

56. Gary Latham and Kenneth Wexley, *Increasing Productivity Through Performance Appraisal* (Reading, MA: Addison-Wesley, 1981).

57. Jonathan I. Klein, "How to Best Achieve Performance Goals—Set Them or Forget Them?" *Management Letter* no. 421 (November 10, 1991).

58. Latham and Wexley, *Increasing Productivity*.

59. Ibid.

60. MacGregor, *Human Side of Enterprise*.

61. Steven Kerr, "On the Folly of Rewarding A While Hoping for B," *Academy of Management Journal* 18 (1975): 769–783.

62. F. J. Roethlisberger and William Dickson, *Management and the Worker* (Cambridge, MA: Harvard University Press, 1939).

63. B. F. Skinner, *The Behavior of Organisms* (New York: Appleton, 1938).

64. Richard L. Solomon, "Punishment" in *Psychology of Learning: Readings*, ed. William L. Mikulas (Chicago, IL: Nelson-Hall, 1977), 15–44.

65. Graham Allison, *Essence of Decision: Explaining the Cuban Missile Crisis* (Boston: Little, Brown, and Company, 1971).

66. Terence Deal and Allen Kennedy, *Corporate Culture: The Rites and Rituals of Corporate Life* (Reading, MA: Addison-Wesley, 1982).

67. Jonathan I. Klein, "Science and Subterfuge," *The Academy of Management Executive* 3, no. 1 (February 1989): 59–62.

68. R. Rosenthal and L. Jacobson, *Pygmalion in the Classroom* (New York: Holt, Rinehart, and Winston, 1968).

69. Thomas Harris, *I'm OK—You're OK* (New York: Harper and Row, 1967).

70. Klein, "Myth of the Corporate Political Jungle."

71. Jonathan I. Klein, "The Case Against Conflict in Organizations," *Management Letter* no. 501 (January 10, 1992).

72. Irving Janis, *Victims of Groupthink* (Boston: Houghton Mifflin, 1972).

73. Solomon E. Asch, *Social Psychology* (New York: Prentice-Hall, 1952).

74. Elisha Y. Babad, Max Birnbaum, and Kenneth D. Benne, *The Social Self: Group Influences on Individual Identity* (Beverly Hills, CA: Sage Publications, 1983), 111.

75. Jean-Paul Sartre, *Anti-Semite and Jew* (New York: Schocken Books, 1946), 52.

76. Jean-François Manzoni and Jean-Louis Barsoux, "The Set-Up-To-Fail Syndrome," *Harvard Business Review* (March/April 1998): 101–103.

77. Ibid.

78. J.A.F. Stoner, "A Comparison of Individual and Group Decisions Involving Risk" (master's thesis, Massachusetts Institute of Technology, Sloan School of Industrial Management, Cambridge, MA, 1961).

79. Jonathan I. Klein, "Rational Integration: Restoring Rationality to Organizational Analysis," *Human Relations* 43, no. 6 (1990): 527–550.

80. Robert Dubin, "Industrial Workers' Worlds: A Study of the 'Central Life Interests' of Industrial Workers," *Social Problems* 3 (1956).

81. Benjamin Lee Whorf, "Science and Linguistics" in *Language, Thought, and Reality: Selected Writings of Benjamin Lee Whorf,* ed. John B. Carroll (New York: John Wiley and Sons, 1956).

82. Asch, *Social Psychology.*

83. Janis, *Victims of Groupthink.*

84. Edward E. Lawler, Lyman W. Porter, and Arnold Tannenbaum, "Managerial Attitudes Toward Interaction Episodes," *Journal of Applied Psychology* 52 (1968): 432–439.

85. Warren Bennis, *On Becoming a Leader* (New York: Perseus Press, 1994).

86. Weick, *Social Psychology of Organizing.*

87. Paul Watzlawick, Janet Beavin Bavelas, and Don D. Jackson, *Pragmatics of Human Communication* (New York: W. W. Norton, 1967), 36.

88. R. N. Osborn, J. G. Hunt, and L. R. Jauch, *Organization Theory* (New York: John Wiley and Sons, 1980).

89. M. T. Hannan, and J. Freeman, "The Population Ecology of Organizations," *American Journal of Sociology* 82 (1977): 929–964.

90. Adam Smith, *The Wealth of Nations* (New York: G. P. Putnam's Sons, 1904).

91. A. C. Pigou, quoted in Paul Samuelson, *Economics* (New York: McGraw-Hill, 1973), 457.

92. Samuelson, *Economics*, 510–515.

93. Drucker, *Management*, 160.

94. Peter Lewis, *The Call of the Wild*. Interview with Sally McManus, 1999, http://www.actu.asn.au/.

95. Communications, Energy and Paperworkers Union, news release, February 13, 1999.

96. The London Greenpeace Group, *What's Wrong With McDonald's?* (London: Report Issued for "World Food Day," Oct. 1, 1986).

97. Linn Washington, Jr., Article in *Philadelphia Tribune*, November 7, 1997.

98. Board of Directors, National Labor Committee in Support of Worker and Human Rights, "Letter to CEO," March 4, 1999.

99. Oil, Chemical, and Atomic Workers International Union, AFL-CIO, news release, February 19, 1997.

100. Stacey Adams, "Inequity in Social Exchange" in *Advances in Experimental Social Psychology*, vol. 2, ed. Leonard Berkowitz (New York: Academic Press, 1963), 267–300.

101. Ross Bergen, The Scott County Emergency Management Agency, personal conversation with author, October 15, 1999.

102. Greg Allen, "Statement to the *Mesa (AZ) Tribune*" *Mesa (AZ) Tribune*, May 30, 1999.

103. Bennis, *On Becoming a Leader*.

104. Bukkyo Dendo Kyokai, *The Teaching of Buddha* (Tokyo: Kenkyusha Printing Company, 1966).

105. Warren G. Bennis, Kenneth D. Benne, Robert Chin, and Kenneth E. Corey, eds., *The Planning of Change* (New York: Holt, Rinehart, and Winston, 1976).

106. Klein, "Rational Integration."

107. Donald Klein, "Some Notes on the Dynamics of Resistance to Change: The Defender Role," *Cooperative Project for Educational Development Services*, Vol. 1 (Washington, DC: National Training Laboratories, 1966).

108. Vincent A. Mabert and Roger W. Schmenner, "Assessing the Roller Coaster of Downsizing," *Business Management* 17 (July 1997): 45.

109. Marilyn Machlowitz, "Management-Business Advice: The Survivor Syndrome," *Working Woman*, February 1983, 18.

110. Karen E. Mishra, Gretchen M. Spreitzer, and Aneil K. Mishra, "Preserving Employee Morale During Downsizing." *Sloan Management Review* (Winter 1998): 83–94.

111. Deal and Kennedy, *Corporate Culture*.

112. Watzlawick, Beavin Bavelas, and Jackson, *Pragmatics of Human Communication*, 271.

113. Jonathan I. Klein, "Parenthetic Learning: Toward the Unlearning of the Unlearning Model," *Journal of Management Studies* 26, no. 3 (May 1989).

114. Bennis et al., *Planning of Change*.

115. Janean Chun, "Try, Try Again," *Entrepreneur Magazine* September 3, 1998.

116. Bill McKelvey, *Organizational Systematics: Taxonomy, Evolution, Classification* (Berkeley: University of California Press, 1982), 299.

117. Ibid.

118. Ibid.

119. Joanne H. Pratt, *Small Business Research Summary* (RS #134, Contract # SBA-6647-OA-91, 1991).

120. Longevity Network, survey, 1999.

121. Robert Burns, *Home-Based Businesses Offer Economic Boon to Local Economies* (College Station, TX: Texas Agricultural Extension Service, Oct. 1, 1995), http://agextension.tamu.edu/distjump.htm.

122. Network Marketing, news release, February 1, 1998.

123. Burns, Home-Based Businesses.

124. Michael Pirrault, personal conversation with author, May 3, 1999.

125. Gordon Kane, *The Particle Garden: The Universe as Understood by Particle Physicists* (Reading, MA: Addison-Wesley, 1993), 21.

126. Von Bertalanffy, Ludwig, "The History and Status of General System Theory," *Academy of Management Journal* 15 (1972): 407–426.

127. P. McGrath, *Newsweek*, October 3, 1988.

128. Isaac Asimov, *Understanding Physics*, vol. I. (New York: Barnes and Noble, 1966), 238.

129. Ibid.

130. Gleick, *Chaos*.

131. Skinner, The Behavior of Organisms.

132. Richard Brealey and Stewart Myers, *Principles of Corporate Finance* (New York: McGraw-Hill, 1981).

133. Robert Miles, *Macroorganizational Behavior* (Glenview, Il: Scott Foresman, 1980).

Bibliography

Adams, Stacey. "Inequity in Social Exchange." In *Advances in Experimental Social Psychology* (Vol. 2), edited by Leonard Berkowitz. New York: Academic Press, 1963.

Allen, Greg. "Statement to the *Mesa (AZ) Tribune*." *Mesa (AZ) Tribune*, May 30, 1999.

Allison, Graham. *Essence of Decision: Explaining the Cuban Missile Crisis*. Boston: Little, Brown, and Company, 1971.

Asch, Solomon E. "Forming Impressions of Personalities." *Journal of Abnormal and Social Psychology* (July 1946): 258–290.

———. "Opinions and Social Pressures." *Scientific American* 193 (1955): 31–35.

———. *Social Psychology*. New York: Prentice-Hall, 1952.

Asimov, Isaac. *Understanding Physics* (vol. 1). New York: Barnes and Noble, 1966.

Babad, Elisha Y., Max Birnbaum, and Kenneth D. Benne. *The Social Self: Group Influences on Individual Identity*. Beverly Hills, CA: Sage Publications, 1983.

Bates, Timothy. *Firms Started As Franchises Have Lower Survival Rates Than Independent Small Business Start-Ups*. U.S. Government Publication (May 1994), http://www.smallbiz.findlaw.com/text/pol_3020.stm.

Bazerman, Max H. *Judgment in Managerial Decision Making*. New York: Wiley, 1986.

Bell, Arthur H. "Gut-feelings Be Damned." *Across the Board* 36, no. 8 (September 1999): 57–62.

Bennis, Warren. *On Becoming a Leader*. New York: Perseus Press, 1994.

Bennis, Warren G., Kenneth D. Benne, Robert Chin, and Kenneth E. Corey, eds. *The Planning of Change*. New York: Holt, Rinehart, and Winston, 1976.

Benson, Ken, ed. *Organizational Analysis: Critique and Innovation*. Beverly Hills, CA: Sage Publications, 1977.

Bergen, Ross (The Scott County Emergency Management Agency). Personal conversation with author, October 15, 1999.

Board of Directors, National Labor Committee in Support of Worker and Human Rights. "Letter to CEO." March 4, 1999.

Braverman, H. *Labor and Monopoly Capital*. New York: Monthly Review Press, 1974.

Brealey, Richard and Stewart Myers. *Principles of Corporate Finance*. New York: McGraw-Hill, 1981.

Burns, Robert. *Home-Based Businesses Offer Economic Boon to Local Economies*. College Station, TX: Texas Agricultural Extension Service, October 1, 1995, http://agextension.tamu.edu/distjump.htm.

Burrell, Gibson and Gareth Morgan. *Sociological Paradigms and Organizational Analysis*. London: Heinemann, 1979.

The Business Team. "The Safe Way to Go Into Business." In *Business for Sale*. San Jose, CA: BTI Group, 1997 (http.//www.business-team.com/opinion.htm).

Case, John. *The Dark Side: The State of Small Business*. Washington, DC: Government Printing Office, 1996.

Chun, Janean. "Try, Try Again." *Entrepreneur Magazine*, September 3, 1998.

Collins, James C. and Jerry I. Porras. *Built to Last: Successful Habits of Visionary Companies*. New York: HarperCollins, 1994.

Communications, Energy and Paperworkers Union, news release, February 13, 1999.

Deal, Terence and Allen Kennedy. *Corporate Culture: The Rites and Rituals of Corporate Life*. Reading, MA: Addison-Wesley, 1982.

Driver, Michael J., Kenneth P. Brousseau, and Phillip L. Hunsaker. *The Dynamic Decision Maker: Five Decision Styles for Executive and Business Success*. San Francisco: Jossey-Bass, 1994.

Drucker, Peter. *Management: Tasks, Responsibilities, Practices*. New York: Harper and Row, 1973.

Dubin, Robert. "Industrial Workers' Worlds: A Study of the 'Central Life Interests' of Industrial Workers." *Social Problems* 3 (1956).

Durkheim, Emile. *The Division of Labor in Society*. Glencoe, IL: Free Press, 1949.

Festinger, Leon. *A Theory of Cognitive Dissonance*. Stanford, CA: Stanford University Press, 1957.

French, J., Jr. and B. Raven. "The Bases of Social Power." In *Studies in Social Power*, edited by D. Cartwright. Ann Arbor, MI: Institute for Social Research, University of Michigan, 1959.

Freud, Sigmund S. *An Outline of Psychoanalysis* (vol. 23). London: Hogarth Press, 1935.

Galbraith, John Kenneth. *The New Industrial State*. Boston: Houghton Mifflin, 1970.

Gibbon, Edward. *The History of the Decline and Fall of the Roman Empire*. New York: Viking Penguin, 1983.

Gleick, James. *Chaos: Making a New Science*. New York: Viking Penguin, 1987.

Gray, Douglas. "Reasons for Success and Failure in a Home-Based Business." *Canada Computer Paper, Inc.* (November 1996), http://www.canadacomputes.com.

Grove, Byron A. and Willar A. Kerr. "Specific Evidence on Origin of Halo Effect in Measurement of Employee Morale." *Journal of Social Psychology* (August 1951): 165–170.

Hannan, M. T. and J. Freeman. "The Population Ecology of Organizations." *American Journal of Sociology* 82 (1977): 929–964.

Harris, Thomas. *I'm OK—You're OK*. New York: Harper and Row, 1967.

Haunschild, Pamela R. and Anne S. Miner. "Modes of Interorganizational Imitation: The Effects of Outcome Salience and Uncertainty." *Administrative Science Quarterly* 42, no. 3 (September 1997): 472–500.

Janis, Irving. *Victims of Groupthink*. Boston: Houghton Mifflin, 1972.

Kane, Gordon. *The Particle Garden: The Universe as Understood by Particle Physicists*. Reading, MA: Addison-Wesley, 1993.

Kerr, Steven. "On the Folly of Rewarding A While Hoping for B." *Academy of Management Journal* 18 (1975): 769–783.

Kerr, Steven and Jonathan I. Klein. "Increasing Employee Motivation and Effectiveness." *The Journal for the National Society of Fund-Raising Executives* (Fall 1984): 22–25.

Klein, Donald. "Some Notes on the Dynamics of Resistance to Change: The Defender Role." *Cooperative Project for Educational Development Services* (vol. 1). Washington, DC: National Training Laboratories, 1966.

Klein, Jonathan I. "The Case Against Conflict in Organizations." *Management Letter* No. 501 (January 10, 1992).

———. "How to Best Achieve Performance Goals—Set Them or Forget Them?" *Management Letter* No. 421 (November 10, 1991).

———. "The Myth of the Corporate Political Jungle: Politicization as a Political Strategy." *The Journal of Management Studies* 25, no. 1 (January 1988): 1–12.

———. "Parenthetic Learning: Toward the Unlearning of the Unlearning Model." *Journal of Management Studies* 26, no. 3 (May 1989): 291–308.

———. "Rational Integration: Restoring Rationality to Organizational Analysis." *Human Relations* 43, no. 6 (1990): 527–550.

———. "Science and Subterfuge." *The Academy of Management Executive* 3, no. 1 (February 1989): 59–62.

Kyokai, Bukkyo Dendo. *The Teaching of Buddha*. Tokyo: Kenkyusha Printing Company, 1966.

Latham, Gary and Kenneth Wexley. *Increasing Productivity Through Performance Appraisal*. Reading, MA: Addison-Wesley, 1981.

Lawler, Edward E., Lyman W. Porter, and Arnold Tannenbaum. "Managerial Attitudes Toward Interaction Episodes." *Journal of Applied Psychology* 52 (1968): 432–439.

Leeper, Robert. "A Study of a Neglected Portion of the Field of Learning: The Development of Sensory Organization." *Journal of Genetic Psychology* (March 1935).

Lewis, Paul A. *Small Business: Preventing Failure—Promoting Success*. Wichita, KS: The Wichita State University Small Business Development Center Publication, 1995.

Lewis, Peter. *The Call of the Wild*. Interview with Sally McManus, 1999 (http://www.actu.asn.au/).

The London Greenpeace Group. *What's Wrong With McDonald's?* London: Report
    Issued for "World Food Day," October 1, 1986.

Longevity Network, survey, 1999.

Luthans, Fred. "Successful vs. Effective Real Managers." *Academy of Management
    Executive* 2, no. 2 (1988): 127–130.

Mabert, Vincent A. and Roger W. Schmenner. "Assessing the Roller Coaster of
    Downsizing." *Business Management* 17 (July 1997): 45.

MacGregor, Douglas. *The Human Side of Enterprise*. New York: McGraw-Hill,
    1960.

Machlowitz, Marilyn. "Management-Business Advice: The Survivor Syndrome."
    Working Woman, February 1983, 18.

The Manitoba (Canada) Nurses Union. *Facts for the Front Lines*, 1999.

Manzoni, Jean-Francois and Jean-Louis Barsoux. "The Set-Up-To-Fail Syndrome."
    Harvard Business Review (March/April, 1998): 101–103.

March, James G. and Herbert A. Simon. *Organizations*. New York: John Wiley
    and Sons, 1958.

McGrath, P. *Newsweek*, October 3, 1988.

McKelvey, Bill. *Organizational Systematics: Taxonomy, Evolution, Classification*.
    Berkeley, CA: University of California Press, 1982.

Miles, Robert. *Macroorganizational Behavior*. Glenview, IL: Scott Foresman, 1980.

Miller, D. T. and M. Ross, "Self-Serving Biases in the Attribution of Causality: Fact
    or Fiction?" *Psychological Bulletin* 82 (1975): 213–225.

Mishra, Karen E., Gretchen M. Spreitzer, and Aneil K. Mishra. "Preserving Em-
    ployee Morale During Downsizing." *Sloan Management Review* (Winter
    1998): 83–94.

Morris, R. *The Economic Theory of Managerial Capitalism*. London: Macmillan,
    1964.

Moskowitz, Merle J. and Arthur R. Orgel. *General Psychology*. Boston: Houghton
    Mifflin, 1969.

Network Marketing, news release, February 1, 1998.

Oil, Chemical, and Atomic Workers International Union, AFL-CIO, news release,
    February 19, 1997.

Osborne, R. N., J. G. Hunt, and L. R. Juach. *Organization Theory*. New York:
    John Wiley and Sons, 1980.

Penrose, E. T. *The Theory of the Growth of the Firm*. London: Macmillan, 1958.

Perrow, Charles. *Complex Organizations: A Critical Essay*. Glenview, IL: Scott
    Foresman, 1972.

Peter, Laurence and Raymond Hull. *The Peter Principle*. New York: William Mor-
    row and Company, 1960.

Pirrault, Michael. Personal conversation with author, May 3, 1999.

Pratt, Joanne H. *Small Business Research Summary*. RS #134, Contract # SBA-
    6647-OA-91, 1991.

Roethlisberger, F. J. and William Dickson. *Management and the Worker*. Cam-
    bridge, MA: Harvard University Press, 1939.

Rosenthal, R. and L. Jacobson. *Pygmalion in the Classroom*. New York: Holt,
    Rinehart, and Winston, 1968.

Samuelson, Paul. *Economics*. New York: McGraw-Hill, 1973.

Sartre, Jean-Paul. *Anti-Semite and Jew*. New York: Schocken Books, 1946.

Seligman, B. B. *Most Notorious Victory: Man in an Age of Automation*. New York: Free Press, 1966.

Skinner, B. F. *The Behavior of Organisms*. New York: Appleton, 1938.

Smith, Adam. *The Wealth of Nations*. New York: G. P. Putnam's Sons, 1904.

The SOHO Guidebook: Starting Your Business (CCH Business Owner's Toolkit). Rolling Meadows, IL: Digitalwork, 1996. (http://www. toolkit.cch.com/text/ pol_0000.asp).

Solomon, Richard L. "Punishment." In *Psychology of Learning: Readings*, edited by William L. Mikulas. Chicago, IL: Nelson-Hall, 1977.

Stoner, J.A.F. "A Comparison of Individual and Group Decisions Involving Risk." Master's thesis, Massachusetts Institute of Technology, Sloan School of Industrial Management, Cambridge, MA, 1961.

Terreberry, Shirley. "The Evolution of Organizational Environments." *Administrative Science Quarterly* 12 (1968): 590–613.

Thompson, James. *Organizations in Action*. New York: McGraw-Hill, 1967.

"U.S. Small Business Administration Report." Cited in *Small Business Resources*. North Oaks, MN: DRI Consulting Publications, 1996 (http://www.dric. com).

Von Bertalanffy, Ludwig. "The History and Status of General System Theory." *Academy of Management Journal* 15 (1972): 407–426.

Washington, Linn, Jr. Article in *Philadelphia Tribune*, November 7, 1997.

Watzlawick, Paul, Janet Beavin Bavelas, and Don D. Jackson. *Pragmatics of Human Communication*. New York: W. W. Norton, 1967.

Weber, Max. *The Theory of Social and Economic Organization*. New York: Free Press, 1947.

Webley, George. "Against All Odds: The Truth About Demos." *Sound on Sound* (May 1998): 166.

Weick, Karl. *The Social Psychology of Organizing*. Reading, MA: Addison-Wesley, 1969.

White, William H., Jr. *The Organization Man*. New York: Simon and Schuster, 1956.

Whorf, Benjamin Lee. "Science and Linguistics." In *Language, Thought, and Reality: Selected Writings of Benjamin Lee Whorf*, edited by John B. Carroll. New York: John Wiley and Sons, 1956.

Why Family Businesses Fail: Survey Results (Storrs, CT: University of Connecticut Family Business Center, 1996).

Index

Abuse, of employees by managers, 62–64, 130

"Agrarian" organization. *See* Organizational types

Allison, Graham, 123

American Management Associates, 211–12

Asch, Solomon, 145, 161

Baldridge, Malcolm, award, 106

Barsoux, Jean-Louis, 153, 154

Behavior, employee, 26; conflict among work units, due to reward for internal, 116–18; co-optation and, 79, 126; culture embedded in, 124; de-skilling and, 77–79; dysfunctional, from promotion to management for performance, 45; ethical license from depersonalization of, 130; evaluation of authorized, 88, 98; halo effect and, 53, 95–96; hubris and, 227; inconsistent with organizational goals, rewards for, 106; misuse of hiring techniques for selecting, 54; negative reinforcement and, 107, 109; neglect of as an issue, by organizational science, 23; neglect of, in formulating strategy, 7; neglect of, in performance appraisal, 100–101; opportunistic, 27; organizational science, 23, 26; ossification of, due to organizational failure, 230–31; perpetuation of dysfunctional, from neglected performance appraisal, 84; professionalism, 130; professionalization, 40–41; punishment and, 111; purposive, 27; as a recommended basis for performance appraisal, 99–100, 140, 244; reward system as a source of, 103, 105; role, 206–7; selection of, as procedures, 41–42; social, 268–70; unsanctioned, 109. *See also* Change, organizational, resistance to; Corporate culture; Ethics; Groups; Institutionalization; Performance appraisal; Politics and political behavior; Pygmalion effect; Reward system; Roles

Behaviorally-Anchored Rating Scale (BARS), 100

Bennis, Warren, 81, 199–200, 243

About the Author

JONATHAN I. KLEIN has served on the faculty at the Graduate School of Management at Rutgers University, where he won the Horace dePodwin Award for research excellence, at Pepperdine University, and at California State University, Los Angeles. Klein currently teaches at the University of Southern California, the California School of Professional Psychology, and at California Lutheran University. In addition, he serves as Director of the Doctorate in Business Administration program at American International University in Los Angeles, and as a consultant to corporate management.

ISBN 1-56720-297-7

90000>

EAN

9 781567 202977

HARDCOVER BAR CODE